E-business Implementation

E-business Implementation

A guide to web services, EAI, BPI, e-commerce, content management, portals, and supporting technologies

Dougal Watt MA, BA, BSc

Routledge
Taylor & Francis Group

LONDON AND NEW YORK

First published by Butterworth-Heinemann

This edition published 2011 by Routledge
2 Park Square, Milton Park, Abingdon, Oxon OX14 4RN
711 Third Avenue, New York, NY 10017, USA

Routledge is an imprint of the Taylor & Francis Group, an informa business

First published 2002

The work of S J Sutherland as editor is acknowledged

British Library Cataloguing in Publication Data
A catalogue record for this book is available from the British Library

ISBN   0 7506 5751 0

The author gratefully acknowledges the use of Microsoft
Corporation Visio™ for the creation of diagrams for this book,
and the assistance of IBM and the Standish Group for their
contribution of material for this book. All product and company
names in this book are trademarked and subject to copyright by the
respective companies.

Contents

Contents

Computer Weekly Professional Series

There are few professions which require as much continuous updating as that of the IS executive. Not only does the hardware and software scene change relentlessly, but also ideas about the actual management of the IS function are being continuously modified, updated and changed. Thus keeping abreast of what is going on is really a major task.

Computer Weekly Professional Series has been created to assist IS executives keep up to date with the management ideas and issues of which they need to be aware.

One of the key objectives of the series is to reduce the time it takes for leading edge management ideas to move from the academic and consulting environments into the hands of the IT practitioner. Thus this series employs appropriate technology to speed up the publishing process. Where appropriate some books are supported by CD-ROM or by additional information or templates located on the Web.

This series provides IT professionals with an opportunity to build up a bookcase of easily accessible, but detailed information on the important issues that they need to be aware of to successfully perform their jobs.

Aspiring or already established authors are invited to get in touch with me directly if they would like to be published in this series.

Dr Dan Remenyi
Series Editor
dan.remenyi@mcil.co.uk

Computer Weekly Professional Series

Series Editor
Dan Remenyi, Visiting Professor, Trinity College Dublin

Advisory Board
Frank Bannister, Trinity College Dublin
Ross Bentley, Management Editor, Computer Weekly
Egon Berghout, Technical University of Delft, The Netherlands
Ann Brown, City University Business School, London
Roger Clark, The Australian National University
Reet Cronk, Harding University, Arkansas, USA
Arthur Money, Henley Management College, UK
Sue Nugus, MCIL, UK
Terry White, BentleyWest, Johannesburg

Other titles in the Series
IT investment – making a business case
The effective measurement and management of IT costs and benefits
Stop IT project failures through risk management
Understanding the Internet
Prince 2: a practical handbook
Considering computer contracting?
David Taylor's Inside Track
A hacker's guide to project management
Corporate politics for IT managers: how to get streetwise
Subnet design for efficient networks
Information warfare: corporate attack and defence in a digital world
Delivering IT and e-business value
Reinventing the IT department
The project manager's toolkit

Overview

Competition within the modern economy has dramatically increased in recent years, as consumers and businesses demand greater choice. In order to survive in this new environment companies must increasingly deliver better customer services and decrease time to market for new and existing products and services, as well as increase collaboration between their employees, partners and suppliers to provide additional efficiency and lower costs. Increasingly, companies are satisfying these business requirements through the adoption of e-business technologies.

This adoption is driven by the increased awareness of the tremendous reach afforded by e-business technologies, and their ability to dramatically increase the efficiency and productivity of existing business processes and systems. E-business technologies provide a single mechanism to reach businesses, consumers, and employees with products and services across local, national and international boundaries in real time and at very low cost.

E-business technologies also provide a powerful mechanism for organizations to automate and simplify business processes used by their internal enterprise systems, and to automate business processes used by external partners and suppliers, or to integrate disparate technology systems after mergers and acquisitions. In addition, e-business technologies are also being utilized for the outsourcing of inefficient or non-core processes in order to gain competitive advantage and allow for greater information flow between trading partners to better respond to changing market conditions.

However, in order to utilize these considerable benefits, companies must understand how to implement e-business technology solutions appropriate to their organization and market segment.

Successful e-business implementation begins with the creation of an appropriate structure for running an e-business project. This structure must be designed to ensure successful delivery for the eventual use of the e-business initiative, and must be capable of delivering the desired business functionality in a timely manner and within budget, while avoiding the high failure rates common to many technology projects.

In addition, a critical element of all successful e-business implementations is the selection of the correct e-business technology solution, which requires an understanding of the e-business technologies and solutions available. These technologies are comprised of one or more solution architectures from the five phases of the e-business lifecycle. This lifecycle typically includes publishing of corporate information through the Internet and Intranets, portals and content management systems, transacting with customers and suppliers over the Internet, integrating internal enterprise applications, integrating external systems with partners and suppliers, and responding dynamically in real time to changing levels of demand through dynamic e-business and web services.

Finally, successful e-business implementation also requires the services of a set of common foundation technologies employed within all businesses and organizations working over the Internet. These technologies include e-business development languages, hardware platforms and their operating systems, security and networking systems, the Internet Domain Name System, and Open Source technologies.

The resulting sets of project management, e-business technology and e-business supporting technology phases, can be assembled into a corporate blueprint, describing the technology and business phases each company can adopt as they progress through the e-business lifecycle. This blueprint provides the core elements of corporate e-business information technology required and is depicted below in Figure 0.1: Blueprint for e-business technology and business adoption.

Figure 0.1 Blueprint for e-business technology and business adoption

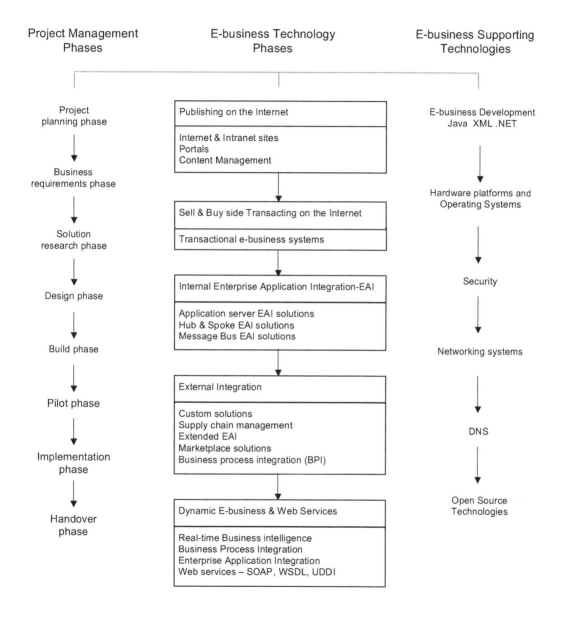

Part One

Project management phases

Structuring an e-business project

When implementing an e-business project a number of processes and structures are required to ensure the project is successful. These include determining the correct structure to guide the course of the project, selecting the appropriate technology to implement, having the correct support technology in place to ensure the implementation will succeed, and choosing the right staff to carry out the project.

Many projects fail because these four elements have not been set up and employed correctly from the beginning. For example, the Standish Group conducted a survey of project failures with 365 organizations of all sizes across a wide range of major industry sectors. Focus groups and personal interviews were also conducted to provide a qualitative assessment of the survey.

Results of this survey showed that over 80 per cent of all projects suffered some form of failure. Only 16.2 per cent of surveyed projects were delivered within time and budget, while 52.7 per cent of projects were delivered but ran over budget, over time and had fewer features than were originally intended. Projects that were cancelled during their development formed 31.1 per cent of the sample.

Project failures included having to restart projects (94 per cent of all projects), cost overruns resulting in an average increase of 189 per cent of original cost, and time overruns, resulting in projects running an average of 222 per cent over original time estimates. Of all companies surveyed, an average of 61 per cent delivered the features originally specified.

The survey found key reasons projects were delayed or failed completely included lack of planning, low user input, incomplete or changing specification of requirements, lack of resources and competent staff, incompetence with technology, unrealistic timeframes and unclear objectives.

A later survey conducted in 2000 by the Standish Group found that 28 per cent of commercial projects were successfully delivered on time and budget with the required functionality. Of the remainder, 49 per cent suffered from partial failure and 23 per cent complete failure. In the government sector 24 per cent of projects succeeded while 50 per cent failed partially and 26 per cent failed completely.

The improvement in figures for project success between 1994 and 2001 was attributed to smaller projects being conducted, which have a higher likelihood of success.

Creating a successful e-business project therefore requires the project be planned correctly from the outset, structured into discrete project steps with identifiable and achievable goals, and the correct staff selected before the project begins.

The following sections discuss these issues, detailing the correct structure and process for conducting an e-business project, and the staff required for fulfilling the project.

1.1 E-business project management

The key to running a successful e-business project is to provide sufficient structure and planning to ensure project success. Success is typically defined as the project meeting its business requirements without running over budget or over time.

Therefore, the project structure should include a set of critical elements that govern the lifecycle of the project and its resulting outcomes. These elements follow the project from its inception to completion, and include the initial project planning, the requirements phase, the solution research phase, the design phase, the build phase, the pilot phase, the implementation phase and the project handover phase. Each phase should be completed with a corresponding set of documents that detail the information gathered in each phase, and the outputs each phase produced.

The initial project planning phase determines the broad outline of the project.

This is used to guide the initial project structure, including an outline of what the project is intended to deliver, and covers preliminary project planning issues such as potential technologies, budget, skills and timeframes.

The requirements phase extends the initial planning to determine the core set of deliverables the project should satisfy, which are in turn used to gauge project success. These cover all areas of business and technology relevant to the company, and are subject to analysis to prioritize the most relevant set of requirements to deliver with available resources.

The solution research phase is used to conduct detailed research into potential technology solutions to fulfil the initial project planning and requirements deliverables. This is then analysed and a set of potential technology solutions researched, with the best solution being recommended to proceed into the design phase.

The design phase takes the recommended solution from the research phase to create a high-level conceptual design for the solution. Following best practice, this design is then audited internally and externally to prove its feasibility, before a detailed design is created to cover the chosen technology solution in more detail, including application design, security systems, and the deployment configurations.

The build phase uses the results of the design phase to create the intended solution. Blocks of functionality are coded, deployed and tested using a build process across development, testing and production environments. The complete solution is iteratively assembled using this process by creating and integrating successive blocks of functionality until all chosen requirements are satisfied by the solution.

The pilot phase deploys an initial version of the completed solution for early testing by stakeholders (the members of staff or partners and suppliers who either sponsor a project or who are most affected by its implementation) and users. This allows the project to tune the solution to better fit requirements and satisfy deployment issues.

The implementation phase expands on the pilot phase to deploy the final solution across the business to all relevant business users. This requires the solution be deployed in a production capacity, capable of supporting all users and workloads, and the training and transition of users from old work practices to the new solution.

The handover phase collates the output of all previous phases into a set of support resources for operational and support staff. It also includes training of support staff, and the creation of final project documentation.

This structured approach to designing and running a project is depicted in Figure 1.1.

Figure 1.1 Structured project planning

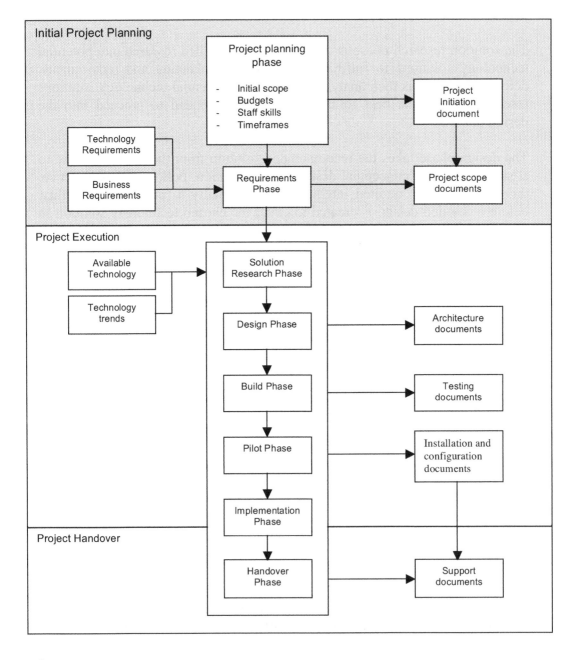

This structured process begins with the initial project planning and requirements phases, and progresses through the main project execution phases until the completed project handover phase, where the project is turned over to internal teams for ongoing support. Each phase requires a set of inputs and produces a set of documented outputs that are required for each successive project lifecycle phase. These well-documented outputs are a fundamental advantage to this approach, and are used for project support, future developments, and auditing purposes.

The following sections discuss the elements of this structured approach to running e-business projects in detail.

1.2 The project planning phase

Before a project begins it is essential to have a broad understanding of the issues the project will address, and how the project will fulfil these issues. These are detailed in the project initiation document, which details the business problems facing the company, a broad overview of potential technology solutions, and estimates of the amount of time the project will take, what it will cost, and what staff will be required. These estimates are intended as a guide to assist in setting up the project, and are finalized in successive project phases.

An internal project manager and an internal or external e-business technical architect typically conduct the initial project planning, with each team member occupying distinct roles. The project manager is responsible for managing and tracking the project to ensure each phase is being delivered successfully. They typically create preliminary budgets and project timeframes in collaboration with the e-business technical architect. The e-business technical architect conducts preliminary research and assessments of the likely technologies necessary to solve the business problem.

The initial project planning is critical to establishing a clearly understood context for the decision-making, through a focus on why there is a need for the e-business project. This involves getting the different stakeholders affected by project decisions or involved in the decision-making process to understand and agree with the problems that are to be addressed. This is critical for 'buy-in' to the project, so that possible conflict between different stakeholders is prevented or minimized.

The core element of the initial project planning is the statement of the nature of the business problem confronting the company. This typically provides the motivation for the company to conduct the e-business project, and the extent to which the company resolves this problem determines the success of the project. It is therefore the focal point for understanding and determining intended technical solutions.

The statement of the business problems should include the nature of the business, the challenges facing it, and what business problems the technology is required to solve. It should also incorporate statements of the medium-term and long-term strategic views of business and technology needs. This ensures that all proposed solutions are aligned with medium-term and long-term plans, thus preventing selection of temporary solutions that will be discarded in future. The statement of the business problem should be expressed in a very simple and clear form, as shown in Figure 1.2.

Figure 1.2 Statement of business problem

> **Nature of Business**
>
> Company **X** is a financial services provider selling packaged pension, insurance and investment products to companies and direct to consumers.
>
> **Business Requirements**
>
> Company **X**'s operating costs are increasing. They wish to restructure their business to use technology more efficiently to save costs and communicate more effectively with their own staff and their customers. They want their technology solution to reflect this.
>
> **The current problem**
> The company has a website and an Intranet site, and want to automate these to increase efficiency and create a cost-effective solution. They want to offer all their products online for self-service to clients, in real time, and utilize existing systems within the business including back-end legacy mainframe applications and their external suppliers of pension and investment products.
>
> **Alignment with medium-term strategy**
> Move to complete automation throughout their business. Enable integration of financial, HR systems, call centres, and marketing systems to provide real-time knowledge of all parts of their business.
>
> **Alignment with long-term strategy**
> They want to be able to provide customers with a real-time customized financial product portfolio that can be changed at any time depending on their circumstances.

Defining the business problem at this stage is also critically important as it provides a baseline to assist in minimizing the risks that may arise from making incorrect decisions during the course of the project. Frequent sources of risk include changes in business issues arising during the project, which in turn invalidate subsequent stages in the decision-making process, and potentially the technology solution selected and deployed.

However, these risks can be mitigated if the business issues have been made explicit at the outset of the project. Any changes in business issues or other requirements during the project can then be compared to the original assumptions, and if they differ significantly, the project can be modified to accommodate them without seriously jeopardizing the outcome.

Once the business problem has been stated, the e-business technical architect conducts preliminary research to provide prospective technology solutions and preliminary budgets and timeframes. Typically, this requires the e-business technical architect to research a range of appropriate design patterns and products from technologies commonly applied to specific business problems. These patterns typically include collections of technology architectures and products, design and development methodologies, and deployment factors utilized in previous e-business projects.

Selection of a range of appropriate design patterns and products is complicated due to the very large volume of technology information available, and the complexities and risks inherent in matching technology solutions to business problems. Therefore, this requires the e-business technical architect to have specialist knowledge, experience and skills of e-business technology, a broad and detailed understanding of the technology industry as a whole, and the ability to match technology solutions to business requirements.

The use of a formal research approach by the e-business technical architect provides several benefits to the project. It offers the ability to shorten the research phase, as the design patterns and products provide a structure to guide research. As the design patterns utilize proven pre-existing successful technology strategies, they lower the risk of making incorrect choices and allow the architect to reduce project timeframes. Finally, the use of such patterns shifts the solution focus away from individual point solutions reactively designed to solve a single business problem, and permits the e-business solution to be synchronized with long-term strategic planning within an enterprise.

This preliminary research must also consider a number of factors that are in turn related to the statement of the business problem. For example, the statement of business problem listed above would influence the technical architect to research e-business design patterns capable of targeting multiple channels, including online and offline channels, and supporting CRM functionality. They would also research solutions capable of integrating with financial services back-end systems, typically legacy AS/400 or mainframe products, and products that can be used with their partners and suppliers. Their choices should also be capable of extension to web services in the future, allowing for alignment of the solution to future medium-term and long-term strategic goals.

The factors affecting the preliminary decisions of the e-business technical architect can be classified into business-specific factors, and general external factors related to industry, vendor and technology trends.

Business factors

Business factors are comprised of business issues specific to the company that may affect initial technology choices. These typically include areas such as the company industry sector, available budgets, current technologies in use, and available staff skills and timeframes.

Industry sector factors are unique to each industry segment a company is active within. For example, manufacturing or retail businesses frequently require real-time information regarding stock levels, while service specific businesses may require a single complete view of all customer information for call centre staff.

Budgets provide limits to the purchase and implementation costs of technologies. They also constrain other resources employed during the project phases, such as skills and levels of staffing employed, and may also influence the availability of resources during later project stages, such as the duration and degree of testing in the build phase.

Initial project planning is also influenced by the technologies currently utilized within the business, due to the large amount of investment a company may already have made in specific areas, and a desire to lower support and administration costs through the reuse of infrastructure. These technologies typically include hardware systems, operating systems, peripherals, and enterprise applications such as business productivity, enterprise resource planning, and e-business systems.

The presence of existing technologies within the business is frequently viewed as an important business factor, and is often given greater weight than critical factors such as the performance or availability of the solution. Overemphasis of this factor may result in the technical architect selecting compatible technologies with resulting tradeoffs, such as increased project timeframes, higher total project costs, and lower levels of reliability, scalability and availability in the final solution.

For example, a company may require a highly available e-business solution to ensure customer satisfaction and maintain high customer retention rates. However, they may have standardized on a particular set of supported technologies that are unreliable for e-business purposes. If the e-business system must conform to these technology requirements, higher levels of system downtime may jeopardize customer satisfaction, resulting in lost business. This may in turn considerably outweigh the savings made from using common but unreliable infrastructure. Therefore, the requirement for the adoption of a more reliable technology should be preferred over selection of common systems.

The mixture of skills available within the company's information technology department may also help to determine what type of technology should be selected, as the department may already have made a significant investment in skills development in this area. For example, if an information technology department has the majority of its development skills in one area, selecting that development technology may be a business factor. However, in a similar manner to the existing technologies within the business, levels of internal skills should not outweigh critical requirements such as the ability to create a suitable e-business solution.

Finally, the total time available for a given project will have a strong influence on the initial project planning. Projects that must deliver functionality within short timeframes will influence decisions towards pre-packaged off-the-shelf technologies capable of meeting business requirements with minimal customization. If a project is allocated long timeframes, decisions can include technologies requiring more custom development. However, long duration projects of over 12 months are not recommended as they frequently lead to cost and time overruns, and result in technological obsolescence.

External factors

External factors are issues outside the business that may influence the initial project planning technology choices. These factors include existing relationships with technology vendors, technologies used by external partners and suppliers, trends within the information technology industry, and technology adoption trends within other business segments.

Frequently a company will have existing relationships with multiple technology vendors. Selecting solutions from a vendor with whom the company has an existing relationship and direct previous project experience can provide a significant reduction in the risks of conducting a project, provided this relationship is close and beneficial to all parties. However, this factor must be balanced against the need to select the vendor technology solution most appropriate to solving the business problem.

Integration of systems with external suppliers of products and services will also influence technology decisions. For example, if a supplier has a proprietary enterprise application integration solution, potential integration technology choices with that supplier may be restricted. Such relationships will also influence the choice of other related technologies, such as security systems, to ensure such close integration will not compromise corporate systems and information.

However, selecting potential technology solutions that are tightly coupled to specific suppliers may increase project risk. This occurs when the solution compromises other internal business factors that must be addressed in the project, and inhibits support for and integration with additional suppliers and future technologies.

Technology industry trends frequently influence the selection of potential technologies due to the expected lifecycle of a technology. If a technology is becoming obsolete, it makes less sense to consider selecting it for a future project. If a technology is becoming more widespread, it may be sensible to utilize it if many vendors will support it. Similarly, technology selections are often influenced by the trend towards adoption of packaged off-the-shelf technology solutions rather than creating proprietary customized solutions.

Finally, trends adopted by competitors also influence preliminary technology decision-making. For example, when many businesses in an industry sector employ the same or similar technologies, companies frequently give these more importance in making initial technology decisions. However, this strategy should be avoided, as each technology should be assessed on its business merits and degree of fit for the company and issues at hand. Alternatively, analysis of how other companies employ technology can indicate the technologies to avoid if there are widespread problems in that industry segment, or how to correctly deploy such technologies to avoid common mistakes.

Following determination of the internal and external factors and their influence on preliminary technology decisions, the e-business technical architect creates an overview of the technology solution proposed to address the business problem. This will typically include a broad overview of the technology functionality required to satisfy the business problem, and the business and external factors. It will also typically include at least three potential solutions from different vendors, and provide an indicative costing for each alternative.

For example, with the example depicted in Figure 1.2, the technical architect's overview may include three proposed solutions for the creation of an internal and external e-business portal solution, integrated with a transactional e-business for customers and internal legacy and partner and supplier systems. These may include specific vendor products and indications of proposed customizations and content development required, and deployment scenarios.

The project initiation document is then created, including the statement of the business problems, the proposed preliminary technology solutions, and estimated budgets, staff skills and project timeframes. This forms the first output generated in the course of the project.

This document should be read and approved by the business and technical stakeholders within the company, as it provides the context for the major decisions within the project. It also provides a mechanism for initial agreement on how the project will be run and what it will deliver. Once this document has been agreed with stakeholders, the project can move into the requirements gathering phase.

1.3 The requirements gathering phase

The business issues introduced in the initial project planning phase provide a general context to the business problem that must be solved. This context must be extended during the requirements gathering phase to provide a more detailed description of all the business and technical issues the project must provide a solution for. These are in turn detailed within the project scope document, which forms the second project output.

During this phase, the project manager is responsible for overseeing the gathering and analysis of the requirements. They must also ensure that appropriate business analysts are hired, and ensure they work closely with the e-business technical architect and business stakeholders. The business analysts are responsible for gathering and analysing the business and technical requirements from business stakeholders and customers using one or more of the methods described below. They must also work closely with the e-business technical architect to ensure the technical issues specific to the company and project are addressed in full. The e-business technical architect is also responsible for analysing these requirements before the subsequent research and design phases, which are used to create the high-level and detailed designs.

Project requirements are the detailed issues that combine to create the initial business problem. These are typically composed of necessary business and technical conditions within the company, or problems experienced with specific business processes by stakeholders. Each requirement imposes specific constraints on the project solution, and must therefore be addressed by the project to ensure project success.

For example, a stakeholder such as an investment manager may use a manual process to assist a customer in choosing an investment product. Customers may wish to have this process automated in a convenient online system, thus creating the requirement for automated product selection using an e-business system.

Detailed requirements are obtained from internal and external sources, including internal company divisions, and external customers and partners and suppliers, and are categorized into detailed business requirements and technical requirements, as shown in Figure 1.3.

Figure 1.3 Common sources of project requirements

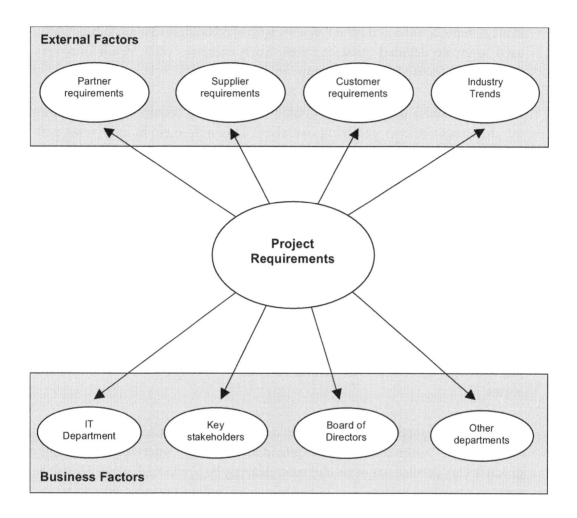

Detailed business and technical requirements originate from the external and business factors highlighted in the initial project planning phase. Once these sources have been identified, their specific requirements are gathered using a range of mechanisms appropriate to the company and business in question. These may include structured questionnaires and interviews with stakeholders, internal reports, strategy documents, and analyst reports.

The methods used to gather requirements will depend on the size of the project and the degree to which it will affect the business. Large and strategically important projects are typically driven from higher levels within the company, often at board level via the chief technology officer or chief information officer. Due to their strategic importance, such projects may require wide consultation within the company, and hence a formal and detailed requirements gathering exercise. This may utilize mechanisms such as published board directives and strategy reports, followed by interviews with stakeholders that are subsequently used to create detailed questionnaires. Such exercises often result in a very detailed and focused set of requirements.

In contrast, small projects with limited budgets may require rapid and more informal requirements gathering exercises. This may include interviews with critical stakeholders, and reference internally published reports and reports from IT analysis firms to gauge 'industry best practice' as a mechanism to shorten the requirements gathering phase.

Structured questionnaires are frequently used to obtain requirements from large numbers of company stakeholders, and typically solicit responses to items such as lists of business objectives, problems with business processes, and proposed solutions. Questionnaires are administered to all stakeholders across company business units, then collated into common problems and desired solutions. Information technology departments should also be included in such questionnaires, as they are normally required to support the solution once it has been implemented and can also contribute relevant technology and business process issues.

Interviews with stakeholders provide a less structured mechanism to gather requirements compared to questionnaires. However, interviews frequently produce very detailed sets of requirements that may be overlooked in questionnaires, such as revealing weaknesses in specific areas within business processes and tools. In addition, interviews with stakeholders may also be employed to create detailed targeted questionnaires for use in widespread requirements gathering throughout the company.

Interviews and questionnaires should also include external stakeholders, such as representative samples of customers and members of partner and supplier companies. Such stakeholders can provide feedback on end-user functionality requirements, and may contribute valuable high-level technical requirements such as desired levels of availability and performance for an e-business system. Requirements may also be gathered through internal reports and strategy documents, including high-level company strategy reports, and business unit documents such as policy and procedure documents. These typically provide short-term, medium-term and long-term goals; objectives and strategies that the proposed solution must satisfy, and may provide critical success factors and performance indicators, such as business improvement targets.

Strategy-based requirements may also originate from the board of directors of a company, which frequently establish broad goals such as 'becoming an e-business leader' in their industry field or 'implementing a supplier trading website with partners'. Due to the pivotal and central place of technology within modern business, technology departments should be represented at board level via CIO or CTO members, and hence provide input into these strategies.

Additional sources of requirements gathering may include specialist analysis firms such as Butler, Forrester or the Gartner Group. Such firms often release reports from in-house analysts detailing the technical and business issues facing companies within specific business segments. These may provide valuable input into the definition of both technical and business requirements.

In general, complex projects that will have a deep impact within the company will require formal and widespread requirements gathering processes. Typically, such projects utilize custom developments to meet these requirements, and utilize formal requirements gathering and description methodologies such as the use case method used in Object Oriented software design. Use cases detail the set of actions and expected responses for each requirement, and are employed for rapid prototyping and simplified development cycles. In contrast, less formal and simpler projects require less involved requirements gathering processes, and typically express the resulting requirements in standard document templates.

Analyse requirements

Once the requirements have been gathered and documented, the project manager, business analysts and the e-business technical architect conduct a requirements analysis using a structured approach. This allows the requirements to be prioritized according to importance to ensure the project can provide the greatest degree of functionality within the available resources. It also provides a mechanism to clarify complex interactions between conflicting requirements by simplifying the amount of detail gathered in the requirements gathering phase.

Requirements are analysed through a process of ranking according to their significance to the project, and the level of risk they represent to the project. Significance is typically determined by the extent each requirement influences decision-making, and thus how critical they are to the final solution. Requirements that strongly constrain a project but threaten project success should be reassessed and modified or discarded if appropriate.

Requirements with high levels of significance frequently include project deadlines, requirement to reuse existing technologies, project budgets, and specific aspects of functionality such as support for payment methods, transaction types or specific customer-driven requirements.

Requirements with lower levels of significance typically include utilizing products from a preferred vendor or consultancy, or from in-house project resources such as existing development and support staff with particular skills.

Ranking of requirements is also affected by less tangible factors. These include factors such as industry trends, competitor trends and corporate preferences in specific technology areas. Such factors should be accounted for when prioritizing requirements, but they do not directly constrain decisions or carry high levels of risk to the project, and can therefore be allocated lower significance levels.

Sources of risk can be determined during the requirements gathering phase through interviews with stakeholders. Risk factors are typically expressed as the threat of the project failing from not satisfying a given requirement, and the specific elements that contribute to risk for that requirement. Formal risk management processes should be incorporated throughout each stage of the project to plan for risks that may arise, using a process of identifying and analysing risks, determining methods to handle risks, and providing ongoing monitoring of risks throughout the project. Risk management typically requires maintenance of a risk register by the project manager, in the form of a database, throughout the project lifecycle.

Once the significance and risk profile of each requirement have been classified, they are placed into an analysis matrix. This locates each requirement within rows and columns corresponding to the source of the requirement (business or external), the description of the requirement, the significance of the requirement, the risk it represents to the project if it is not fulfilled, and details of factors contributing to this risk.

An example of such a requirements matrix would typically include the elements depicted in Table 1.1.

Table 1.1 Requirements analysis matrix

Source	Requirement description	Significance	Risk	Risk Issues
Business	Must be delivered in 6 months	1	High	Must beat competitor to market
	Must integrate with partner X	1	High	They supply some critical financial products
	Budget capped at $3 000 000	1	Medium	Project very important therefore budget can grow
	Integrate with internal CICS financial system	1	High	Core products sourced from this system
	Strategic goal to adopt industry standard technology to lower costs	1	Low	Current trends support this form of development
	Availability	1	High	Must be continually available to service customer requests
	Scalability	1	High	Must account for varying levels of customer demand
	Security	1	High	Must prevent compromise of solution from internal and external sources
	Corporate guideline to use Unix based solutions	2	Low	Extensive in-house support and widespread industry support for Unix products
	Corporate hardware standard is for Sun SPARC systems	2	Low	As above
	Internal skills in Unix, SPARC, and COM technologies	2	Low	Can outsource development and support skills or retrain staff
	Integration with existing COM e-business system desirable	3	Low	Will not affect project launch date
External	Technology industry trends (list)	2	Low	Industry standardizing on Java e-business technology
	Current vendor relationships (list)	3	Low	Can readily utilize other companies
	Current supplier relationships (list)	3	Low	Can readily utilize other companies
	Competitor trends (list)	4	Low	Competitors utilizing similar technology

The requirements analysis matrix is included as the final section of the project scope document. It should incorporate enough detailed information to permit the e-business technical architect to begin the design phase of the project.

An example scope document is depicted in Figure 1.4.

Figure 1.4 Decision output: project scope document

Project Scope Document (title of document)

Table of Contents (list of all document headers)

Introduction
Briefly state the purpose of the document, and summarize the contents.

Objectives
State what the document is intended to achieve, i.e. the need to resolve the business problems being faced.

Document History
As this document will change over time, include version information in a table here with document author and the reasons for making changes, e.g. adding a new section.

Related Documents
In a table, list any other documents that are referenced within this document. E.g. published reports used.

Overview
State the key issues facing the business, why these require a technology decision, and how this will solve the issues.

Business Requirements
Discuss the source of the business requirements, how they were gathered, and discuss each requirement in logical groupings (e.g. business and external factors).

Technology Requirements
Discuss the source of the technology requirements, how they were gathered, and discuss each requirement in logical groupings (e.g. internal and external factors).

Requirements Analysis
Place each requirement into matrix of source, name, influence type, importance and risk. Include verbal summary of results of this analysis

Source	Requirement description	Significance	Risk	Risk Issues
Business	Must be delivered in 6 months	1	High	Must beat competitor to market
	Must integrate with partner X	1	High	They supply some critical financial products
	Budget capped at $3 000 000	1	Medium	Project very important therefore budget can grow
	Integrate with internal CICS financial system	1	High	Core products sourced from this system
	Strategic goal to adopt industry standard technology to lower costs	1	Low	Current trends support this form of development
	Availability	1	High	Must be continually available to service customer requests
	Scalability	1	High	Must account for varying levels of customer demand
	Security	1	High	Must prevent compromise of solution from internal and external sources
	Corporate guideline to use Unix based solutions	2	Low	Extensive in-house support and widespread industry support for Unix products
	Corporate hardware standard is for Sun SPARC systems	2	Low	As above
	Internal skills in Unix, SPARC, and COM technologies	2	Low	Can outsource development and support skills or retrain staff
	Integration with existing COM e-business system desirable	3	Low	Will not affect project launch date
External	Technology industry trends (list)	2	Low	Industry standardizing on Java e-business technology
	Current vendor relationships (list)	3	Low	Can readily utilize other companies
	Current supplier relationships (list)	3	Low	Can readily utilize other companies
	Competitor trends (list)	4	Low	Competitors utilizing similar technology

Summary
Summarize the findings of the document.

1.4 The solution research phase

Once the business and technical requirements have been determined, the solution research phase is conducted to produce a set of recommended technical solutions to solve the project requirements. The preferred solution then forms the basis of the proposed high-level design.

The e-business technical architect conducts the solution research phase. This involves a process of selecting sources of information about proposed solutions, conducting research and compiling information on the technology products and their vendors using these sources, and evaluating the results of this research against the initial scope and project requirements. This process is depicted in Figure 1.5.

Figure 1.5 Technology solution research process

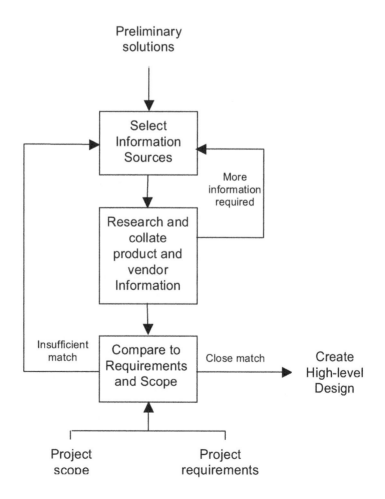

The e-business technical architect determines appropriate information sources for research based on the three initial technology solution overviews created in the project initiation phase. Typical sources for research include print and Internet magazines, print media such as trade publications in relevant areas, vendor websites, and market research reports.

Solution information is gathered and collated from these sources, including core functionality, product technologies and deployment options, and the product architecture. Analysis of this information by the e-business technical architect will typically employ multiple analysis techniques gained within previous projects. These include methods such as function point analysis comparing product functions to required functions from the requirements matrix and scope documents, analysis of vendor and industry analyst evaluations, assessment of user reports, previous experience with products, and the vendor factors. If a solution does not provide sufficient functionality, additional information must be gathered, or alternatively the solution must be discarded and a new solution selected and researched.

The process of technology solution research and selection is one of the most important decisions made during the project lifecycle, as it is crucial to project success to ensure the correct technologies are selected. E-business technology continually changes, and therefore selecting the wrong technology may result in systems that fail to work, or provide only a partial solution to business problems.

Technology selection should also account for existing corporate business and technology strategy, and other projects and technologies deployed within the company, to ensure that solutions can be integrated into other corporate systems. Appropriate selection also minimizes 'orphaned' solutions where technology is deployed that rapidly becomes obsolete and unsupported by vendors, resulting in lack of support and difficulty in obtaining product updates, and therefore increasing the operational cost to the business.

Following this process, the e-business technical architect should produce a final detailed recommendation for the proposed technology solution, and two alternative recommendations. Each recommended solution should be ranked according to the extent to which they fit the project scope and requirements. If the solution research phase cannot clearly distinguish between proposed alternatives, it is recommended that a small-scale proof of concept project be conducted using the recommended technology solutions to allow the e-business technical architect to more accurately determine the most appropriate solution.

Vendor selection

The role of solution vendors is an important element in product research, selection and resourcing for an e-business project. Vendor suitability for a project is determined by a set of factors, including suitability of products and services offered by the vendor for the project requirements, the viability and history of the solution and vendor, the cost of their solution and ongoing support, and the vendor's levels of customer service.

The suitability of vendor products and services to the business and technical requirements of the project is a key factor in ensuring project success. Selection of inappropriate vendor solutions is a common problem, and frequently results in a solution incapable of supplying the required functionality, necessitating additional and unexpected custom work to fit the solution to the project requirements. This also frequently results in increased costs and time overruns for projects, and requires high levels of support for the incorrect solution. It is therefore important to choose a suitable vendor and solution that closely matches project requirements, and has minimal need for customization.

Vendors should also be assessed to determine their ongoing viability over the following years in order to provide continued support, bug fixes and new features for current and outdated products. This ensures the solution can generate a reasonable return on investment before its replacement with newer, upgraded systems. Vendor viability typically includes the financial viability of the vendor, with a focus on selecting vendors and products with high or increasing market share to ensure their products will not be discontinued.

The viability of a solution can also be increased if vendors have widely available and well-supported products. Such products are sold and supported by multiple independent vendors, with consultants specializing in the product widely available from vendors and independent contractors. In addition, training in such products is typically readily available for internal staff. These factors allow companies to switch vendors to find suitable service and support levels, which in turn decreases vendor lock-in and reduces the risks to the project.

The strategic viability of products and vendors should also be considered. Vendors should demonstrate a history of innovation in e-business, and articulate a clear strategic direction for their products, including adoption of emerging technologies and standards, and targeting of specific market segments with appropriate features. This direction should also be aligned with the company strategic direction to ensure compatibility.

A vendor's strategic vision should also remain consistent over time and focus on providing business value for customers. Vendors attempting to profit at the expense of customers through frequent strategic shifts, licence changes, or forced product upgrades through incompatible product features should be avoided.

Once a product offering the required features has been selected from a viable vendor, the cost of solution should be determined. Typically, up-front purchase costs represent only a small percentage of the total cost of the solution. It is therefore imperative to determine the complete lifecycle cost of the solution from initial purchase to eventual replacement. Lifecycle costs include factors such as the ongoing cost of product maintenance, support and upgrades, security costs, training costs, and the usability of the solution, which affects employee productivity and customer satisfaction.

Reputable vendors should also be able to provide a detailed breakdown of their solution costs during early negotiations. This allows for price, performance and feature comparisons between competing products. Vendors also frequently offer discounts for start-up companies, the purchase of additional products and services, global licensing of products across multiple business units in large companies, and for companies subscribing to development programmes. Therefore, when obtaining quotes from vendors, companies should capitalize on such incentive programmes to ensure they obtain the best price for the chosen solution.

When evaluating vendors and vendor solutions, it is also recommended that trial copies of products be obtained either during the initial negotiations with the vendors, or from website downloads. This allows a company to conduct tests of features and integration capabilities, and assists in the determination of cost factors such as security, support, and usability. Availability of trial copies may also indicate vendor confidence in their products, and a willingness to build market share by seeding the market with product knowledge and skills.

Finally, the level of customer service provided by the vendor should also be considered during vendor selection. This includes factors such as providing professional service at all times, the sales experience for prospective customers matching the level of their technical after-sales support, vendors returning calls promptly and providing sufficient information to assist in decision-making (including knowledgeable technical staff), and providing guaranteed delivery dates for products and services. Such dates are critical during project execution to ensure valuable staff members do not have to wait for vendors to deliver project resources. Similarly, it is recommended that all dealings with vendors be conducted with equivalent levels of professionalism from the company to foster a good long-term working relationship.

1.5 The high-level design phase

Once the solution research phase has finalized a recommended technology solution the project progresses to the creation of the high-level design phase using the results of this research. The high-level design provides a formal overview of the technical components of the solution necessary to meet the required business and technical functionality specified in the requirements analysis.

The e-business technical architect is responsible for the creation of the high-level design. This occurs through analysis of the recommended solution to produce a set of functional and operational design components satisfying the business and technical requirements of the project.

High-level functional design components consist of software solutions that will be used to provide discrete groups of business functionality corresponding to stakeholder requirements. For example, a high-level functional design for a transactional e-business system may consist of a set of software components providing data storage, catalogue management, transaction processing, payment processing, interface management, and security. Each component is an independent entity that offers services to other components, with the complete set of components satisfying the business and technical requirements.

The appropriate high-level functional components are determined through an analysis of the project requirements, the interactions users will have with the e-business system and the features and systems offered in the proposed technology solution. Functional components may be provided through purchase of packaged solutions, or development of the appropriate components.

The operational components of the high-level design describe the physical aspects that govern how the functional design will be deployed, and are selected during the solution research phase. These typically include operating systems and hardware servers, development tools, network and security systems, and performance and availability levels. For example, the transactional e-business system described above may require an operational design consisting of specific hardware servers, operating systems, and network and security devices assembled in a network configuration to provide high availability and performance. Typically, the operational servers are used to host the functional design components.

Operational components are also determined from further analysis of technical and business project requirements, and from the functional design, which may indicate the need for additional systems.

Both operational and functional components may be simplified during the solution research phase by selecting solutions supporting multiple operating systems and/or development languages. This removes potentially restrictive dependencies between design components, such as specific products selected to provide functional components requiring specific operating systems. Removing such dependencies in turn allows the e-business technical architect more scope to optimize the functional design to suit requirements, and the operational design to support different deployment, performance and availability requirements.

Once analysis of the functional and operational design components is complete, they are included in the high-level design document. This document is intended to provide an overview of the design for internal and external audit, and to guide the subsequent creation of the detailed design and build phase.

The high-level design should therefore be written in a manner suitable for a technical and non-technical audience, and provide sufficient detail to justify the choice of design components while avoiding detailed discussions of implementation-specific issues such as detailed functionality or configuration and deployment information. Once complete, the high level design allows the e-business technical architect and project manager to finalize the project budgets and timeframes according to the chosen solutions and design.

The audit phase

Following completion of the high-level design phase, it is strongly recommended that the high-level design document be submitted to an external firm for analysis. This provides an independent audit for the design to ensure each requirement has been met, and to minimize the risk of making incorrect decisions. Specialist analysis firms such as the Butler Group or Gartner are recommended for this function, or alternatively another external e-business technical architect.

In addition, an internal audit of the high-level design is also recommended to gain stakeholder buy-in and ensure the proposed solution will be acceptable to relevant stakeholders. This internal audit also provides stakeholders with necessary feedback from internal staff to ensure their business requirements will be met.

1.6 The detailed design phase

Once the high-level design has been audited and approved, the detailed design can be created by the e-business technical architect. This design provides a detailed set of specifications of the functional and operational components of the design, which are then used by developers, implementation staff and web designers to create and test the system during the build phase.

The detailed functional design provides an in-depth description of the functional software components (known as the software component model) providing the functionality specified in the requirements document. This includes descriptions of the software components, the interactions between components (which components use other components), their software interfaces (their expected inputs and outputs), and descriptions of the externally observable behaviour of the components, typically described using 'use cases' and 'collaborations' created from the requirements analysis. Use cases specify how an external individual or system would interact with the solution, for example how a user would purchase a product from an e-business site. Collaborations specify the interactions between components over time, and are used to express the dynamic behaviour of the functional components. Each element of the detailed functional design is typically expressed using the Unified Modelling Language (UML) system of notation, providing a common language for the project team.

Functional components are structured through analysis of the required functionality and selected software solutions. The e-business technical architect assigns specific units of functionality to discrete software components using a range of design principles. These include distributing functionality between components into distinct layers, including presentation user interfaces, business logic and data access, and internal and external integration systems. It also requires avoiding redundancy and duplication in components, the incorporation of legacy systems and other corporate applications, and consideration of operational service level requirements such as performance, security and availability.

This analysis should produce clean separation between the application business logic, presentation, event management, data access, and integration components. This separation in turn permits the different groups of project staff to work on separate components in parallel during the course of the project, thus decreasing the time taken to create the solution. In addition, it permits each component to be modified separately from the others, allowing for rapid changes during the build phase such as the addition or alteration of solutions features. It should be noted that in addition to in-house development of functional components, much of the required functionality may be purchased as packaged solutions and integrated with custom project-specific code.

The detailed functional design components are also used to create test cases, which consist of specific sequences of steps and their related conditions used to test the expected behaviour of functional components. Creating test cases early in the build phase ensures that testing is closely aligned to the development of the solution, and allows for rapid and interactive modifications to systems to fulfil the specified requirements.

The detailed operational design consists of a set of components responsible for how the system will be physically deployed, including specific products such as hardware servers, network devices, security devices, and the physical placement of these components within the company. These components are typically expressed using network structure diagrams, depicting the location and connections between operational components, the functional components deployed across these, and specific configuration documentation.

In addition, the operational design includes non-functional issues such as the performance, availability, and security of the solution, support processes and procedures for the ongoing operation of the solution, and internal and external technology requirements such as preferred operating systems. These aspects of the design are typically expressed through service level agreements (SLAs), and support documents such as installation and configuration documents.

The detailed operational design must be synchronized with the functional design to ensure the design is capable of satisfying the non-functional aspects of the design, such as performance. This requires the e-business technical architect to analyse the flows of data within the solution according to user activity and data source, the deployment configurations of packaged products, and the non-functional operational requirements. This process should occur simultaneously with the functional design to ensure that operational design factors are built in to the complete solution from the outset.

The detailed design must also specify project change control mechanisms. These include software code and document management products such as the Open Source CVS, the Rational Clear Case product, or Microsoft Visual

Studio/SourceSafe. Such tools provide a central repository for all project code, and can enforce rigorous change control of functional component source code to ensure the correct code is utilized and deployed during the build phase. In addition, change control procedures should also be specified for operational systems (such as server configurations), and project documentation. This provides an audit trail for changes made during the project, and ensures that arbitrary, unnecessary and potentially problematic changes are not enacted by project or company staff.

The resulting detailed design provides a blueprint for the creation of the solution in the build phase. However, it should include sufficient flexibility to allow for modifications during the build phase, such as restructuring the deployment of functional components across operational systems for performance. It should also support future enhancements as requirements evolve, such as the addition of new components or modifications to existing components.

1.7 Build phase

Once the detailed design has been approved, the build phase begins. This phase involves creating a working solution to meet the project requirements, using the specification supplied by the detailed design document.

During the build phase, the e-business technical architect ensures that the development and testing of a production-ready solution is managed and implemented correctly according to the detailed design document. This includes tracking technical milestones to ensure design components are correctly delivered on time, ensuring the performance, reliability and security of the complete solution is maintained, and enforcing technical change management to minimize errors during development.

Similarly, the project manager oversees the build phase as part of the ongoing management of the project. This includes ensuring staffing, resourcing and client issues are managed, that project milestones are met, and that project risk issues are addressed as they arise.

The build phase begins with implementation staff members skilled in the appropriate technologies and products installing the detailed operational components of the design into the development, testing and live production environments before application development commences. These include components such as web servers, application servers and packaged business logic products. It also includes source code control servers used to store the software created by the development team in a central repository, and computers and tools used by members of the development teams to code the business logic, databases, integration, and presentation layer systems. In addition, network and security systems are installed across the design layers, and consist of network hardware such as switches and routers, and security systems such as firewalls, intrusion detection systems, and server hardening procedures.

The development, test and live environments, build phase tasks, and staff members responsible for these tasks are depicted in Figure 1.6.

Figure 1.6 Environments and processes used during the build phase

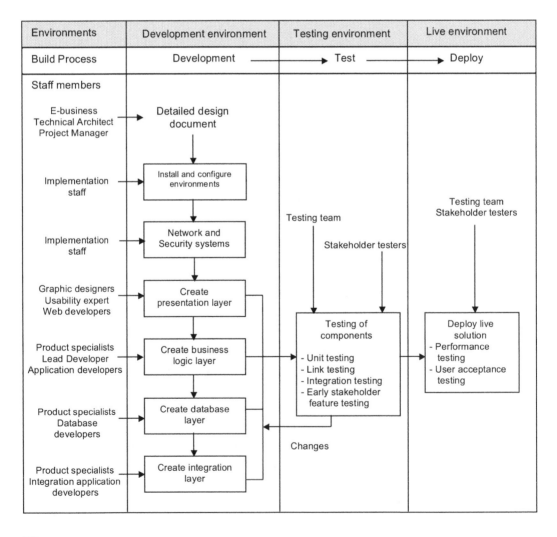

Once the operational systems and environments have been installed, development of the detailed design commences. This includes parallel development of the functional components in presentation, business logic, data and integration layers, the testing of these components, and their deployment and tuning across operational components.

The functional components developed in the presentation layer are located on web servers, and consist of the web pages that customers see when they connect to the e-business site. Graphic designers create the appearance of this layer through the design of graphical images and the layout of page elements. Web developers then code the site content into this design using technologies such as HTML, DHTML, JavaScript, JSP and ASP, through a range of tools such as Macromedia Dreamweaver and Microsoft Visual Studio. A usability expert is also typically employed to work with the graphic designers and web developers to ensure the presentation layer is simple and easy to use for customers, thus ensuring customer retention. Finally, the presentation layer should be constructed to support all common Internet browsers running on Macintosh and PC platforms to ensure all customers can access the e-business site.

The functional components developed in the business logic layer are used to process customers' requests and apply business-specific rules to appropriate data to produce the required output. These components consist of software code created through custom development or packaged products, and are created by application developers according to the detailed functional design. Once created, components are deployed on application servers according to the operational design. Typically, the business logic layer consists of either open solutions based on J2EE application server products such as WebSphere, iPlanet or BEA WebLogic, or proprietary systems based on C, C++ and COM/DCOM such as many client-server ERP, CRM and financial products. In contrast to open solutions, proprietary – systems typically require an additional integration layer to enable them for customer use over the Internet.

Creating transactional Internet-enabled business logic requires the use of specialist-packaged products or development of custom written code. It is recommended that specialist products that fit requirements be adopted to ensure the solution can be implemented within a short timeframe, thus not delaying the project in the build phase. Additional functionality not included in such products can then be created through customization. Alternatively, if the project requirements cannot be satisfied through deployment of a packaged solution, custom development should be undertaken in the build phase, preferably using open solutions.

The building of the business logic layers requires a database layer for the storage and retrieval of information, such as e-business catalogues and customer and order information. This database layer is located on dedicated hardware servers, and consists of database software installed onto these servers and externally attached storage systems. The database layer is installed and configured by implementation staff members with knowledge of the database product selected in the detailed design. Once these have been installed, specialist database developers work with the application developers to create the design of the database structures to be used by the business logic layer.

Additional systems may be required to participate in the e-business system, such as proprietary products or existing legacy systems. This is achieved through development of an integration layer during the build phase, according to the specifications of the detailed design document. The integration layer is located on separate hardware servers, and consists of integration software products and integration code. This layer is built in parallel with the business logic layer by implementation staff knowledgeable in integration software and integration application developers, and typically requires input from legacy system and product support staff.

Development of design components within each layer is conducted with the participation of testing team members, who work closely with all team members to ensure test plans are written for each component as they are developed. Each test plan documents the component to be tested, the testing conditions in use during the test, the expected input and output for each component, and the results of each testing phase.

As each solution component is completed in the development environment, it is migrated into the testing environment for unit testing to ensure it functions according to the detailed design specifications. The test environment contains duplicated hardware, software, network and security systems from the development environment, and allows for testing to be isolated from development and therefore conducted independently and in parallel.

Following successful completion of unit tests, components are link tested together with related components to ensure correct communication between components. Integration testing is then conducted on the completed set of solution components to determine that the solution satisfies the detailed design requirements. Components are then migrated into the live environment for performance testing to ensure the solution can meet expected levels of demand. This environment consists of the solution components that will be used once the system receives stakeholder approval. If a component fails any stage of the testing process it is returned to the development environment for appropriate changes then retested.

Once the components have passed integration and performance testing, user acceptance testing is conducted in the live environment with a representative group of stakeholders to ensure the solution meets their requirements. Once this is successfully completed, the solution is signed off by stakeholders and becomes ready for deployment into the pilot phase.

It is recommended that user testing by a small group of stakeholders also be conducted during development as this allows the solution to be tuned to more closely meet user requirements. It also allows the project to accommodate any requirements missed during the initial project phases or any subsequent changes in requirements. However, large-scale changes such as switching development methodologies or dramatically altering component functionality, are not recommended as they may seriously impact the successful delivery of the project.

Finally, during the build phase each team member contributes towards the project documentation set. This includes the creation of the test plans and their results, creation of installation and configuration documents for the design components, and a preliminary set of operational management documents detailing how to manage the complete solution. These documents are progressively amended until the handover phase as operational experience is gained with the solution.

1.8 Pilot phase

Once the solution has been built and tested, and passed user acceptance, a pilot is conducted by a representative sample of end users who will utilize the solution in their daily work.

The project manager, technical architect and testing staff assess the ongoing results of this phase, and any modifications that may be required are submitted through the build phase processes to the appropriate staff members. The project staff members also begin training internal support staff in the operation and management of the new solution. This requires input from all project team members, and should be monitored by the project manager and e-business technical architect.

At this stage in the project lifecycle, all functional requirements of the solution should have been delivered. However, solutions frequently require modifications to ensure smooth deployment. These typically involve fixing minor bugs missed during testing, or small changes to the solution to more closely fit requirements. They may also include modifications due to operational issues such as performance, availability and scalability, which may require additional work before the system is put into full live production.

The pilot phase also provides a valuable opportunity to test the transition to the new system for internal staff, and for integrating the new technology with existing systems. Frequently new solutions are swapped in overnight with minimal or no training for staff, with resulting confusion and loss of productivity. Deployment of the solution in a limited pilot allows the business to determine how best to adapt staff work processes to the new system to ensure a smooth transition and to determine training requirements and prepare training materials. It also provides a mechanism to determine how other business technology systems will be affected by the transition to the new system, and allows time to adapt these if required to ensure all technology related issues are solved before implementation.

At this stage in the project lifecycle, major changes to functionality should be avoided, as these will require considerable additional work in new design and build phases, and typically result in considerable delays and greatly increases the chances that the project will not complete successfully.

Such changes can be avoided through management of stakeholder expectations and by ensuring that the correct processes are used throughout the project. This includes involving stakeholders in the initial project planning and requirements gathering phases, by ensuring that the design and auditing phases are properly conducted, and by involving stakeholders in early testing of the solution. Stakeholder management also requires creating awareness of the serious repercussions introduced by requesting major changes in the latter project phases, and by shifting requests for changes or additional functionality into subsequent projects.

1.9 Implementation phase

The implementation phase follows successful deployment and use of the solution in the pilot phase. This phase involves deployment of the solution into 'live' production environments across the company to all appropriate end users and other stakeholders. At this stage in the project lifecycle all requested functionality should be addressed and the stakeholders should have signed off approval for the solution.

Staff members required during the implementation phase typically include infrastructure, implementation and support staff to roll out and tune solution components, development and testing staff to provide additional development and testing services if required, and oversight by the e-business technical architect and project manager. In addition, team members are required to update project documentation throughout the implementation phase.

The implementation phase occurs through a staged deployment of the e-business solution to groups of users, rather than to all users simultaneously. This ensures a manageable transition to the new system without straining available resources and adversely affecting business continuity or affecting existing processes.

This staged deployment in turn requires a set of infrastructure and user deployment processes. Infrastructure deployment processes allow for staged deployment of additional or new hardware and software systems to end users if required, such as new desktop computers and associated systems. User deployment processes are designed to maximize user productivity, and include granting user access to the live production environment, and providing support for users during rollout of the solution, such as training users before changeover to the new system, and providing ongoing assistance once users have migrated.

Finally, during the changeover period the new solution should be monitored for each group of users as it is deployed. This ensures that issues occurring during changeover can be tracked and addressed before subsequent deployment of the solution to additional user groups. This requires infrastructure, development and testing staff be available to optimize performance of the solution as it comes under increased usage, and to correct minor bugs that may occur within the solution.

1.10 Handover phase

Once the solution has been successfully implemented, it is formally handed over to internal staff for ongoing maintenance and support. Project handover involves a process of knowledge transfer, including knowledge of the technical design and implementation, project outcomes, support processes and procedures, and the completed documentation set.

Project handover should include a fixed period of support from critical project members with considerable project input, such as the e-business technical architect and lead developer. This ensures the availability of critical project resources for ongoing knowledge transfer back into the company, and assistance with any technical issues that may arise following implementation.

The final element of project handover requires publishing the complete project documentation set within the company. This provides a reference covering the project history, technical decisions, and solution design, and the deployment and support configurations for internal staff and stakeholders. All documentation and project source code should be supplied on CD-ROM and on the company's Intranet site, allowing ready access for company support staff.

1.11 Project documentation

Following project handover and completion, documentation is required as a knowledge repository for the project, and for the developments of subsequent versions of the e-business system requested by users. In such cases, the documentation provides a detailed understanding of decisions that were made, and the manner in which technologies were implemented, to ensure they do not introduce problems into stable live production systems.

Due to their role in designing and implementing the solution, the e-business technical architect has overall responsibility for the creation and delivery of project technical documentation. Similarly, the non-technical project documentation is the responsibility of the project manager. Non-technical project documentation includes documents concerned with the ongoing management of the complete project by the project manager such as training plans, the project risk register, meeting minutes between project members and company staff, budgets, and the project plan.

The completed documentation should include all outputs created during the project lifecycle. These include the project initiation document, the scope document, the design documents, test plans and test results, installation and configuration documents, and support and training documents. It should also include the source code repository maintained throughout the project.

The project Iinitiation document introduces the reasons for beginning the project, and suggests a proposed solution. These issues are covered through an introduction to the project consisting of an overview of the business issues facing the company, and a general discussion of the high-level business and technical requirements for the project. The discussion of the proposed solution should cover project management and technical aspects, including the preliminary project plan, budget, an assessment of staff skills required for delivering the proposed technology solution, and a preliminary timeframe for the project.

The scope document provides the detailed context to why the project is required and what it should deliver. It expands on the overview of business issues facing the company to include the detailed requirements of all project stakeholders, including internal stakeholders within the company and external users and partner and supplier companies. Requirements are gathered from relevant company and customer sources, divided into business and technical requirements, and summarized through a requirements analysis matrix. A risk management register also accompanies the scope document detailing the risk issues facing the project and risk management plan to cope with these.

The high-level design document provides an overview of the proposed solution. It should incorporate the functional design components, which describe the groups of features provided in the solution, and corresponding operational design components, which describe products and technologies chosen to supply these features. The vendors and product evaluation and selection criteria determined during the research phase may also form part of the high-level design, or be included as a supporting document for complex projects with large numbers of requirements to satisfy.

The detailed design documents describe the blueprint to build the solution through detailed functional and operational design components. Detailed functional design elements include software components, their interactions and interfaces, which are expressed using detailed UML use cases, data models, and component class model diagrams. Detailed operational elements in this design include descriptions of infrastructure systems such as hardware server systems, network systems, security systems, and specific deployment configurations, which are expressed using UML diagrams, network diagrams, and installation, configuration and operation documents for each operational system. The detailed design documents also describe the source code management tool deployed in the project, and the change management processes used to maintain the solution source code and project documents.

The test plan documents detail the testing procedures and tools used during the build phase. These include the test scripts used to test individual components against their intended design, test scripts for communication between components using specified interfaces, and test scripts for the correct functioning of the complete solution against the design specifications and stakeholder requirements. Each test script also includes documented results of each phase of testing.

The installation and configuration documents allow staff members to recreate the solution from its constituent functional and operational components. These include installation processes for operational components such as servers, network devices, development systems, security systems, and software. They also include the subsequent configuration of these once they have been installed, such as performance tuning, load balancing configuration and security hardening, and the setting of run-time parameters.

Finally, the support documents should detail the operational management and support processes and tools required for the ongoing operation of the solution. These include software management systems, such as HP OpenView, and their appropriate configuration, and daily operational processes such as diagnosis and problem resolution, content migration, or security checking processes. Support documents are created during the pilot phase by project staff, in consultation with company support staff. Once the project enters the implementation phase, support documents are refined to accommodate additional support and management requirements discovered during this phase.

Successfully conducting an e-business project requires hundreds of decisions be correctly made throughout each project phase. This in turn requires considerable specialist input from staff members who must plan, design, test, build, integrate and implement the many complex technologies required during the project. Therefore, one of the most critical elements in the success of an e-business project is the quality and skill level of staff members involved.

However, correctly resourcing an e-business project is complicated due to a number of factors, including the current skills shortages within the e-business industry, the rapid pace of change in the technology sector, and the complexity and variety of technologies involved. In addition, the cost of e-business project resourcing is an important factor in the budget as it typically exceeds the hardware and software costs of the project.

Therefore, it is important to understand the types of staff required and their aptitudes and abilities, when to deploy them, and how to source them in order to obtain the correct number of skilled staff appropriate to the project while managing costs and project risks.

2.1 Selecting project staff

Information technology staff can be classified into two general categories, including project staff, and operational staff. Project-based staff are dedicated to the implementation of new technology systems, and are frequently sourced from outside the company. In contrast, operational staff members are dedicated to supporting and maintaining existing company business systems and infrastructure, and are frequently sourced internally. Therefore, when conducting an e-business implementation project it is important to utilize specialist project-based staff who are experienced in new technologies to design and build the solution, and existing operational staff to support and maintain the final solution.

However, selecting the appropriate project and operational staff for each project phase is complicated due to existing hiring and human resources practices, which often utilize stereotypical criteria to select staff members. Such criteria are often not suitable for e-business staff members, who typically defy normal selection criteria.

For example, many of the most successful and influential people in the information technology industry have non-stereotypical backgrounds. Bill Gates co-founded Microsoft after dropping out of university, while Shawn Fanning founded the ground-breaking Napster music sharing business at the age of 19. Bob Metcalfe was an academic who left the Xerox PARC research centre after creating Ethernet networking and founded the 3COM network company, and Jerry Yang and David Filo founded Yahoo while still at university.

Therefore, staff selection necessitates analysing a candidate's skill level without recourse to traditional stereotypes such as age, qualifications, experience, appearance, cultural fit and length of time in projects to determine suitability.

Typically, skilled e-business staff can be distinguished by their tendency to create optimal solutions by balancing risks and rewards to achieve the best possible solution for the task at hand. Such people typically demonstrate rapid delivery of projects in short timeframes, have up-to-date skills, are able to make fast and accurate decisions, and are able to learn new skills quickly. Frequently such staff members are also highly creative and dynamic, have strong problem-solving ability, and are able to create a fast and accurate solution from the business problem at hand. They are usually team players, as their motivation is derived from improving their knowledge and skills, not from competing with their own team members.

In contrast, staff who have spent years delivering a single project with large amounts of staff are typically indicative of a project that has run over time and budget, and should be avoided. Such staff members frequently come from highly structured environments within hierarchical organizations, with a focus on delegation of responsibility through hierarchical management processes, rather than making the fast and complex decisions necessary in successful e-business projects.

Therefore when making staffing decisions careful selection should be utilized to ensure the staff selected are well suited to fast moving implementation projects and have the broad skills necessary for successful e-business implementation.

When assembling an e-business project team, the most critical roles are typically the e-business technical architect, the project manager and the lead developer. Selecting these individuals requires an understanding of the aptitudes and abilities appropriate to each role.

The e-business technical architect

The e-business technical architect is the technical design authority for the project and is responsible for the design, selection and management of the implementation of the solution according to their detailed design. As this input constitutes the core of the project solution, the e-business technical architect is one of the most important roles within the project team.

To ensure project success it is therefore important to hire the services of an expert e-business technical architect with outstanding technical vision. This individual should demonstrate an in-depth and expert knowledge of all aspects of e-business solution selection, design and implementation including technology products, platforms, security, applications, networking, infrastructure and integration. They should also be able to evaluate these issues to achieve a solution that offers the best functionality and value for money for the company.

Therefore, the e-business technical architect should demonstrate a very technical and hands-on approach. This requires they be capable of implementing the systems they design such as installing servers and coding software, rather than just designing systems on paper for others to implement. Typically, they will have implemented complex e-business projects across different parts of the e-business lifecycle, and can work at a rapid pace to deliver projects in less than 12 months, with teams of fewer than 20 staff.

The e-business technical architect must also demonstrate understanding of the business issues facing a company, and the appropriate business uses for technology solutions. They should be used to having their designs externally audited, produce excellent documentation, have a passion for e-business and project success, and be comfortable mentoring other team members. They should also provide excellent references for past work.

As well as the skills listed above, an e-business technical architect should also possess a range of personal qualities to enable them to be highly effective in their role. These include being able to achieve goals on time and in accordance with their stated deliverables, being non-competitive and non-hierarchical, being able to admit mistakes, and being able to create a productive and honest culture. Other personal qualities include reliability, having excellent time management skills, being honest and a good communicator, and being prepared to accept responsibility and put themselves on the line for their decisions. Finally, they should possess high energy levels, have high intelligence and problem-solving ability, the ability to get on with others and work as part of a team, as well as demonstrating strong leadership to technical staff.

The project manager

The project manager also has a critical position within an e-business project. This role focuses on the organization and delivery of the project, and typically includes budget management responsibility for the project. The project manager must work closely with the technical architect and stakeholders from the company to ensure the project is on target for delivery.

To ensure project success the project manager must possess good technical ability and broad knowledge of e-business technologies and platforms, including a strong understanding of e-business concepts and terminology. The more technical the project manager and the more passionate they are about e-business, the greater the likelihood of project success.

The project manager must also understand project management techniques suited to e-business gained through delivery of previous projects with fewer than 20 staff within a 12-month period. They should also have experience with change management and risk management within these projects, and understand how to create a project offering value for money. As they work closely with technical staff, it is also vital that the project manager has a strong understanding of how to fit technology to business requirements and understands the requirements and motivations of technical people. They should therefore be able to follow the instructions of the e-business technical architect to support and resource the technical staff in the course of their work. These skills should be supported with excellent references for their previous work.

A project manager should also possess specific personal qualities related to their position. These include being able to achieve goals on time, delivering on their stated intentions, and being reliable and punctual with excellent time management skills. They should also be non-competitive, flexible, non-hierarchical, and be a good communicator who gets on well with others. The project manager should foster an open non-blaming culture, and project honesty, leadership, and a focus on being a team player. They should therefore be able to admit mistakes and be prepared to put themselves on the line for their decisions. Finally, they should have high intelligence and strong ability to solve problems as they occur, and have a high energy level to drive the project to completion.

The lead developer

The lead developer is also a critical role in the e-business project. This role is responsible for providing specific technical expertise during the build and subsequent phases of the project, and for programming the solution designed by the technical architect. They typically lead other development staff and work closely with the technical architect.

To ensure project success, the lead developer should possess expert knowledge of all aspects of programming in the relevant development languages selected for the project. They must also be very technical, hands on, and understand multiple technology platforms and development technologies. Typically they will have broad experience gained through working on multiple e-business development projects, have worked in different industries, be used to working with fewer than 20 staff, and be accustomed to fast delivery of projects in under 12 months. They should be capable of producing excellent documentation and adhering to source code and change control procedures, and be able to demonstrate a passion for e-business development. Finally, they should be able to supply excellent references in support of their previous work.

A lead developer should also possess a range of relevant personal qualities, including being able to deliver work on time, delivering on what they say, and being reliable and punctual with excellent time management. Other personal attributes include being honest and able to admit mistakes, being focused on their work, non-competitive, non-hierarchical and receptive to suggestions from others. The lead developer must be capable of working as part of a team, get on well with others in a non-blame-centred culture, and mentor other developers. They should also be prepared to put themselves on the line for their work, and have high energy levels, high intelligence, and good all-round problem-solving ability.

2.2 When to deploy project staff

Resourcing appropriate staff for an e-business project requires correct planning and timing for when to hire project and operational staff. This issue is critical to project success, as projects frequently run over time and budget through delays in hiring staff onto a project, hiring staff before they are required, or by hiring staff with inadequate skills during the project. In addition, hiring too many staff onto a project may also negatively impact the project through increased management overhead and an increased risk of hiring inexperienced or poor staff. This may also in turn increase pressure and conflict for expert skilled staff, who must monitor inexperienced staff to locate and rectify mistakes in their work.

E-business projects therefore benefit from smaller numbers of highly skilled staff, frequently restricted to no more than 20 staff members at each stage. However, some projects may require additional staff numbers, such as large content-based projects requiring additional content developers, or large-scale projects with considerable custom development that require additional developers. Staffing numbers can be maintained at appropriate levels by avoiding duplication of resources in the same role, especially duplication of the e-business technical architect, project manager, and lead developer. Instead, productivity should be increased by obtaining the best resource for each role, by avoiding hierarchy and political conflict in the project, and through the use of correct process and due diligence throughout the project.

In addition, staff levels can be managed by employing specific staff members only when needed for specific project phases, and by reducing staff levels as phases complete. This is depicted in Table 2.1.

Table 2.1 Typical project lifecycle staff matrix

Project phase	Internal operational staff	External project staff
Project planning	CTO/CIO Marketing director E-business director Operational director Project manager Other key stakeholders	E-business technical architect
Business and technical requirements	CTO/CIO Marketing director E-business director Operational director Project manager Business analysts Other key stakeholders	E-business technical architect Business analysts (if not available from within the company)
Solution research phase	Project manager Key stakeholders	E-business technical architect
High-level design	Project manager Key stakeholders	E-business technical architect
Audit	Internal auditor	External auditor
Detailed design	Project manager Key stakeholders	E-business technical architect
Build phase	Project manager Support staff Content publishers Key stakeholders	E-business technical architect Lead developer Application developers Product specialists Testing staff Graphic designer Web developers Usability expert Installation staff Technical project manager if required Integration specialists if required
Pilot installation and testing	Project manager Support staff Content publishers Key stakeholders	E-business technical architect Lead developer Application developers Product specialists Test staff Graphic designer Web developers Usability expert Installation staff Technical project manager if required Integration Specialists if required
Implementation	Project manager Support staff Content publishers Key stakeholders	E-business technical architect Lead developer Application developers Test staff Graphic designer Usability expert Infrastructure staff Installation staff Technical project manager if required Integration specialists if required
Handover	CTO/CIO Marketing director E-business director Project manager Operational director Support staff Content publisher Other key stakeholders	E-business technical architect Lead developer Installation staff

As new staff members are deployed into each project phase, it is recommended that they be assessed to determine if they have the aptitudes and abilities required for their role and function within the project environment and team. This trial assessment period should cover one to two weeks, with each team member required to deliver a set of outputs appropriate to their role. For example, the e-business technical architect should begin research and analysis of solutions early in the initial project planning phase, and produce preliminary versions of technical documentation. Similarly, the project manager should start work on the project plan, project scope and risk register as soon as they start.

In addition, trial assessment of outputs should include performance by staff members on tasks appropriate to their role, such as the installation and configuration of systems. If team members cannot perform such tasks, take a long time to deliver such tasks, or avoid making decisions around such tasks, they may have insufficient skills to deliver their elements of the project. This may in turn compromise the project through poor decision-making, lengthened timeframes, and increased costs. If staff cannot deliver appropriate outcomes, they should be retrained or removed, and new staff recruited.

2.3 Obtaining project staff

Operational and project-based staff can be resourced from three sources, including internally within the company, from self-employed contractors, or from external consultancy firms. Alternatively, projects may assemble a composite team from a combination of these three sources.

Internal staff members are typically recruited from existing internal divisions within the company, often via human resources departments. Self-employed contractors can be obtained via external agencies or through major online IT job sites. In addition, a wide range of consultancies can be used to resource a project through project outsourcing or by providing specific project member resources.

Consultancies are available in a broad range of sizes, including very large international firms, medium-sized firms, small firms often operating at a national level, and micro consultancies with a handful of staff. Consultancies frequently work together on projects to mitigate industry skill shortages and reduce the costs of maintaining large amounts of project-based consultants who need to have specific expertise. However, when working with all consultancies, a range of strategies should be employed to maximize the value obtained to ensure greater likelihood of successful project delivery.

Consultancies should be selected to ensure best fit with the project requirements, according to a number of criteria. Due to the complexity and high failure rates in e-business projects, it is important to hire a consultancy specializing in e-business projects and project staff. They should also demonstrate experience conducting similar projects successfully, and be prepared to provide contacts within previous clients to discuss their previous work.

The consultancy should also be dedicated to project-based work rather than operational support and be able to provide skilled consultants at the top of their field. It is advisable to check the quality of staff assigned to the project which may require meeting essential project team members and ensuring they will be dedicated full time to the project. It is also recommended that minimal amounts of administrative and non-technical staff be utilized on the project to avoid bureaucracy and diversion of resources into a delegation-type structure.

Companies should avoid consultancies that focus on coding and development and create poor quality high-level and detailed designs. This approach typically results in the creation of completely customized solutions with minimal use of commercial off-the-shelf technology, which in turn results in vendor lock-in for support contracts to maintain the ongoing viability of the solution. Such development-focused consultancies should therefore be avoided.

It is also recommended that where possible, only one consultancy be engaged to work on a project at a time. Projects utilizing multiple consultancies frequently incur considerable management overhead, and lead to political conflict and lack of accountability for project roles, responsibilities and deliverables. They also frequently lead to the selection and deployment of incompatible technology solutions, or solutions with high maintenance and support requirements, and may therefore seriously jeopardize project success.

Finally, the selection of a consultancy should be geared towards firms willing to create a strong and lasting working relationship that is beneficial to both parties. This ensures better results during the course of the project, and simplifies working together on future projects.

Companies should be prepared to pay a fair price for e-business resourcing services, as inexpensive bids or low hourly rates for staff are typically indicative of low levels of skill. Selecting such consultancies or consultants will typically lead to less competent staff being hired onto the project resulting in delayed projects, failure to achieve project objectives, and cost overruns.

Once a consultancy has been selected, a detailed understanding of project deliverables should be created and agreed by both parties before contracts are signed. It is recommended that a company hire a consultancy on a stage-by-stage basis, with the consultancy committed to single phases at one time. Each stage should then be successfully completed before giving signed approval for successive stages to ensure ongoing control over the project.

The agreement should also allow the company to maintain some control over the technical direction of the project to manage their risk and exposure to the consultancy. This may include conducting some preliminary technical work before engaging the consultancy, such as creating an audited design, to provide a detailed specification of project deliverables. In addition, the company should provide some project members who have an understanding of the business and technical requirements, such as their own project manager and e-business technical architect. This allows the company to reduce project risk by monitoring the progress of the consultancy and ensuring successful delivery against the requirements and design.

However, dividing project responsibility among in-house staff and a consultancy requires a strong degree of collaboration between all parties to prevent the project from failing due to political conflict. Therefore, special attention should be paid to the skill and personal attributes of such staff members involved in interacting with the consultancy.

Once a consultancy has been selected, contracts should be drawn up and signed by both parties. These should be simple, short and in plain English to enable all project staff to clearly understand the project terms and conditions. Penalties should be included if the actions of the consultancy cause the project to run over time and budget. However, contracts should be equitable for both parties to foster a beneficial working relationship. Payment should be made at the end of each project phase or set of deliverables, as this typically leads to better pricing from the consultancy.

Finally, the ongoing operation of the project requires regular meetings between the consultancy and senior stakeholders and technical staff. These are typically weekly and cover ongoing administration, technical planning and management. However, attention in such meetings should not be solely dedicated to problem resolution, as this may foster a negative focus on the working relationship between both parties.

Part Two

E-business technology phases

3 The five phases of e-business adoption

Successful e-business implementation requires a detailed understanding of the technology solutions appropriate to different business scenarios. This enables an e-business technical architect to research and select appropriate e-business solutions and designs for an e-business initiative.

A recent study by IBM (Seeley, 2001) surveyed 21,000 companies across the world to determine the extent of their adoption of e-business technologies. Results from this survey showed that companies adopted common sets of e-business solutions corresponding to a range of business scenarios.

The study classified e-business solutions into five phases, comprising an e-business lifecycle. This lifecycle follows a company's progression from adopting e-business technology to reach more customers in a more efficient manner through to the final goal of optimizing all internal and external systems and processes to respond in real time to the changing demands of customers (Seeley, 2001). This progression through the five phases of e-business adoption is depicted in Figure 3.1.

Figure 3.1 The e-business lifecycle

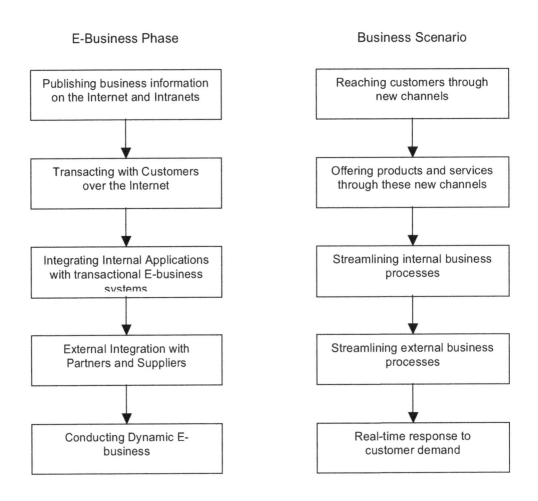

The e-business lifecycle starts with Internet publishing, where the company gains a presence on the Internet through publication of marketing and corporate materials, and uses internal Intranets to publish corporate information to staff. Internet publishing also includes the use of corporate portals to simplify publishing and includes information from corporate applications, and the use of content management systems to create and manage large volumes of rapidly changing content for distribution to multiple channels. This phase allows a company to realize new channels to communicate with customers and their own internal staff, and achieve considerable savings from shifting the presentation and distribution of information from paper-based forms to Internet-based content.

As a company gains more experience and understanding of the benefits of e-business technologies to reach new channels, they progress to using these channels for transacting business directly with their customers. These transactions typically take the form of providing existing and new products and services.

The transaction phase is then extended to the internal application integration phase. This phase focuses on deploying Internet technology further into the business to realize efficiency gains within existing internal processes. Disparate corporate systems are integrated to automate transactional processes required for online transactions, such as account settlement and invoicing. Integration is also pursued to improve the speed and efficiency of internal processes to make the company more efficient and productive, and hence more competitive. Internal integration is also used to integrate companies during corporate acquisitions and mergers.

The fourth phase focuses on integrating internal corporate systems with external partners and suppliers to achieve further efficiencies in areas such as order processing, invoicing and fulfilment. This phase seeks to realize greater corporate efficiencies and savings through refinements to internal processes and external interactions with partners and suppliers.

Ultimately, the company seeks to become completely responsive to customer demand through the ability to conduct dynamic e-business. The aim of this fifth phase is to achieve a tight focus on the needs of the customer by synchronizing changing customer demand with internal processes and external partner and suppliers to better meet changing customer needs.

However, IBM discovered that over 80 per cent of the 21 000 companies surveyed were still in the first two phases of e-business. In addition, EAI Journal (Editorial, 2001) reported the results of a survey by Hurwitz of 600 enterprises, which found that only 10 per cent had integrated their most mission-critical business processes, and 45 per cent had not started an integration strategy. The results from these surveys indicate there is still considerable scope for the adoption of advanced e-business technologies within business.

The following sections discuss these five phases of e-business adoption. Each section introduces the set of interrelated issues required for implementing e-business at each stage of the e-business lifecycle. These issues include the business background motivating adoption of each e-business phase, the benefits of adopting each phase, the critical technologies comprising each phase and the features and functions required when selecting products for each phase. The discussion of each phase also includes high-level designs pattens, the key benefits and limitations of the technologies, and finally, common vendors offering products suitable for deployment in e-business projects in each phase.

4   Phase 1: Internet-based e-business publishing

Internet-based publishing is the first phase of the e-business lifecycle. This phase involves a company providing corporate and marketing information to customers over the public Internet and through Intranets to their own staff on private internal corporate networks.

The benefits of Internet and Intranet-based e-business publishing include providing companies with a simple and inexpensive mechanism for information distribution to their target audience of customers, partners and suppliers, and internal staff. In contrast to most traditional channels Internet and Intranet e-business publishing has the ability to reach a widespread audience, and allows information to be created and published online considerably quicker than traditional means. It can also reach a much larger audience for less cost, and removes the high cost of creation and distribution of paper-based publishing methods.

Content published online can be targeted to reach multiple audiences through different channels such as mobile phone or digital TV with minimal changes. It can also simultaneously reach audiences locally, nationally and internationally. Additional functionality can be added to published information to provide business benefits beyond traditional media, such as searchable telephone lists, or online training systems. Correcting and updating Internet-based publications is also quicker, simpler and much more affordable than traditional publishing mechanisms.

Internet and Intranet publishing can also be used to augment existing manual publishing processes. For example, paper-based company reports are required by regulatory authorities to be sent to shareholders. Such documents can be published on Intranets and Internet sites in addition to their printed form, thus reaching a much wider target audience. Additional financial statements or environmental compliance reports can also be made available to groups who would not normally receive such information but who may have an interest in it. This then assists a company in maintaining a public presence and brand.

For example, a company publishes large volumes of information to customers via multiple channels, including mobile, email, an Internet site, print and digital TV, on new products and services. Internal staff require access to this information, as well as staff-specific internal content such as product development plans, company newsletters, staff phone directories, and customer service information from across the business. This information must be accessible from financial systems, marketing systems, CRM systems, and e-business systems. This publishing process is depicted in Figure 4.1.

Figure 4.1 Internet-based e-business publishing

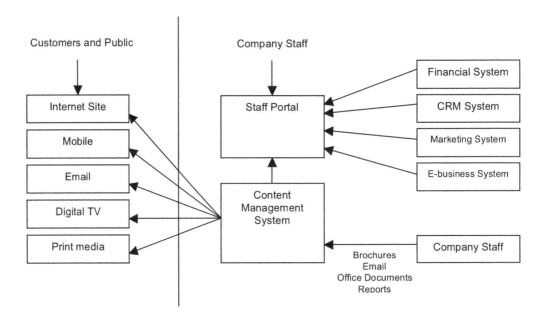

In the preceding example, the company utilizes a content management system to provide customers with changing content across all channels. An internal portal system provides employees with this content from the content management system, and customer and other business information from multiple internal sources. This provides customers with the content they require and staff with information required for their jobs from all areas of the business.

4.1 Key technologies used

In order to publish content online, companies require a solution capable of creating, managing, and delivering content in multiple formats to internal staff and externally to customers and suppliers.

Internet – and Intranet-based publishing involves assembling information from different sources, transforming it into Internet-ready content, transmitting it to users, and displaying the content. This process is depicted in Figure 4.2.

Figure 4.2 Online publishing process

Each step in this process relies on a set of common, freely available standards and technology components that define the Internet.

The Internet was initially developed in the 1960s to connect researchers between universities in the USA, with participation and sponsorship from the Defense Advanced Projects Research Agency (DARPA) now called ARPA. This early system consisted of multiple interconnected networks running different data transport protocols. As networks expanded and multiplied, a common protocol was required to ensure all participants could communicate using the systems available at that time, including email, shared files, and remote computing resources access systems. This led to the evolution of the TCP/IP networking standard, and its widespread adoption in the 1980s.

Defining the standards responsible for the fundamental infrastructure of the Internet occurs through submission of proposals to the Internet Engineering

Task Force, a non-profit body responsible for network and infrastructure standards on the Internet. This group votes to accept new standards based on technical merit, with standards published through freely available RFC (Request for Comment) documents.

Through this process, researchers gradually added additional services on top of the TCP/IP transport protocol, such as the World Wide Web system invented in the early 1990s by Tim Berners-Lee at the CERN-institute in Switzerland. This system described a simple mechanism for the transport and display of information across TCP/IP network, using the Hypertext Transport Protocol (HTTP).

The HTTP protocol was designed to transport 'Hypertext' documents, written in the HTML display language. HTML, derived from the high-end SGML language (Standard Generalized Mark-up Language) provided simple 'tags', or annotations within documents to describe how document content should be displayed. Special tags pointed to other related documents, creating an interconnected 'web' of documents, hence the name World Wide Web. The web browser, a software application dedicated to rendering HTML content on screen, then handled display of the document content. Transport of HTML documents to web browsers utilised the services of simple web server applications, dedicated to serving pages via the HTTP protocol.

In contrast to other content display and transport systems, the HTML/Hypertext system was designed to be independent of underlying operating systems and platforms, and accessible from any connected network. This resulted in a simple and affordable system for providing information, and led to the rapid uptake of Internet technologies by business following popularization of the Netscape Web browser by Netscape Communications Corporation in 1994.

HTML documents also offer the ability to include non-textual content within the document, such as images and sound. Common image formats include the GIF (Graphics Interchange Format) and JPEG (Joint Photographic Experts Group) formats. Common audio formats include MP3 (Motion Pictures Expert Group Audio Layer 3), and video formats include the MPEG 2 and 4 (Motion Pictures Expert Group Layers 2 and 4) formats, AVI and Windows media, and Apple QuickTime formats.

Subsequent developments of content standards are overseen by the World Wide Web Consortium (W3C). In a similar process to that used by the IETF, this group assesses and approves recommendations for new Internet content standards. Once approved, these new standards are made available to individuals or companies free of royalty payments. Vendors can then implement these standards within their products, resulting in a broad base of compatible products from many vendors. This results in increased competition within the industry and the delivery of higher quality products. It also ensures consistency and compatibility between competing products.

In addition to these standards and applications, Internet-based publishing relies on the content searching function provided by search engines. Search engines allow users to locate content either in Intranet systems, on Internet sites. The search engine locates and classifies the content, and creates a summarized index of all content attributes such as date created, author, type of document, size and location, contents of document. Users enter search queries into the search engine, which searches through the index for all occurrences of the search query and returns the relevant page and its link.

4.2 Types of publishing systems

Three different technology solutions have evolved to provide online publishing functionality, with each solution targeting different publishing requirements. These include custom Internet and Intranet publishing systems, corporate portals, and enterprise content management systems. Each system is differentiated by the mechanisms they employ to manage different forms of content, which include static and dynamic application-based content. Static content typically includes largely unchanging written content or images presented as a series of pages. Dynamic application-based content consists of information sourced from data stored and maintained within enterprise applications.

Custom Internet and Intranet systems were the first online publishing systems used. They systems are assembled from web servers, tools to create and manage HTML content, and manual processes required to publish content. Such systems provide simple functionality for creating, managing and displaying static content. Custom Internet and Intranet systems are generally suitable for businesses with small amounts of static page-based content that changes infrequently. These solutions are generally unsuitable for the display of application-based content, as this requires considerable additional customisation to integrate with enterprise applications, and is more suited to a commercially available portal product.

Portal systems evolved to address some of the limitations of early custom Internet and Intranet solutions, such as heavy reliance on error prone manual site publishing processes. Portals automate these processes within a single product, and allow a company to efficiently aggregate and display large volumes of static and application-based corporate information. This information is displayed to Internet and Intranet – users as customizable elements within a web browser interface. Portal systems are suitable for businesses where employees require Intranet access to large volumes of application-based corporate information, and large volumes of static page-based information that undergoes a moderate degree of change. They are also suitable for Internet sites where customers require large amounts of static page-based content and some application-based content with a moderate degree of change. If this content is undergoing rapid addition, deletion or modification, the portal system should be integrated with a dedicated enterprise content management system.

Enterprise content management systems address a different set of publishing requirements, centred on storing and displaying huge volumes of rapidly changing content. These systems evolved from early document management systems that were designed to scan, store and manage documents, removing the need for paper-based business processes. They were then extended to support multiple document types and manage rapidly changing content within Intranets and Internet sites.

Content management systems are suitable for custom Intranets and Internet sites where employees and customers require access to large amounts of rapidly changing of static page-based content, but no application-based content. They are also suitable for integration with portal systems to support large volumes of rapidly changing static and application-based content. If large volumes of transactional e-business or very high volumes of application-based content are required on an Internet site, integration is typically required with enterprise application integration technologies.

4.3 Custom Internet and Intranet publishing systems

Internet sites are comprised of linked HTML pages of related content, such as descriptions of a company's products and services, and public company information. Internet systems allow companies to reach their customers and suppliers with relevant information in an affordable and simple manner. They also provide a convenient central point for information distribution and management, allowing a company to maintain a consistent public image and brand.

In contrast, Intranet sites consist of a similar system, but with content specific to the needs of internal staff. Intranet sites are available to staff within the company over their internal private networks, and provide a centralized source of corporate information.

Custom Internet and Intranet systems are designed to satisfy the online publishing requirements of small – to medium-sized volumes of content, or for companies wishing to experiment with this medium on a small budget. They provide a quick entry into e-business publishing and are very affordable and simple to create with the skills required to create such systems and publish content readily available. Content can be published to either system depending on the nature of the content and its intended audience. Typically companies restrict Intranet content to internal use only, while public content is for Internet use.

For example, a company maintains an Internet site for customers and an Intranet site for staff. Content is authored using a number of tools, tested to ensure it is correct and displays correctly, then published to the appropriate Internet or Intranet site. Users connect to either site and browse content by following links, or alternatively by searching for content. This process is depicted below in Figure 4.3.

Figure 4.3 Internet and Intranet publishing process

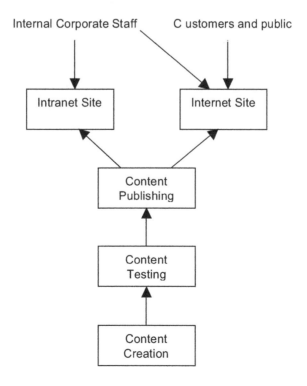

In the preceding example, content is created from corporate information sources such as internal reports, and authored into Internet formats and linked into a series of content pages. The content is then tested to determine that it will display properly, and published to the appropriate Internet or Intranet site. Internal staff can view either site, while customers and members of the public are restricted to the Internet site.

4.3.1 Key technologies used

Custom Internet and Intranet sites utilize core Internet components including web servers designed to service HTTP requests for HTML content, web browsers for content display, and sets of tools to publish content in the different Internet content formats, such as HTML editors to create and manage pages. Sites should also include search engines to allow users to search for relevant content.

What to look for in online publishing products

Online publishing products require support for a structured site creation process. This includes steps for the creation of site content, content testing, site management, and site publishing.

Creation of Internet and Intranet sites progresses from an initial site layout template. The template details the major categories of content to be displayed on the site, and is structured as a hierarchical layer of pages grouped by topic. The home page, represents the first page on the site a visitor will encounter, and must therefore display all the content areas in a simple and readily accessible form. Often this page will include frequently changing topical content to maintain user interest and encourage repeat viewing. Successive layers of the site structure guide site visitors to different areas of content, with cross-links to other site areas. This allows users to browse content in an efficient and fast manner.

It is recommended that a site usability expert should be employed to create the site layout template and website content. This role involves guiding development of the site to ensure that content is manageable and easy to find for users, and that customers have a positive experience when visiting the site and are therefore more likely to return.

The site layout is populated with content using content creation tools. These include HTML editors, with the ability to create site pages, embed images in pages, and create links to audio and video content. Images, audio and video require initial formatting into the correct Internet standard formats using image, sound or video manipulation tools. This process also ensures that the files are optimized so they load quickly into a user's browser.

The HTML editor should include site management functionality, to facilitate maintenance of the site layout. This tool maintains a database of the site structure, page content and assets (including images, audio and video files), and the links between pages. If a page is moved within the site, the site management system restructures each page to accommodate the change. This dramatically reduces the amount of manual changes required when alterations are made to the site, and minimizes errors in content. Advanced products will also assist in managing the complete website production process, including providing team-based collaboration and communication, and file management facilities.

Once all pages are complete, the site is published to an Intranet or Internet web server using file transport systems such as the File Transfer Protocol (FTP) or WebDAV (Distributed Authoring and Versioning). Publishing to a web server may be supported by additional functions such as site management engines, and integrated search engines. In addition, delivery of video content may be provided through specialist web servers supporting real-time delivery, or streaming, of video and audio.

Web servers may also include support for scripting languages, which are used to provide interactive functions in the sites. These typically include functionality such as serving content in multiple languages to users from different countries. Site scripting systems also allow sites to be connected to database back-ends to provide a simplified, structured mechanism to store site assets and content. This also allows for simplification of the publishing process. As page links are contained as references within the database, and not encoded within each page, changes to site structure do not require manual changes within each page. Common dynamic scripting languages include the simple PHP (Personal Home Page) system designed for websites, PERL (Practical Extraction and Reporting Language), a highly advanced scripting language ideally suited for processing textual information, and the JSP (Java Server Pages) and ASP (Microsoft Active Server Pages) scripting systems.

Web servers can also be extended through the addition of software written to support web server-programming interfaces. These interfaces allow web servers to provide additional automated functionality, such as online forms to solicit customer feedback. Common web server programming interfaces include the advanced Java Servlet standard, or proprietary programming languages such as the ISAPI (Internet Information Server Application Programming Interface) and NSAPI (Netscape Application Programming Interface) standards.

Internet and Intranet systems must also include management and administration functions to enable the capture and reporting of site usage statistics. These typically involve additional applications that read web sever log files and generate reports on the nature of user accesses to the sites. This information is invaluable in determining the usage patterns of customers, and hence optimize a site to better suit their needs.

Finally, Internet and Intranet search engines, available as part of the web server or as standalone servers, should provide the ability to search all content types on the site, including HTML pages and downloadable content such as Adobe PDF or Microsoft Word files.

4.3.2 High-level designs of Internet and Intranet systems

Designs for Internet and Intranet systems must provide availability and scalability to ensure continual content provision, and to support content creation and management processes.

Availability and scalability are provided using one – or two-tier web architectures. One-tier architectures feature deployments of single web servers, with reliability features such as RAID 5 storage systems to preserve operation of the system in event of disk failure, and error correcting memory to minimize system downtime resulting from memory failure. Scalability is provided by a combination of multi-threaded web servers and multi-processor server hardware.

Two-tier architectures extend the previous one-tier design to include a back-end database for reliable and scalable storage and generation of site content. Additional availability and scalability features include the use of database clustering for higher performance and fail-over support.

The scalability and reliability of either architecture can be extended using network load balancing of multiple web servers. This requires extension of content publishing to all servers simultaneously, with identical content stored on each server.

High-level designs must support the e-business content publishing process, from authoring to testing to deployment. Once site developers have authored content, it is placed into a development environment, which is a copy of the live Internet or Intranet system used for developing new content and features.

Content is previewed in the development environment to ensure it functions correctly, and then migrated to a staging environment. This environment is identical to the development environment, but used by business staff responsible for the sites for viewing, testing and approving Internet and Intranet content. This enforces a change control process to ensure that only correctly functioning and approved content is made available to end users. It also allows for separate development of advanced functionality, such as online forms, to minimize potential impacts on live systems.

Once content has been approved, it is migrated to the production environment to become 'live'. Users then access the production server to view the new content. Access to development and staging servers is prevented for casual users to maintain the security of unapproved content.

Limited security can be enforced within the design using access control lists (ACLs) on the web server. These restrict user access to regulated content by prompting users for their username and password. Security of content in transit between a user and a web server can be assured using SSL technology to encrypt all communication.

All designs require an understanding of hardware, network and DNS design issues, and network, host and application layer security. For a detailed discussion of these issues, see part three.

The following designs depict online publishing systems for one-tier corporate Internet and Intranet sites, and two-tier database driven Internet and Intranet sites. Each design includes the ability to support extension through additional functionality, including facilities such as automatic content migration, search engines, and advanced dynamic content types such as online forms.

High-level design for one-tier Internet and Intranet publishing solution

A standard design for a combined corporate Internet and Intranet site is depicted in Figure 4.4. This design is suitable for small to medium sized static page-based content requirements, and is capable of supporting web server and search engine software from different vendors.

This design incorporates development and test servers within the corporate network, an internal Intranet server, and an Internet server within the De Militarized Zone (DMZ) for secured public access. The DMZ restricts external user access by allowing access to the production web server while denying access to internal corporate systems.

Content is created on development servers and migrated to staging servers for testing. Once approved, content is migrated to the production Internet or Intranet web servers. Migration to the Internet site may require additional network ports opened on the firewall to allow one-way traffic between the Internal and DMZ networks from the staging to live servers.

An Internet search engine for indexing and searching the Internet site is located on the DMZ, with a similar Intranet search engine located on the internal corporate network. A single staging search engine is required for staging Internet and Intranet sites hosted on the corporate internal network. A development search engine is not required, as site developers rarely require this functionality. It is recommended that live web servers be deployed with live search engines on separate hardware, as search engine content indexing can seriously impact web server performance.

All Intranet servers are located within the corporate network behind the firewall. Although these servers are not exposed to the public Internet, they should be configured with standard high security features in the event that they are shared with partners and suppliers through a private Extranet. In such circumstances, the servers participating in the Extranet should be placed within a separate DMZ network.

Note that development and staging servers can incorporate both the Intranet and Internet sites on the same hardware through a process known as multi-homing. Multi-homing is supported by all major Internet server software products, and allows for consolidation of sites and the elimination of redundant hardware. When deploying multi-homed sites, it is recommended that each site utilize the same server IP address, to minimize waste of IP addresses. This also simplifies DNS records and DNS management, and permits simple future migration of sites to new server technologies.

The combined Internet and Intranet design is depicted in Figure 4.4.

Figure 4.4 High-level design for combined Internet and Intranet one-tier e-business publishing system

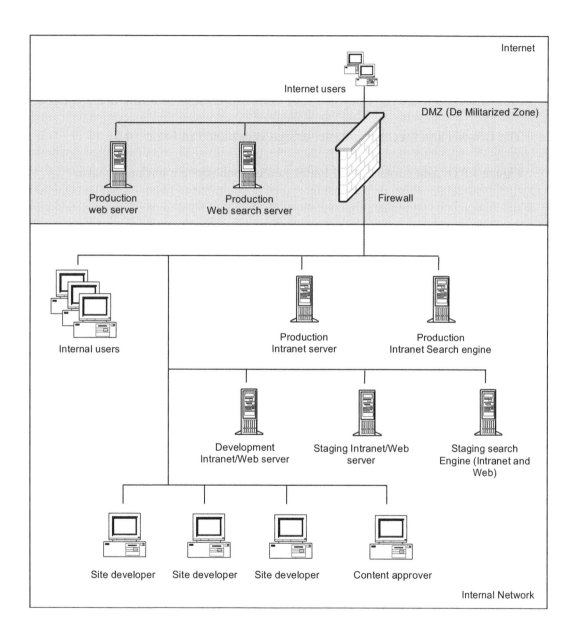

High level design for two-tier Internet and Intranet publishing solution

This design extends the one-tier Internet and Intranet design depicted above using a two-tier web architecture for Internet and Intranet sites. This design includes an additional tier used to store site content within a database for retrieval in response to user requests.

As with the preceding designs, this configuration utilizes multi-homing to locate development and staging Internet and Intranet sites on the same systems. In addition, development and staging environments consolidate the content database within the same server to minimize unnecessary infrastructure, as they do not typically experience high-performance demands compared to the live systems.

The two-tier Internet and Intranet design is depicted in Figure 4.5.

Figure 4.5 Dynamic Internet and Intranet online-publishing e-business system

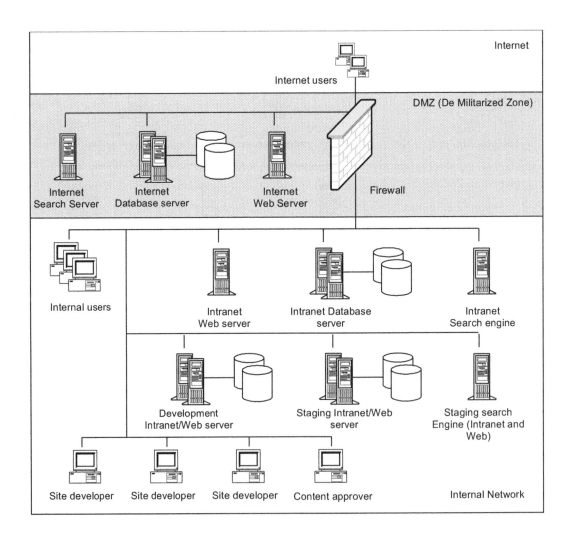

4.3.3 Benefits and limitations of Internet and Intranet publishing solutions

Custom Internet and Intranet publishing systems offer affordable and simple technology to create and publish static content. They typically have minimal hardware and software requirements, and can be extended to support advanced functionality, such as search engines or online forms.

However, these systems suffer from a number of limitations such as lack of control over content, including lack of document versioning, automated authoring and approval workflow processes, and the ability to automatically convert documents into multiple publishing formats. Therefore, as the volume of content, its rate of change, and site complexity increase, the manual site creation and maintenance processes create a bottleneck for publishing and maintenance.

Using site management tools may alleviate some of this bottleneck, but as content volumes increase the costs and features of advanced software such as portal systems and enterprise content management systems typically outweigh these limitations. Portal and content management systems also dramatically reduce the number of errors in the content production process.

In addition, larger companies typically require that staff from several divisions publish content online. Using custom Internet and Intranet systems limits the ability to distribute this publishing function throughout the company, due to the need for specialist online publishing skills. This function is normally held within a specialist-publishing unit with the required expertise, which can become a bottleneck for large volumes of rapidly changing content.

Custom Internet and Intranet systems also frequently prove inadequate for accessing and displaying application-based content. This typically requires considerable customized development effort to extend Internet and Intranet software, using proprietary web server development interfaces such as NSAPI, ISAPI or Apache modules. This approach results in 'fragile' systems that must be manually altered to compensate for changes to internal enterprise applications. In contrast, vendors typically maintain their portal products to remain current with enterprise application integration solutions and enterprise applications such as CRM or ERP systems.

4.3.4 Vendors of Internet and Intranet software

Table 4.1 lists software products used in Internet and Intranet e-business publishing systems. It should be noted that due to the large number and complexity of vendors available, this list is not exhaustive and should be used as a guide only before detailed product research is undertaken.

Table 4.1 Vendors of Internet and Intranet publishing products

Vendor	Internet and Intranet publishing products
HTML editors	
Adobe	GoLive
Macromedia	Dreamweaver MX
Microsoft	FrontPage
Image editors	
Adobe	Photoshop, Photoshop Elements
Corel	CorelDraw Graphics Suite
Macromedia	Fireworks
Open Source	GIMP (GNU Image Manipulation Program)
Site management	
Adobe	GoLive
Macromedia	Dreamweaver MX
Browsers	
Netscape	Netscape Communicator
Microsoft	Internet Explorer
Omni Group	OmniWeb
Opera	Opera
Web servers	
Apache Group	Apache Web Server
iPlanet	iPlanet Enterprise Server
Microsoft	Internet Information Server (IIS)
Search engines	
AltaVista	AltaVista Enterprise Search
Autonomy	Autonomy
Inktomi	Inktomi Search Engine
Verity	Verity Search Engine

4.4 Portal systems

Portal systems are integrated online publishing solutions, which typically contain most of the functionality required for publishing static and application-based content to Internet and Intranet sites. This functionality is often available through rapid out-of-box deployments.

Portal systems provide advanced integration and publishing functionality to amalgamate all sources of corporate information. This is then published as customized content accessed by users through web browsers, which the portal can update in real time to staff members via an Intranet, or to customers and external partners and suppliers via the Internet or an Extranet. Portals are designed to support large amounts of both static and application-based content published over an Intranet and large amounts of static content and moderate amounts of application content over the Internet. They can also manage moderate amounts of rapidly changing content, or can be integrated with content management systems for more demanding content requirements.

Portal systems provide considerable benefits within an organization for the management and distribution of information. Because they contain features to automate the distribution of critical information throughout the enterprise, portal systems save users considerable time when locating and accessing company information. They provide a centralized, easily managed source of consistent corporate information and corporate identity for workers distributed across different locations, and provide central access to corporate information for roaming/remote access users. They also reduce the costs for management of knowledge and information within the company and for its partners and customers (Borck, 2000).

Portal systems also allow companies to save on software installation and support costs. Companies typically spend considerably amounts of time managing multiple interfaces into enterprise information sources on staff computers. These include separate database clients, email clients, file browsers, and mainframe clients (Bhatt and Fenner, 2001). Consolidating access to these information sources into a browser reduces the need to install and support many potentially conflicting products, and reduces licensing costs. They are also increasingly being used to transfer work processes that formerly relied on paper-based information into the new Internet and Intranet systems (Mears, 2001c).

For example, a company uses a portal system to provide access to corporate email, Internet and Intranet content, electronic employee message boards, business intelligence reports from corporate systems such as data warehouses,

CRM, and ERP systems, and give users the ability to publish Intranet content from anywhere within the company. This process is depicted in Figure 4.6.

Figure 4.6 Corporate information access via a portal solution

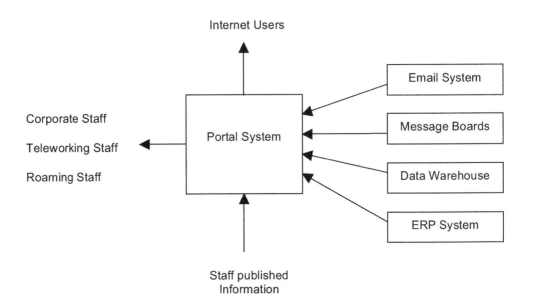

In the preceding example, Internet and Intranet users access the portal and select content areas of interest. The portal then assembles these into customized pages using predefined templates, or alternatively users select how the information should display in their pages. Pages may include components of static, page-based content such as quarterly reports published into the portal by internal staff, and application-based content components, such as a query interface into a CRM system. The portal solution displays the static content within the user's browser, and retrieves the application content as requested, such as when a user requests customer details. Internet users are typically given restricted access to fewer application-based content items for security reasons.

4.4.1 Key technologies used

Borck (2000) classified portals into either consumer portals providing news, email, and search engines to Internet users, or enterprise portals providing personalized views of corporate data, collaboration systems, and access to corporate applications and processes.

Consumer portals are typically used to provide consumer-centric systems for Internet users (e.g. www.yahoo.com or www.hotmail.com) and are typically not used by companies, and thus not discussed in this book.

Enterprise portals are created with similar technologies to Internet and Intranet designs. Users interact with the portal via an HTML/DHTML web interface provided by a web server. This server in turn communicates with the back-end portal server, which manages portal business logic functions, user and security services, content storage systems, and integration systems (Homan, Sanchez and Klima, 2001). Portals are typically created as two or three-tier Internet applications, using either COM/DCOM technology, or Java J2EE technology to provide application logic.

What to look for in a portal solution

Selecting an appropriate portal product is complicated by the rapid market-driven changes in vendor products, and the large number of portal product– vendors, currently more than 100 (Mears, 2001c). In addition, products are described using multiple classification systems (see Fitzgerald, 2001; Mears, 2001c; Upton, 2001). However, analysis of portal features indicates these different categorizations are merging as vendors adopt similar features to their competitors, and the portal marketplace matures.

Portal product selection requires careful understanding of product features and enterprise requirements. However, not all products are capable of supporting all enterprise class features. This may result in a company selecting multiple products to meet the requirements of different company divisions. However, this is not a recommended strategy, as it results in isolated systems with pockets of data serving specific users, and may result in problems integrating between the different portal products.

Enterprise portal products typically provide seven components to provide a comprehensive set of portal services. These include integration services, personalization services, content management services, collaboration services, business intelligence features, administration and user management services, and security systems.

Integration services allow the portal to integrate with existing corporate information sources such as databases, existing websites, legacy mainframes, and ERP systems. This integration is typically achieved through vendor-specific proprietary integration adapters, which connect the portal product to each enterprise information source. However, such connector systems may lack integration features required to retrieve information from applications distributed across the company, necessitating standalone Enterprise Application Integration systems. Integration services should also provide single sign-on for all corporate applications through the corporate directory services. This allows users to log in to the portal, which uses their credentials to access permitted corporate systems.

Personalization services allow staff members to select and display the information relevant to themselves through customized home pages. Personalization services are typically made available through subscription and notification processes, which notify the user when a new or changed information resource has become available in the portal. Personalization services should be integrated with the portal security systems to ensure controlled access to application information.

Content management services allow the portal to integrate sources of content. This service is comprised of a set of technologies including directory services, search services, and content publishing features.

Directory services provide a directory server, such as LDAP, to store metadata, which is used to define the types and locations of information resources within the enterprise. This provides a centralized means to locate resources through a structured overview of the total enterprise resources, including diverse resources such as Internet and Intranet sites, legacy systems, ERP systems or CRM systems.

Search services build searchable indexes of content such as internal and external websites. Employees subsequently conduct searches on these indexes to quickly locate relevant information.

Publishing features allow users to enter and manage different forms of information in the portal. Template driven publishing is the preferred method, incorporating predefined templates used to enter information. This reduces the publishing burden for non-technical users, and allows for efficient distribution of the publishing functions throughout the enterprise. Templates should be created through included application development tools, along with graphical utilities to integrate templates with appropriate data sources. Products should also include predefined business logic components for automating common publishing tasks.

Collaboration services provide systems to increase employee productivity using workflow and interaction tools. These include email tracking and indexing, workplace communities for shared discussions and virtual meeting rooms, and task lists.

Business intelligence services provide tools to analyse information held in the system, including accessing data warehouse, online analytical processing, and data mining functions from existing corporate resources. This service is an important aspect of portals, as it allows employees across a company access to vital analytical information.

Portal administration is best achieved through a web browser, and should integrate with corporate directory servers. It should also support single-sign-on (SSO) allowing one-time entry of usernames and passwords to access resources. This may be required for accessing the portal from different locations (e.g. Internet and Intranet), and for integration with other corporate systems, or with partner/supplier systems.

User management services provide membership services for the creation and management of users and their access rights in the portal. These are then used by the security services, which provide the ability to regulate access based on the user identity and type of information being accessed.

In addition to these seven components, it is also recommended that portal solutions utilise or support J2EE-based application servers. This ensures the solution can utilize the J2EE Java Connector Architecture and Java Message Service for direct integration with Enterprise Application Integration systems for higher performance, scalability, and reliability.

Support for J2EE application servers also permits companies to capitalize on more rapid vendor development of the portal solution features. This occurs through the vendor utilizing development productivity improvements offered by Java, and by being able to rely on the underlying application server reliability, scalability and availability facilities.

4.4.2 High-level designs for portal systems

Enterprise portal systems utilize two – or three-tier Internet application architectures. This allows portal solutions to incorporate availability and scalability features, and integrate with existing Internet and Intranet infrastructure systems.

Typically the first tier is responsible for delivering content to a user. This presentation layer can deploy content in multiple formats for different devices such as HTML for web browsers, WML for WAP phones, or SMS text messaging.

Typically the second tier houses the portal server business logic, which utilizes the seven portal components discussed in the preceding section to transform static and application information into content for display via the presentation layer. The user management and security functions are enhanced through integration with corporate directory servers, which store user information and security attributes. Data processed by the portal server is stored in the third tier database system.

The portal server also includes application integration systems to interface to back-end corporate applications. These systems are typically integrated into the second, business logic tier, and employ custom-built integration adapters. Alternatively, products based on J2EE application servers utilize industry standard integration technologies such as JMS and JCA to achieve integration with a wide range of enterprise applications and data sources.

Portal designs frequently require very high scalability and robustness, as they are typically deployed as mission-critical business tools and therefore face considerable performance demands. Scalability and robustness are achieved through the use of scalable clustered database back-ends for content storage, and network load balancing for very high scalability and availability of first tier web servers. In addition, second tier portal servers may be clustered for redundancy and increased performance, or alternatively use J2EE application servers for transaction management, application integration, and clustering of portal functions across multiple servers for very high scalability and availability.

These high-level designs allow for reconfiguration of the different layers to support the requirements of different portal products. For example, some products may be deployed using a one-tier architecture, with all functional units deployed on one server. This architecture is recommended for development and staging environments, as it reduces hardware and management requirements. However, this configuration does not provide enough scalability or reliability for live production systems. Two-tier designs may also be used in some products, but are typically less scalable than three-tier designs. This design variation evolved from early Internet architectures utilizing proprietary solutions directly integrated with web server programming interfaces, and is currently being superseded by modern three-tier architectures.

Portal designs also support provision of content to external partners and suppliers or to customers through private Extranet networks. This design variation utilizes high security connections between participant firewalls, with additional authentication systems to validate the identity of participants, and authorization systems to control access to subsets of the total portal information.

Similarly, portal content available to customers over the Internet incorporates security systems to restrict access to critical portal content and components. This is achieved through network security systems, and access control within the portal product. Typically, products define a subset of total content available to Internet users, and make this available through dedicated portal servers in the secure DMZ network.

The following designs provide two-tier and three-tier architectures for Portal products. Due to the considerable variety of products, these designs are offered as a reference guide only.

High-level design for moderate usage two-tier portal solution

The two-tier portal design depicted in Figure 4.7 is intended for portals subject to moderate to medium levels of usage. This design is intended to give access to corporate content for internal employees via an Intranet, external partners and suppliers via an Extranet, and select customers or roaming employees over the Internet.

Presentation and business logic functions are incorporated into the portal servers, with data storage provided by separate storage servers. The internal portal server is for use by employees, and partners and suppliers connecting via a secure Extranet connection. A search server indexes all portal content and allows user searching for relevant content.

The internal portal server connects to the portal integration server to retrieve information stored within the enterprise applications. Content authors and approvers create and approve other content for display through the portal. They also define and approve content suitable for publishing to customers over the Internet. The internal portal server then publishes this content to the Internet portal server.

This design also offers integration between the portal and back-end corporate applications such as ERP systems, financial systems, and CRM systems. If additional integration is required, enterprise application integration systems can be incorporated. Security is provided through the DMZ network, firewall, and internal network intrusion detection servers. These monitor all network traffic to detect suspicious activity. Authentication of users and authorization of their access to information is provided through integration with the corporate directory server using the LDAP protocol.

This design also provides a customer internet portal through a first tier presentation server in the DMZ. This server connects to the internal portal server to retrieve content and utilise portal services. This allows the company to simultaneously target internal staff, while providing external customers with an appropriate subset of the total corporate. Additional security systems are required to restrict access to the internal portal server, including firewall control rules and intrusion detection systems. A search server is also included in the DMZ, which incorporates a subset of the internal search server indexes, allowing customers to search for relevant customer content. This design is depicted inFigure 4.7.

Figure 4.7 High-level design of two-tier portal solution

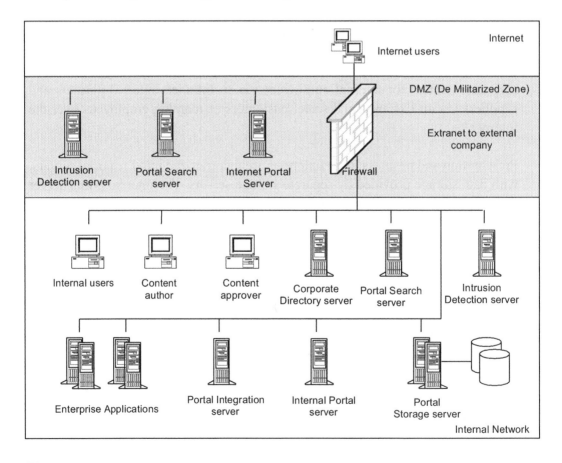

Variations on this design allow for higher availability and scalability. For example, if the portal is considered mission critical and downtime is not permitted, high-availability continual operation can be ensured through multiple clustered portal and integration servers. This requires a network load-balancing design. In addition, the database server can be clustered using operating system/file system clustering and a parallel database product.

High-level design for high usage three-tier portal solution

The three-tier portal design depicted in Figure 4.8 is intended for high usage portals with integration with many enterprise applications. It is also intended for companies intending to deploy multiple 'virtual' enterprise portals, consisting of several portals dedicated to different topics. Such virtual portals are typically hosted on the same hardware to minimize administration and expense.

This design builds on the two-tier design by separating presentation and application functions into the first and second layers, with storage functions residing in the third layer. Additional functions such as enterprise application integration and security and user management server are also included, along with a separate access logging server, used to record and report on portal usage, for increased performance.

The third tier contains the data storage server. This tier provides storage for content managed by the portal solution, and is clustered on multi-processor servers for increased performance and scalability. In addition, multiple databases can be deployed for different elements of the portal such as document storage and collaboration applications, allowing each database to be tuned for different performance requirements. This tier also contains the portal-logging server to record accesses to portal content for management reporting.

Security and user configuration information is provided through the same mechanisms used in the two-tier design, including LDAP directory servers, firewalls, and intrusion detection servers.

This design also includes separate search engines with their own databases. These products are designed to search large volumes of information from multiple internal and external sources, and thus require separate storage due to the considerable size of the content indexes they generate. They also offer high scalability and reliability using multiple search and index servers.

Figure 4.8 High usage three-tier portal design

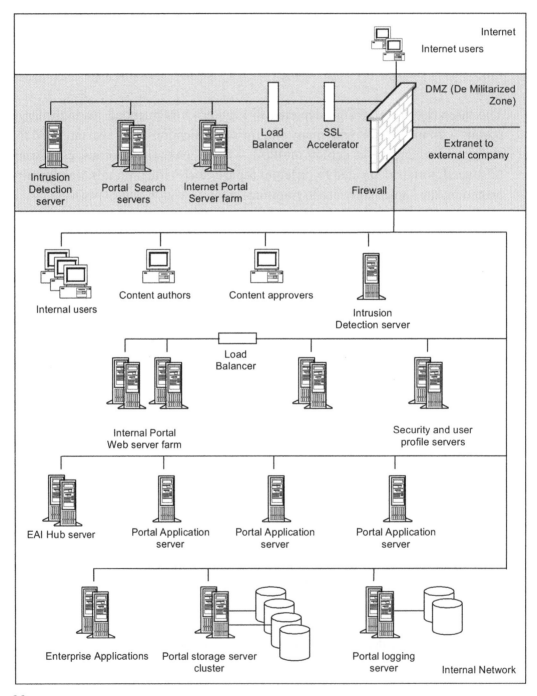

As with the design above, this architecture allows access to the portal for internal employees via an Intranet, external partners and suppliers via an Extranet, and customers and employees over the Internet.

However, this design differs in the use of multiple first tier presentation servers utilizing network load balancing, and multiple clustered Portal business logic servers. This design also provides for highly scalable enterprise application integration through the use of a central enterprise application integration (EAI) 'hub', which acts as a routing and distribution centre for messages between applications.

4.4.3 Benefits and limitations of portal solutions

Portals provide an ideal mechanism to centralize and manage employee access to corporate information. They also provide a simple solution to distribute e-business publishing throughout an enterprise and to provide automated publishing of content to Internet and Intranet sites.

However, portal solutions may be limited in their ability to integrate with enterprise applications. Portal integration modules are typically proprietary to portal vendors and may not suit all corporate integration requirements. Portal integration systems are also typically designed primarily for simple information retrieval from the enterprise applications and the portal, and may therefore lack high scalability and extensibility required for high-performance demanding environments. This in turn may result in restrictions to the amount of corporate information they can provide to users.

4.4.4 Vendors of portal solutions

Table 4.2 lists enterprise portal solutions and vendors. It should be noted that due to the large amounts of vendors and products available, this list is not exhaustive and should be used as a guide only before solution research is undertaken.

Table 4.2 Vendors of enterprise portal solutions

Vendor	Enterprise portal solution
ATG	ATG Enterprise Portal
BEA	WebLogic Portal
BroadVision	Enterprise Portal
Brio Software	Brio Portal
Epicentric	Epicentric Foundation Server
Hummingbird	Hummingbird Portal
IBM	WebSphere Portal and Enterprise Information Portal
Microsoft	Sharepoint
Open Source	Jahia and Jetspeed
Oracle	Oracle 9iAS Portal
Plumtree	Plumtree Corporate Portal
PeopleSoft	PeopleSoft Portal Solutions
SAP	mySAP Enterprise Portal
Sybase	Sybase Enterprise Portal
Sun Microsystems	Sun ONE Portal Server
Tibco	ActivePortal
Viador	E-Portal

4.5 Content management systems

Content management systems are designed to allow companies to create and manage very large volumes of rapidly changing static content, and reformat it for use across different channels such as Internet, Intranet, mobile, digital TV and print media.

Therefore, companies in industry segments where huge volumes of content are generated, such as media organizations and publishing companies producing large websites, frequently require content management systems. These also include companies with extensive information products, and specialist companies, such as aerospace or pharmaceutical companies, who create and consume huge quantities of structured information such as research studies or computer aided designs (CAD).

Such companies require systems to manage the thousands of items of rapidly changing content they create (Doculabs, 2000). Content is typically created in multiple formats, including company brochures, corporate reports, and online media files such as video, audio and web pages. It is also typically converted from original source formats into several target formats for distribution through channels such as television, print and the Internet. This in turn requires many members of staff to contribute to the creation and subsequent formatting of this content, which necessitates sophisticated tools to manage the content as it moves between workers.

These requirements typically exceed the ability of existing Internet, Intranet and portal systems to manage, due to the rapidly changing volume of content and the sophistication of work practices needed to produce the finished content. From their roots in earlier dedicated document management products, content management products evolved to provide solutions capable of handling any content format.

Content management systems provide a number of advantages to companies faced with demanding content requirements. They allow content to be 'repurposed' (reformatted) for simultaneous delivery to multiple channels such as CD-ROM, print, Internet, email, SMS and WAP. This in turn allows a company to target content to different staff and customers for increased productivity of staff and increased uptake of content by consumers. They also offer sophisticated 'workflow' capabilities, where content is routed between multiple contributors such as authors and editors, thus providing a high degree of control over the creation, management and distribution of content.

These abilities allow organizations to realize substantial benefits through reductions in manual content creation and management practices. Time-consuming manual systems used to create, format, and display content can be made more efficient by increasing the degree of automation of each step. This results in improved employed productivity, reduced content creation and management costs, and allows companies to offer more complex information-based products and services. Such systems also allow targeting of content, allowing customers, staff and partners to locate and use relevant information in the form they require without tying up staff in manual searches or content reformatting.

The total cost of ownership of corporate information assets is also lowered through content management tools due to the simplification of content creation and management across different online and offline channels. Using a single Content Management solution rather than multiple manual systems for each channel results in lower infrastructure, administration and support costs, reductions in staff training through standardization, and more consistent and error-free output.

These benefits can provide compelling savings. For example, the Giga group (Moore, 2001a) estimated that shifting content management from manual systems to packaged content management systems could reduce maintenance costs by one third and reduce labour costs in content authoring and design by half. They also estimated this could reduce operational web publishing costs by half, reduce the business risk of publishing erroneous or out-of-date content, and increase sales, revenues and profits.

For example, a media company uses a content management system to create and manage content for distribution to television, digital TV, multiple partners Internet sites, mobile devices and print media. This process is depicted in Figure 4.9.

Figure 4.9 Managing content across multiple channels

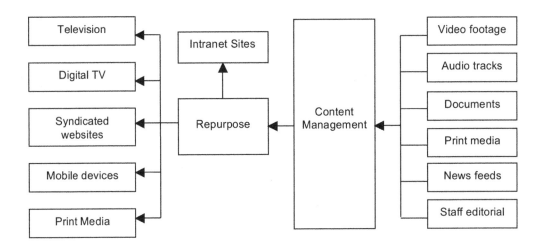

In the preceding example, corporate information from multiple sources is entered into the content management system to produce relevant content for target markets. It is then repurposed into suitable display formats for a wide range of devices and channels, and delivered to consumers.

4.5.1 Key technologies

Content management systems are designed by vendors using either traditional client - server technologies, or modern Internet-based technologies. Traditional client - server products employ two-tier architectures with proprietary client and server products that are highly dependent on each other, and dedicated to specific client platforms. For example, many products utilize server applications written in the C++ language for Windows NT and Unix servers, with client tools written in C++ running on specific platforms such as Windows or Macintosh.

Recently, many vendors have adopted J2EE-based architectures for their products (Aberdeen Group, 2001). Such vendors have moved away from traditional client - server product approaches consisting of toolkits requiring considerable customization, towards scalable and extensible architectures supporting traditional content management functions and Internet technologies such as personalization, catalogue management, and recommendation engines.

Many vendors have also decoupled their repositories from dependence on proprietary client tools and monolithic server systems, and added compliance with Internet standards. This allows users to access the content stored in the repository from standard Internet browsers used on all client platforms. This evolution has in turn led to new generations of products featuring browser-based workflow, website and content management, and the ability to integrate with a variety of third-party products.

What to look for in a content management system

Content management vendors initially targeted their products at the different market segments they traditionally represented, including document management products, e-business content management products, and web content management products.

Document management products were designed for the management of large numbers of corporate documents. These typically include FrameMaker documents for book publishing, corporate documents such as Microsoft Office Word and Excel, and print media publishing documents such as QuarkXPress for Magazine production.

E-commerce content management products were created by vendors of E-business products who added content management functions to enable their solutions to manage large catalogues and website content.

Web content management products were designed specifically for the management of web-based content for very large Internet and Intranet sites. Such products targeted sites requiring management of thousands of pages of rapidly changing content.

More recently, the shift by vendors to offer near complete compliance with Internet standards has led to consolidation around a common set of core technologies and features. This has resulted in products condensing into two market segments, including generalized content management products offering content management features suitable for deployment in many situations, and integrated e-business content management products offering e-business applications built on a content management infrastructure (Aberdeen Group, 2001). These converged products now encompass the enterprise content management (ECM) field.

Content management products typically offer a common set of components to support the full content management lifecycle. This lifecycle follows content from initial creation to consumption by end users, and includes phases for the creation, management and delivery of content. These stages are typically provided through four content management components. These include an end user – client interface, a content storage repository system for structured content storage, a file store for maintaining unstructured documents and website content, and a content management server to provide the workflow and content management functions.

The client interface provides access for users into the system, allowing them to view content, upload content into the content management server after its creation, and perform administration functions. Interfaces include web browsers or traditional desktop client software. Use of browser-based systems typically offers the advantages of minimizing training requirements, and reducing support costs incurred by installing and supporting proprietary desktop client software.

The user interface must support integration with common desktop tools used in content creation and modification. These include Internet content creation tools such as HTML editors, traditional corporate document production tools such as Microsoft Word, and traditional print media production tools such as QuarkXPress. It should be noted that not all products support integration with print publishing applications.

The user interface must also provide support for all target content delivery formats, such as Java, HTML pages, JPEG and GIF images for Internet content, PDF for business content, and QuarkXPress, InDesign, FileMaker or PDF for print documents. The product must also offer predefined templates for content creation by non-technical users, and allow such users to define and assemble their own templates.

Once created, content is uploaded into the content storage system. This component includes a file store for storage of unstructured items of content such as corporate documents and images, typically as files in a traditional hierarchical file system. It also includes a database repository for the storage of structured content and information about content, known as metadata.

Metadata is used to identify, categorize and locate each item of content and link related items together. Products should support metadata customization by users to enable the product to fit the information structures within the organisation. This requires determination of the structure of its metadata by analysing what metadata is required for each type of content to be published. This classification should be extensible, and extend to all aspects of the business. Metadata must then be assigned to existing content before importing it into the content management system, with automated tools used for large volumes of content. Similarly, the system must support importing existing content into the repository, via automated tools for large volumes.

The repository should utilize industry standard relational database products, and support expiration and archiving of out-of-date content. Other features should include library functions such as document history, check in and out, document profiling and versioning to enable sophisticated management of content. Versioning is a critical element of the repository, as it allows for the creation of multiple versions of content, with rollback and roll-forward between versions as content changes are made. Versioning should be at a granular element level, such as a single image, and at higher levels such as an entire page or website. Metadata tagging should be applied to content as it is imported into the repository, to classify the content for more accurate targeted searches.

The content management server is used to manage content throughout the content lifecycle. This component provides business logic to support services required by users, including publishing of content, workflow and collaboration for users working on related content simultaneously, and system functions such as managing library services, database connectivity, and security. Automated workflow is a critical function of the content management server, as this facilitates content production. Workflow requires allocation of appropriate rights to users, thus defining user permissions to create and approve content as it moves through the content lifecycle. It also requires automated tools to route the content between these users based on the nature of the content and its intended destination.

The content management server must also support the removal of expired content to ensure published content is 'fresh'. The system should support manual and automated removal of old content or content that is no longer required, which in turn requires tracking and auditing of content.

Content delivery requires content be physically deployed to end users electronically, or packaged into physical form for eventual shipment to users. The system must therefore support all required forms of deployment, such as websites, FTP, email, or syndication to other websites, such as news providers. This requires the repository support storage of content in an XML format in multiple languages, to facilitate simple repurposing of content into multiple target formats such as HTML for Internet browsers or WML for WAP phones. It also allows for targeting of content for different international markets. When content is repurposed into Internet formats, the solution must support website management functions such as checking page links, and delivery of real-time content.

In addition to the components discussed above, content management solutions must provide management systems to ensure their continued efficient operation. These include the ability to monitor the performance of the solution and of components such as data storage subsystems, or Internet sites. This allows for real-time assessment of performance, and highlights any issues in the ongoing management of the solution. Management functionality should also include logging of the content management lifecycle functions, to provide analysis and business reporting and direct assessment of the results of structural changes to content, such as alterations to a site affecting customer traffic.

4.5.2 High-level designs of content management systems

Content management solutions are designed around two-tier or three-tier application architectures. Typically, two-tier products utilize client - server systems with dedicated client interfaces and back-end content management server and database server systems. The more common three-tier products typically utilize standard three-tier Internet architectures with web server front ends, middle tier applications and back-end data repositories.

As they may be deployed across large enterprises, content management solutions must provide sufficient scalability for the size of the company while allowing for any expected growth. They must also be capable of integration with enterprise resources such as databases and application servers, and should support industry standard security management such as LDAP and single-sign-on mechanisms to integrate with corporate security systems.

Scalability is typically provided through standard network load balancing of front-end web servers, and clustered content management servers and repositories. The most scalable products feature federated designs, which group content management servers and repositories into distributed hierarchical structures with central management. Such products typically also offer automated replication of content between distributed repositories. This allows the solution to scale across organizational and geographical boundaries to support the largest organizations.

Integration requirements are best met through industry standard Internet-based technologies such as Enterprise Java Beans and J2EE-compliant application servers. These systems support integration with a wider range of corporate applications than products based on proprietary architectures, while offering very high scalability and reliability. They also provide standardized mechanisms for repurposing content via XML and conversion servers such as WAP gateways.

Application server-based products also permit vendors to reduce their development effort by using the underlying services of the application server with little additional development effort. This in turn allows them to concentrate on creating additional features in their products. This is reflected in the increasing integration of additional functionality within content management products. Vendors now offer solutions with catalogue management features, content-based collaboration systems for portals or supply chains, mobile commerce applications, and vertical industry products such as financial or pharmaceutical industry content management solutions. Such integrated products are worth consideration for companies with little or no existing e-business infrastructure, or for companies requiring industry-specific solutions.

The following design provides a three-tier architecture for content management systems. This represents a reference design, illustrating the major deployment configurations suitable for such products. Two-tier designs are not depicted due to the predominance of three-tier architectures in modern content management products.

High-level design for high usage three-tier content management solution

The three-tier content management solution depicted in Figure 4.10 is designed for high levels of content creation, repurposing and consumption across multiple channels and Internet and Intranet sites.

This design incorporates presentation web servers in the first tier providing content to web browsers through Internet and Intranet sites. This tier also includes specialist presentation servers used for content repurposing, such as mobile gateways for SMS (Simple Messaging Service) and WAP (Wireless Application Protocol). In addition, a separate Intranet web server is provided to provide the management interface for workflow definition, and to accept content submissions from contributors.

The content management services, including workflow, collaboration, library services, security and integration services, are provided on the second tier. These include application components developed in Java or languages such as C++ Microsoft COM components.

The second tier interacts with additional systems such as the third tier repositories, internal EAI deployments used to send content to other enterprise applications, and proprietary client desktop applications such as image scanning packages or desktop publishing software. Integration is also required with content archiving systems, such as optical storage jukeboxes used in the long-term storage of important content. Security is provided through integration of content management server systems with corporate directory servers such as Novell Netware or Microsoft Active Directory.

Additional security can be provided using an additional content repository and content management Server in a second internal DMZ network. The primary content management server on the corporate network populates relevant Internet content into this system through a one-way process. When Internet users access the Internet site, the internal DMZ servers generate all content. As content is not retrieved from the internal network systems, their security is preserved.

The third tier incorporates the content management repository, used to store and retrieve content. This layer includes structured relational databases, and unstructured storage systems such as file and print servers used for storage of corporate files in traditional client - server environments.

Availability and scalability features include network load balanced web server farms, and clustering of content management servers and repository servers. Additional availability is provided using federated servers, with additional systems distributed throughout the organization to support clusters of users at remote business units. Development and staging environments are not depicted in this design; however, these should be maintained as separate systems to enhance the stability of all live systems.

This design is depicted in Figure 4.10.

Figure 4.10 High-level design of three-tier content management solution

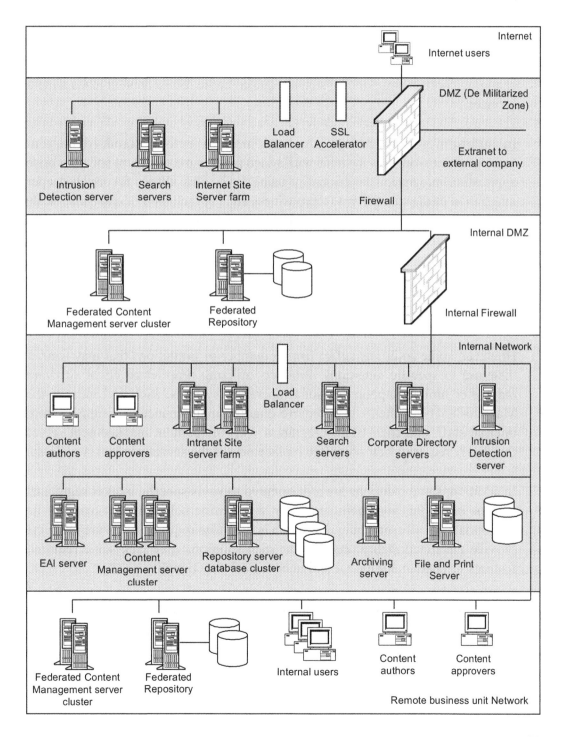

4.5.3 Benefits and limitations of content management systems

Enterprise content management systems provide a very powerful solution for demanding content requirements of modern businesses. They are ideally suited for the creation and management of large volumes of content in many formats, and for repurposing content to different channels. They also provide valuable services to Internet and Intranet sites requiring large volumes of rapidly changing content, and portal systems requiring more robust content management services.

In addition, some vendors are beginning to extend standard content management workflow systems with added process management and enterprise application integration functionality using Java. This allows for much deeper integration of the solution into the business and the inclusion of enterprise-scale content management across corporate business processes. Other developments include creation of specialist versions of content management solutions targeted at specific industry segments, providing considerable packaged functionality and faster implementation timeframes. These developments ensure that adoption of an Enterprise Content Management solution should position companies well for future e-business efforts in subsequent phases.

However, some solutions suffer from a number of limitations that may restrict their use to specific situations. Products utilizing proprietary client software may offer limited support for some operating systems, such as Linux or the Macintosh. These clients also require ongoing maintenance and support from internal staff, and their tight integration with the content management server frequently requires their complete replacement if the server product is updated.

In addition, some solutions are still oriented towards specific market segments, such as providing document-centric or web-centric solutions that may not be appropriate for all companies. Research is therefore required to ensure products provide the functionality required, as such solutions may lack some required features or contain additional and unnecessary functionality.

Other limitations to enterprise content management solutions include the need for considerable up-front planning before implementation. Corporate organizational issues and processes must be determined before solutions are implemented. These typically include issues such as determination of corporate metadata policies (to ensure consistent descriptions for all corporate content), thorough definition of import and conversion requirements to enter existing content into the solution, and policies and procedures for creating, handling, consuming and distributing content. They also include integration requirements with desktop applications such as desktop publishing products, and how content expiry will be handled.

4.5.4 Vendors of content management systems

Table 4.3 lists software products used in enterprise content management solutions. It should be noted that due to the large amounts of vendors and products available, this list is not exhaustive and should be used as a guide only before solution research is undertaken.

Table 4.3 Vendors of enterprise content management solutions

Vendor	Content management solution
BroadVision	One-to-One Content & Publishing Centre
Divine	Enterprise Content Center, Participant Server and Content Server
Documentum	Documentum 4i
Filenet	Filenet Web Content Management and Panagon
Gauss	VIP Enterprise
HummingBird	Fulcrum KnowledgeServer and DOCS document and content management solutions
IBM	IBM Content Manager
InterWoven	TeamSite
Microsoft	Content Management Server
OpenPage	ContentWare Enterprise Edition
Open Source	PostNuke and PHP-Nuke
Open Text	Livelink
Stellent	Content Management
Vignette	Vignette Content Suite
Zope	Zope Content Management Framework (Commercial and Open Source)

Phase 2: Transacting with customers

Transacting with customers is the second phase of the e-business lifecycle. This phase involves an organization offering products and services for sale to their customers over the Internet. These customers can include any entity the organization conducts business with, including retail consumers in the traditional business-to-consumer (B2C) model, or with other businesses in the business-to-business (B2B) model.

This phase represents an extension of the publishing model into commerce capabilities, as it allows customers to view content related to specific products and services and then to conduct a transaction for these. It is also typically implemented as an extension to online publishing.

Transacting with customers through e-business systems provides considerable benefits to organizations, including decreased costs of sales, greater responsiveness to customers, greater product reach, and more accurate targeting of sales to customers.

Transactional e-business decreases the cost of conducting business using automated systems. This reduces the need for routine processing carried out by staff, such as order taking, order confirmation and order processing, and allows inventory to be more efficiently managed. In addition, some transactional systems provide the opportunity to obtain reduced prices for supplies.

Responsiveness to customers is increased through the ability to react more quickly to changing customer demand, and by decreasing the time taken to bring products and services to market.

Customer reach is also increased by using the Internet as the mechanism to reach an almost unlimited number of potential customers anywhere in the world, and at any time of the day.

Finally, the recent inclusion of content management and personalization features into vendor products has given rise to transactional e-business solutions offering more accurate real-time targeting of products and services to customers. Content management and personalization features allow companies to run transactional sites with large volumes of content targeted to the specific needs of individual customers. This in turn leads to increased acquisition and retention rates for customers, and greater customer loyalty. It also allows companies to increase revenues through facilities such as targeted cross-sell (selling similar products), up-sell (selling more expensive products), and provision of targeted online marketing campaigns.

For example, a company uses a transactional e-business product to sell services and products online to business and consumer customers. A customer connects to the corporate site to browse content, and follows links to select related products and services for sale. When they choose products, the site recommends related products they may also wish to purchase. Once they have confirmed their order, the customer enters payment details and the order is confirmed. This process is depicted in Figure 5.1.

Figure 5.1 Transactional e-business process

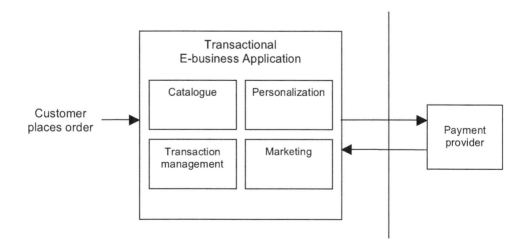

In the preceding example, the transactional e-business system contains several functional modules to provide the required commerce features. These modules track the customer browsing behaviour to improve their transactional experience. Catalogue functionality is used to present static or dynamic catalogues of products and services. This module is supported by the personalization and marketing modules, which provide product recommendations that would be of use to the customer. The transaction management module controls the customers purchasing, and handles taking payment and processing this through an external or internal payment provider system.

The preceding discussion details the sell-side transactional e-business model. However, transactional e-business also includes a buy-side. Buy-side e-business is the process whereby a company engages in business-to-business transactions with suppliers and trading partners. Buy-side transactions occur either through manual processes or automatically though software products. Manual processes require companies to adopt manual processes to purchase goods and services online, while automatic buy-side commerce requires integration of existing corporate systems and processes with the systems of suppliers and trading partners.

5.1 Key technologies used

Transactional e-business solutions typically utilize one of three sets of technologies. These include proprietary systems based on scripting languages, products based on the de facto industry standard Java technologies, or products based on Microsoft technologies such as the COM/DCOM object standards, or the emerging .Net infrastructure.

Proprietary systems arose from early transactional e-business systems that were designed to provide simple e-commerce facilities (Fenner, Meister and Patel, 2001). These early systems were typically written in a wide variety of programming languages such as PERL or Microsoft ASP, and often lacked highly reliable or scalable features and had few integration options with external applications.

More recently, most vendors have standardized their products around the de facto industry standard Java 2 Enterprise Edition (J2EE) technology. Vendors have adopted this platform to simplify their development efforts by using the services provided by the underlying J2EE application servers. This has removed the need for vendors to develop reliability, scalability and availability features in their products, and thus allowed them to concentrate their development effort on incorporating additional product features such as integrating transactions with content, personalizing the transactional process, and providing enterprise class integration systems.

Finally, a number of products have been developed using Microsoft object technologies such as COM/DCOM, but it is expected that such products will migrate to the emerging .Net application development platform as it replaces existing Windows server programming interfaces.

What to look for in a transactional e-business solution

Transactional e-business systems were initially developed with broad sets of features to sell products and services to specific customer segments, including business-to-consumer (B2C) and business-to-business (B2B) markets.

However, many businesses now view their customers from the perspective of their interactions with the business across multiple channels such as Internet, email, telephone, and direct marketing. This view focuses on providing transactional services to any customer through any channel, rather than the customer segment. In addition, many businesses transact with customers across both the B2C and B2B customer segments, and therefore require products with functionality suitable for both.

Because of this customer driven demand, the e-business industry has now folded the business-to-consumer and business-to-business terms into the sell-side e-business model. This term shifts the focus of e-business from customer segments to the process of selling products and services, which more accurately describes the aim of transactional e-business. Vendors are therefore increasingly incorporating broader functionality into their products to facilitate transactional e-business simultaneously across all customer segments to multiple channels.

However, although most vendors now describe their products in terms of the sell-side model, many products may still reflect their development history and provide more features targeted to a specific customer segment. Consequently, many products are differentiated into 'standard' sell-side e-business offerings targeting B2C and some B2B customers, and business-focused e-business offerings incorporating additional B2B functionality on top of their standard products, such as contract negotiation or additional business-specific payment options such as purchase orders.

Selecting a product with the greatest degree of required e-business functionality is therefore critical in order to reduce the need to develop missing features, and to integrate different products from third-party vendors. It is therefore recommended that a product be selected that is capable of targeting both business and consumer customer segments, as most businesses deal with both segments. In addition, many products and services are applicable across both customer segments. This reduces the need to buy separate products to satisfy the requirements of both customer segments, which would result in greater complexity and operational cost.

All sell-side transactional e-business products should provide features supporting the five core e-commerce processes common to all forms of sell-side commerce, including marketing, shopping, buying, fulfilment and customer service.

Marketing processes are used to present targeted products and services to customers to increase sales. This function is typically provided through product catalogue systems, merchandising systems, and personalization systems.

Catalogue systems provide users with groups of related products and services for purchase. This requires catalogue management features such as the ability to offer personalized catalogues to specific customers, catalogues predefined by administrators, multiple catalogues for different categories of customer, and integration with external catalogue management products for large catalogues.

Merchandising systems offer pricing and discount functionality for catalogue items. Multiple pricing and discount models should be supported, such as flat pricing for all customers, personalized pricing and discounts for specific users or groups. Merchandising is also achieved through campaign systems, which offer product recommendations through personalization systems.

Personalization systems allow transactional e-business sites to tailor content to the individual customer in an effort to increase sales. Personalization systems include the ability to sell more products through cross-sell and up-sell capabilities. Cross-sell involves selling related items to customers, while up-sell involves selling more expensive products in place of the customers' choice. Personalization typically includes the additional ability to recommend substitute products in the event an item is out of stock.

Personalization systems should include the ability to analyse data from customer interactions with the system in real time. These should include explicit sources, such as user filled forms, and implicit sources, such as the links a user follows. Transactional content is then personalized using this information through collaborative filtering mechanisms. These provide real-time product recommendations based on observing similar behaviours in other customers, and via rules-based mechanisms using product-customer rules explicitly defined by administrators. Information collected through these systems is also frequently used to drive further revenues through offering valued-customer targeted pricing, or through online advertising or direct mail/email marketing campaigns.

Marketing systems should also include support for other countries through internationalization systems, including supporting multiple dates, currency and taxation formats, and support for providing content in different languages.

Shopping processes allow customers to browse and search for products and services. Browsing functionality is provided through catalogues, and searches through included search engines. Search techniques should include plain language queries, simple text queries, and complex methods such as Boolean logic searching using words such as 'and', 'or' and 'not' to narrow searches.

Shopping is also increasingly being offered through alternative methods such as auctions, gift registries or collaboration, to provide customers with additional shopping options. Auction functionality should target the business and consumer segments through multiple auction models, such as open-cry, Dutch and sealed bid auctions. Open-cry auctions allow customers to see bids during the auction, in contrast to sealed bid auctions where only the seller sees customer bids. Dutch auctions are similar to the open-cry method, but start at higher prices and work downward. Alternative shopping functions include gift registries for purchasing for special events and collaboration or guided shopping, with two users shopping simultaneously.

Buying processes allow customers to purchase products and services through a variety of mechanisms. This function is provided through a transaction management system, which should offer payment processing in a variety of formats such as credit/debit cards and purchase orders for business customers. It should also offer functions such as saved orders and reorders, and include taxation and shipping charge calculation using taxation and shipping methods specific to different regions and countries. Payment processing may be handled by internal systems, or via integration with external third-party systems.

Buying systems require integration with inventory systems to allow customers to determine if items are in stock before purchasing. This may be provided through interfaces to dedicated internal inventory systems, or included within the transactional e-business product.

The fulfilment process ensures that products are selected from warehouses, packed, and sent to customers. As these are manual processes, typically handled by third parties, fulfilment functionality should track the status of items while in transit to provide improved customer service.

Customer service processes enable the e-business to manage customer enquiries and customer orders. This typically involves updating and amending stored customer profile information such as passwords and addresses, manually creating and processing orders for customers, determining customer order status, and processing goods returned by customers. It can also support manual amendments to customer orders such as allowing customer support staff to make price amendments to customer orders.

In addition to this core set of functions, products targeting business customers may be required to support dedicated functionality appropriate to this market segment (see Varon, 2001).

Products often represent business customers on an 'account' basis, with each account representing a single company. Each account will include a hierarchy of staff members who have permission to approve purchasing. Products should therefore offer account-based pricing and catalogues, allowing for negotiated discount levels. Payment systems also incorporate account-based mechanisms such as payment on account and invoice basis, cheque payments, and purchase orders.

Business specific functionality may also include support for negotiation processes through RFQ (Request for Quote) processes for requesting quotations from other businesses, and RFI processes (Request for Information) for the supply of information required to make a business decision. They may also include the ability to define and exchange contracts and negotiate terms and conditions for purchasing goods and services.

Finally, all transactional e-business solutions should provide simplified administration and management interfaces for business users. They should offer the ability to define business operational roles such as shop/store administrators and customer support staff, enter customer details, define pricing models and catalogues appropriate to customers, and manage customer service functions. Products should also allow for the creation and management of sales and marketing functions.

5.2 High-level designs for transactional e-business solutions

Designs of transactional e-business solutions must provide high availability and scalability to ensure continual operation of the e-business, and continued performance to handle fluctuating customer demand.

Customers may originate from any time zone or country, and they increasingly expect e-business systems will be continually available to service their needs. System downtime therefore results in lost business, and reduces repeat business. Designs must therefore support high availability to ensure the solution continues working in case of failure of one or more components.

Systems must also cope with unpredictable levels of demand for their services. Frequently, new e-business projects may experience very rapid increases in demand that they are unable to support, resulting in system overloads and crashes. Often this will require a complete redesign and build of the e-business system. It is therefore imperative that the system be capable scaling from an initial modest load to support large increases in site traffic in the future.

Sufficient scalability and availability is typically provided using three-tier web architectures. This architecture design separates operational systems for presentation, business logic, and database systems, allowing each layer to be scaled according to demand, and incorporating multiple systems in case of failure.

Multiple presentation web servers are deployed using network-level server load balancing to distribute requests for web pages across multiple servers. These servers in turn communicate with the second tier e-business logic servers, which contain the business functionality of the solution such as marketing and buying components. Logic servers then communicate with a third tier database server cluster used to store configuration information and customer data.

Most transactional e-business systems based on object-oriented Java 2 Enterprise Edition (J2EE) or COM/DCOM technology support this architecture (Fenner, Meister and Patel, 2001; Kramer, 2001a; Kramer, 2001b). Of these, Java is the most common technology in use in the majority of transactional e-business products as it typically provides the highest performance and availability.

In contrast, proprietary products based on scripting languages utilize lower performance two-tier web architectures, as they cannot distribute application components across multiple servers. These designs typically feature integrated first tier presentation and business logic systems, and separate second tier database systems.

Other functions that form an important part of transactional e-business architectures include providing high-security, integration capabilities, and extensibility of the solution.

Security is frequently neglected when designing e-business architectures, rendering systems vulnerable to attack and compromise. This has serious implications resulting from breaching data protection laws, and from the resulting loss of customer trust. Regulatory data protection requirements for security vary between countries, with many countries requiring customer data to be stored and used with the highest possible security, and only for the original purpose for which it was gathered. Preserving customer data security is also critical to maintaining customer trust, and hence repeat business. In addition to data appropriation by hackers/crackers, companies must ensure that data is not sold to other companies for other purposes such as direct marketing.

Transactional e-business architectures therefore require a system of distributed security to safeguard all stages of the customer's interactions with the system. Industry best practice dictates deploying multiple firewalls for access control, intrusion detection for the detection and response to hacking/cracking incidents, server hardening to safeguard systems, and the use of encryption technology to protect customer data.

Encryption of stored customer data can be handled by the e-business application when it writes information into its database. If an unauthorized entity gains access to the database they cannot then acquire customer information such as credit card numbers. Encryption is also required when a customer purchases goods and services, to prevent unauthorized access to sensitive credit/debit card numbers in transit between the customer computer and e-business application. This dictates the use of Secure Sockets Technology (SSL), which is built in to all modern web servers. SSL technology sends a digital certificate from the web server to the customer's browser, which the browser uses to encrypt the communication. Certificates are purchased from a Certificate Authority (CA) such as Verisign, by sending a certificate request along with details about the company. The certificate then issued will uniquely identify that site. All certificate requests should be made for 128-bit security, currently the strongest level of commercially available SSL security.

However, use of SSL technology may result in problems with performance. When a browser connects to an SSL enabled server, the server must carry out intensive calculations to generate the required level of encryption. This may result in dramatically decreased performance on that server if it is subject to large volumes of customer traffic. For sites expecting or experiencing high levels of SSL traffic, it is recommended that SSL encryption and decryption be offloaded onto dedicated SSL appliances. These appliances sit behind firewalls and in front of the web servers, and handle all encryption and decryption, thus relieving the web and application servers of this processing.

Architectures must also support integration with a number of internal and external systems. Integration is frequently required with external systems from banks and credit card vendors to facilitate final payment processing. Alternatively, internal financial systems may be used to settle business accounts through mechanisms such as payment on invoice. Integration may also be required with external personalization system from third parties to utilize customer demographic data. Alternatively, personalization systems may interact with existing corporate directories containing user information. This in turn requires secure communication systems, and securing of internal directory servers using server hardening and firewalls.

More advanced integration may be required between the transactional e-business product and internal enterprise application integration systems, or business process management systems. This allows the solution to incorporate functionality such as providing real-time inventory levels within product catalogues.

Solutions developed using Java technology offer the greatest integration ability with such advanced systems, due to their support for integration standards such as the Java Connector Architecture and Java Message Service. These allow the J2EE application server to connect directly to many enterprise applications, or alternatively to integrate directly with many middleware and process management products. In contrast, proprietary and COM/DCOM-based products may require additional customization to support integration with such systems.

Alternatively, transactional e-business architectures allow the core products to be extended to support new features required to satisfy changing business requirements. For example, as an e-business experiences growth, additional systems such as content management systems may be required to enhance the e-business offering to customers. As many of the leading content management products are written in Java, J2EE-based transactional e-business products represent the most extensible systems capable of direct addition of such products to the same hardware systems.

Adopting such a product also allows for extension of the architecture to support emerging standards such as web services, which are currently supported by application server products. Such development is enhanced using the wide variety of Java development resources available. In contrast, many proprietary scripting products require considerable customisation to integrate with web services, while existing object-based COM/DCOM will typically require rewriting using the Microsoft .Net system.

Finally, the architecture should include development and testing environments to support the creation and management of site content, and development of additional site functionality. This should include change management features to manage the large amount of content, tools, and application code transactional e-business environments generate. More advanced products supporting advanced features should include an integrated development environment and a broad range of tools to facilitate such developments.

High-level design of low to medium-level transaction volume e-business solution

The following design is intended for transactional e-business systems supporting low to medium levels of transactions. Companies with undemanding e-business requirements, who often adopt proprietary scripting, often use such systems, or alternatively, low-end COM/DCOM-based products.

This design employs a two-tier architecture with combined business logic and presentation functions in the first tier. The presentation functionality is provided by a web server, with the business logic hosted on the same server using an application server for J2EE-based systems, an integrated scripting engine for proprietary systems, or Microsoft COM transaction manager for COM/DCOM systems. The second tier provides a database for storage of product configuration data and customer profile data.

This design provides limited availability and scalability features by distributing customer requests to servers using network load balancing in the first tier. However, this technique will rapidly exhaust the performance of the second tier database as the multiple, independent tier one systems contend for database resources. Availability for the database in the second tier is provided through a fail-over cluster. In case of failure of a database, this transfers database functionality to a parallel, standby database server with a copy of all data.

However, for systems using COM/DCOM or J2EE-based products, this design can be expanded to the high-performance three-tier design. This requires separation of the first tier functions into two separate tiers for presentation and business logic, and the addition of live database clustering.

Security systems are provided through the techniques discussed previously, with the addition of a secured Extranet network connecting the transactional e-business system to the third-party payment provider.

Finally, a development environment is included to prototype new content and systems for the live production site. This environment includes a reduced set of all system components, typically on one server for simplicity.

This design is depicted in Figure 5.2.

Figure 5.2 High-level design for low - medium level transactional e-business solution

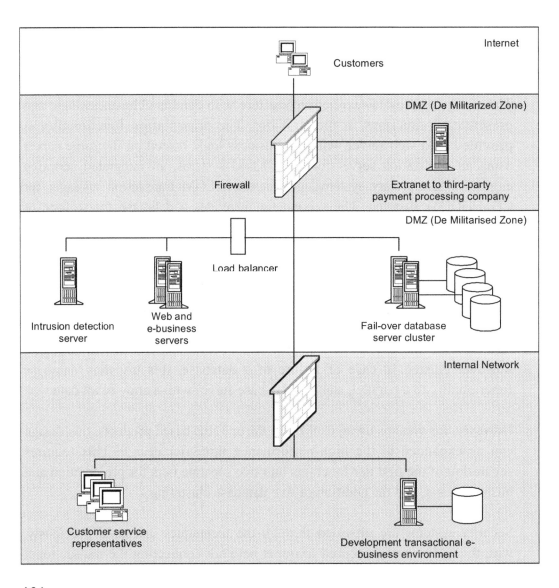

High-level design of medium to high-level transaction volume e-business solution

The following design is intended for transactional e-business systems supporting medium to high levels of e-business transactions. Such systems are often used by companies with demanding e-business requirements such as multiple e-business sites serving customers across several countries. Such systems are typically deployed using high-end COM/DCOM-based products, or Java-based products.

This design employs a more complex three-tier architecture. A web server farm consisting of a set of web servers 'hidden' behind a network load-balancer provides the presentation functionality. The second layer includes multiple copies of core business logic components hosted across several servers. Requests from web servers are distributed to these components to balance customer demand. The third tier includes an active database cluster, which distributes a single database image across multiple servers and storage systems for very high performance and availability. This design can therefore be scaled as customer demand increases, by adding additional systems within each tier.

Additional scalability and availability is provided through a load balancer cluster, with active/active devices functioning in parallel, and multiple SSL accelerators to offload encryption from the web and e-business servers. Additional servers for personalization and catalogue management are included within the DMZ to off – load these resource-intensive functions from the business logic servers. The complete product catalogue is maintained in a separate server within the corporate network, and content published to the DMZ catalogue server to maintain security.

Integration can be provided through inclusion of Java Connector Architecture and Java Message Service components within the e-business application server cluster. In addition, content management systems can be integrated using these technologies, or installed directly onto the cluster servers.

Security systems expand on those of the low – medium-level design through the addition of a second internal intrusion detection server, and the inclusion of directory servers. An LDAP server within the DMZ provides for centralized management of customer information. This is in turn synchronized with an internal enterprise directory server to provide centralized management of all corporate resources such as internal users and their computers and customer data.

Finally, an expanded development environment is included, offering development and staging systems. These allow for uninterrupted development cycles for new content and systems and for independent testing of performance and approval of content and systems ready for publication to the live production site.

This design is depicted in Figure 5.3.

Figure 5.3 High-level design for high-level transactional e-business solution

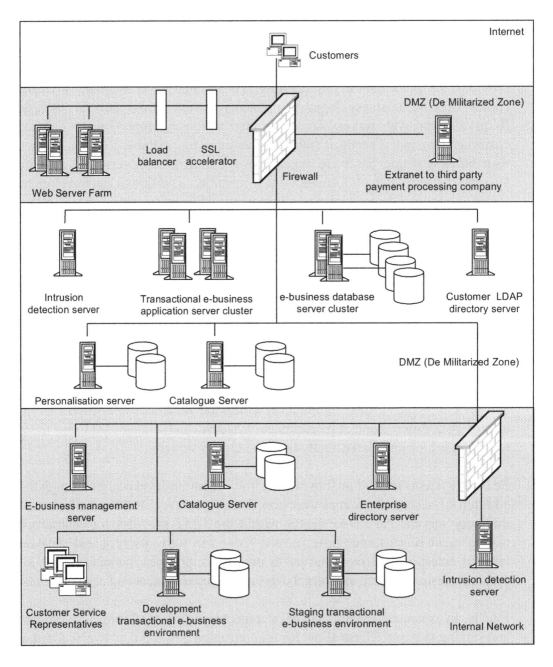

5.3 Benefits and limitations of transactional e-business systems

Modern transactional e-business systems contain rich sets of functionality ideally suited for a range of e-businesses. They typically include most of the functionality required for trading online for either purely Internet-only businesses or traditional businesses wishing to establish an online presence.

Many products are now very flexible, and include store templates to enable users to quickly create customized transactional sites with minimal programming knowledge. They also support consumer – and business-oriented functionality allowing the business to target both types of customer.

Higher-end products often include large numbers of components in the one package, such as integrated database and application servers, and site development tool sets offering page construction utilities, site management utilities, catalogue managers, and coding tools. The higher cost of such products is frequently offset by the convenience and savings achieved through acquiring all the necessary tools from one vendor rather than purchasing potentially incompatible products from multiple vendors with lower-end products.

Some of the more limited e-business products based on COM/DCOM and proprietary technologies typically have a lower up-front cost compared to higher-end products, but may lack more advanced features, and therefore may not be applicable to all business requirements. For example, they may lack templates, require additional customization and development before deployment, require the addition of third-party products such as taxation and payment engines, and may require purchasing additional subsystems such as database servers.

Such products may therefore be suited to organizations wishing to experiment with e-business or organizations with an existing commitment to these technologies. However, such products may not be capable of deployment into enterprise class scalability and availability configurations.

Products offer different levels of support for extension and integration to support emerging technologies. Products based on J2EE technology offer the strongest expansion and integration features of all transactional e-business products, followed by COM/DCOM products. Proprietary products typically offer very limited facilities in these areas, and require extensive customization.

Most transactional e-business products include some content management features, typically to provide support for functions such as catalogue creation, and management of product catalogues. However, additional content management functionality such as management of media assets or business documents required for RFI/RFQ processes is becoming increasingly important as content assumes a greater role in business. Proprietary products may lack the ability to integrate such functionality, and product selection should therefore consider the ease of integration between transactional e-business systems and web or document management products.

They may also lack suitable integration facilities to support expansion as business requirements grow. Subsequent integration with additional third-party products such as content management systems or enterprise application integration systems may therefore require expensive and time-consuming customization.

If advanced content management features are required, a number of vendors offer content management systems based on the same core technology deployed in their e-business products. Some products also include direct integration with external content management products from leading vendors. Therefore, if content management is a transactional e-business requirement, products from these vendors are recommended.

In addition, some vendors of Java-based products offer systems tailored to specific market segments such as the travel industry, or specific business-oriented functionality such as support for purchase orders. If the intention is to target such segments, it may be more appropriate to select products from vendors who offer such products.

Finally, some transactional e-business products are not capable of hosting multiple e-business sites, such as separate stores, on the same physical hardware. Products should therefore be assessed to determine their ability to support multiple transactional e-business sites per server, and the associated cost.

5.4 Vendors of transactional e-business systems

Table 5.1 lists vendors of transactional e-business systems. It should be noted that due to the large amounts of vendors and products available, this list is not exhaustive and should be used as a guide only before solution research is undertaken.

Table 5.1 Vendors of transactional e-business systems

Vendor	Transational e-business system
Actinic	Actinic Catalogue and Business
ATG	ATG Consumer Suite and Enterprise Commerce Suite
Blue Martini	Blue Martini Commerce
BroadVision	BroadVision Business Commerce, Retail Commerce, and Billing
IBM	WebSphere Commerce Suite and IBM WebSphere Commerce Suite Business Edition
Intershop	Enfinity and Intershop 4
InterWorld	Commerce Exchange
Sun Microsystems	Sun ONE BillerXpert, Market Maker, and BuyerXpert
Microsoft	Commerce Server

6   Phase 3: Internal enterprise application integration

The third phase of e-business is internal enterprise application integration (EAI). This phase involves connecting internal enterprise applications such as financial, ERP, CRM, and manufacturing systems with each other and with transactional e-business systems.

Enterprise application integration systems offer an excellent mechanism to increase the corporate return on investment for existing internal enterprise applications. This is provided by integrating older applications with e-business systems, or through providing new products and services to customers by integrating existing applications with minimal extra development effort. These applications are typically deployed to customers as 'self-service' applications, and utilize EAI systems to integrate transactional e-business functionality with internal application functionality to lower customer service costs and acquire additional customers.

Examples of self-service applications include providing customers real-time information on what products are available for immediate purchase, up-to-date pricing of products to let customers quickly find the best deal, and offering credit or loyalty cards. Consumers also increasingly demand self-service applications across different industries such as online banking, insurance, share trading, travel and retail.

Companies frequently have older applications that are required for the running of the business. EAI enables these systems to be reused via integration with newer enterprise applications, without subjecting them to costly high risk rewriting. It also provides a rapid mechanism to integrate the internal enterprise systems of new companies or divisions that have been acquired through mergers and acquisitions.

Internal enterprise application integration also allows companies to remove time-consuming and error-prone manual processes, such as re-entering orders from transactional e-business systems into internal financial systems. This allows companies to provide new products and services to customers by wrapping a transactional e-business front-end onto existing internal applications, integrate legacy applications with new enterprise applications, and increase efficiencies in internal applications through greater use of automation.

EAI can also increase the speed with which products and services are delivered to customers, allowing the company to respond to changing customer demand more rapidly and therefore increasing sales. For example, implementing real-time updates of inventory levels from daily or weekly batch or manual processes allows customers to know that a product they purchase is immediately available for delivery, which is more likely to result in a purchase decision.

Another advantage of EAI is to increase the volume of transactions that can be performed with no increase in staff effort, and remove unnecessary steps in order processing. These in turn directly decrease business costs and increase profits. For example, many transactional e-business sites manually re-enter orders into internal applications. Directly integrating the existing back-end systems into the transactional e-business front-end will result in dramatic increases in efficiency.

Enterprise application integration therefore provides a powerful tool to increase efficiencies, and gain and retain customers by increasing their satisfaction and hence loyalty. This in turn allows a company to respond to competitive pressures more effectively.

For example, a company may have a transactional e-business system that allows customers to order products from their site. Orders are processed manually by staff members who enter payment details, and the type and quantity of products ordered into internal financial applications and manufacturing systems. This manual process contains considerable opportunity to create errors during data entry and is highly inefficient, as it requires staff be dedicated to performing simple order processing tasks.

Using internal enterprise application integration (EAI), a customer's order information can be sent directly to the internal financial and manufacturing systems to calculate and process the customer's payment and begin the manufacture of their product. The manufacturing system can then automatically update the financial system with details of the product parts used during manufacture for reordering, as shown in Figure 6.1.

Figure 6.1 Order processing using enterprise application integration

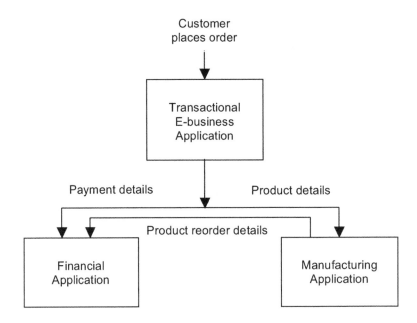

Using EAI technologies, the company can also provide their customers with new products and services, such as offering credit or loyalty cards online through integration of existing financial credit card approval systems with the transactional e-business application. This enables the company to provide services that are more efficient to their customers by simplifying their purchasing and finance requirements into one site, and results in labour cost savings. This process is depicted in Figure 6.2.

Figure 6.2 Offering additional products and services via enterprise application integration

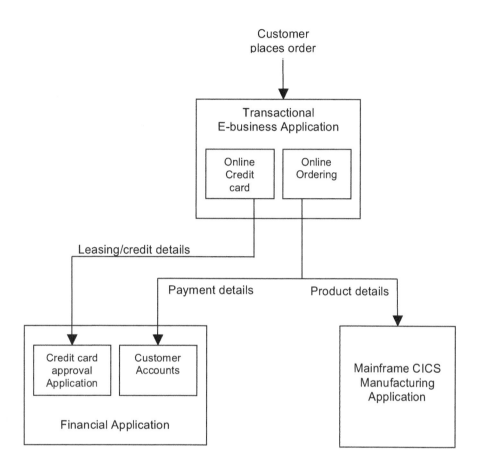

6.1 Key technologies used

In order to integrate internal enterprise applications, companies require a solution that can interact with transactional e-business systems using Internet standards, and with existing internal enterprise applications using the many proprietary technologies contained in such applications.

Software vendors have therefore developed a range of technologies to integrate these systems. These solutions have evolved to cover a very wide range of integration functionality required between internal systems and transactional e-business applications. These include platform integration, data integration, component integration, and application integration solutions, as depicted in Figure 6.3.

Figure 6.3 Technology solutions used in enterprise application integration

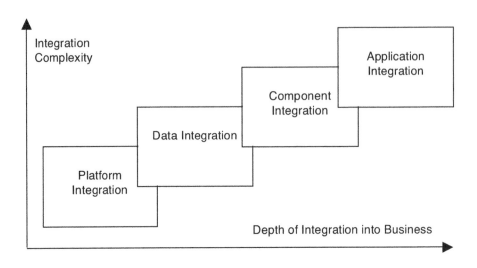

Platform integration technologies are designed to integrate different types of hardware, operating systems, and specific applications at a very low level. This is achieved through a range of technologies including simple messaging systems, object request brokers (ORBs), and remote procedure calls (RPC's). These products are either used for very simple integration between a few specific pieces of applications, or are used as components within more sophisticated integration solutions that require integration with specific proprietary technologies.

Data integration technologies are designed to operate directly on enterprise data stored in databases. These include dedicated database gateways via SQL commands, or ETML (Extraction, Transforming, Moving and Loading) tools to extract data directly from underlying databases, thus bypassing the enterprise applications themselves. Both types of data integration product suffer some limitations, including reliance on synchronous access to data which may not be appropriate in all integration scenarios, and requiring an understanding of the underlying database schema and maps. Data integration solutions are often used to integrate legacy systems such as old mainframe applications. As these systems cannot easily or affordably be rewritten to use newer technologies, this form of integration allows the application to be bypassed and its underlying database accessed directly.

Component integration technologies are collections of platform and data integration services housed within a centralized integration server. These products often feature connector-based architectures using messaging backbones. In contrast to the previous integration solutions, component integration technologies work at a higher level to remove some dependencies on underlying technologies. This can insulate the integration solution from potential changes in applications, or from complexities resulting from the introduction of new applications.

Application integration technologies are designed to provide near real-time integration through advanced data processing and routing functions layered on top of the previous three categories of integration technologies. This is achieved through data transformation message brokers, rules-based data routing, and integration with high-level proprietary application interfaces through packaged connectors (Stokes, 2001). These features allow application integration solutions to rapidly integrate with existing enterprise applications without requiring costly and time-consuming assembly of integration tools from multiple vendors, as required for the above solutions.

Four different categories of products have arisen to provide enterprise application integration solutions, with each solution using a different combination of these integration technologies. These categories include point-to-point customized solutions, and three forms of 'Middleware' solutions.

6.2 Point-to-Point point EAI solutions

Due to a lack of packaged solutions, early enterprise application integration initiatives required the creation of proprietary 'point-to-point' architectures between applications. To enable applications to communicate together, these solutions required customization of each integrated application using the platform and data integration technologies discussed above. This resulted in applications maintaining multiple connections to other integrated applications, as depicted in Figure 6.4.

Figure 6.4 Point-to-point enterprise application integration

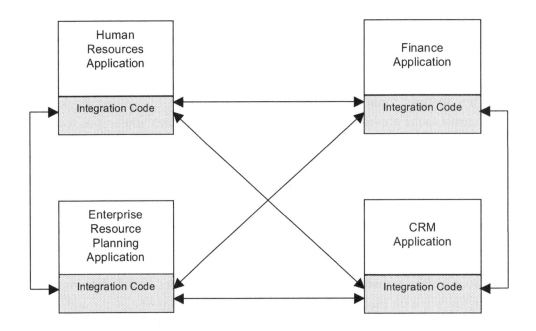

These customized solutions were designed to integrate critical packaged enterprise applications, such as ERP systems, with legacy systems or other packaged applications. The integration typically focused on low-level technical aspects such as making applications understand other application-specific data formats. This technical focus resulted in the creation of decentralized application-to-application solutions, which lacked central management.

Such early integrations allowed companies to create highly customized solutions dedicated to the requirements of their internal applications. However, this architecture proved to be inadequate long-term solutions for enterprise application integration, as it required very detailed knowledge of the proprietary technologies used in each application, to create links to other applications. Maintaining each application link therefore consumed considerable time and development resource, and resulted in the creation of 'fragile' solutions, where minor changes in applications, or the addition of new applications, required expensive and time-consuming rewriting of each integration link. In addition, failure in one application could cause the whole integration solution to cease functioning due to their close coupling. This form of integration also created solutions that could not support more advanced functionality, and could not scale well to support high levels of traffic between applications.

Because of the limitations of point-to-point integration efforts, modern integration architectures are designed to employ mechanisms that are more sophisticated for enterprise application integration. These systems, called 'middleware' EAI solutions, reduce the effort required to integrate applications, and create more manageable and robust integration solutions with greater scalability and responsiveness to changing corporate requirements.

6.3 Middleware solutions

The most common form of application integration solution are the Message-oriented middleware EAI products. These products manage and route all communications, in the form of messages, between applications through an intermediate software layer– the so-called middleware layer.

Each integrated application communicates with the middleware layer through application-specific connectors (or adapters) installed into the Middleware product. Adapters act as translation tools between the communication protocols and messages issued by each application and the internal messaging system used by the middleware product for its own internal communication. This process is depicted in Figure 6.5.

Figure 6.5 Functional components of message-oriented middleware integration solutions

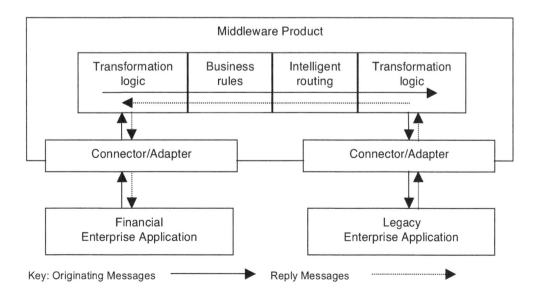

In the middleware integration solution depicted in Figure 6.5, a message is sent from a financial application to the Middleware product using a specific adapter that understands the proprietary connection interfaces of the application. This ensures that minimal changes are required to the application to enable it to participate in the integration. The connector then translates the application messages into the message structure used within the middleware product. The different functional layers within the middleware product interpret the destination of the message and apply predefined business rules and transformation logic to render the message into a format understood by the target legacy application. The response message is then sent to the specific legacy adapter, which communicates using the specific legacy application integration interfaces.

Integration connectors/adapters provide the middleware solution with considerable flexibility and extensibility. When a new application is integrated, the appropriate connector is 'plugged in' to the middleware layer, allowing the new application to participate in the complete integration solution. Development of the integration solution is also simplified using adapters. Developers typically have to understand only the middleware architecture and development systems, not multiple detailed application-specific technologies, as the adapters handle such issues. Such solutions can typically provide 70 to 80 per cent of the required integration capabilities out-of-the-box, resulting in considerable time saving when integrating applications (Sanchez, Patel and Fenner, 2001a and b).

Message-oriented middleware integration products are categorized into three different solution types based on the performance and scalability requirements and design of the integration solution. These include application server middleware designs, hub and spoke message-oriented middleware designs, and message bus message-oriented middleware designs.

6.4 Application server middleware solutions

Application server middleware designs are generally suited for less demanding integration initiatives with fewer applications and less message passing compared to hub and spoke and message bus solutions. They are frequently used to provide enhanced customer services through integration between transactional e-business systems and internal applications such as financial systems, customer databases or ERP systems.

These middleware solutions are a form of component integration, using J2EE-based application servers as the central point of integration between enterprise and e-business applications. Communication with applications occurs via standard packaged JCA (Java Connector Architecture) integration connectors that can be deployed in any J2EE compliant application server, simplifying integration development efforts and lowering integration risks. These provide access to enterprise applications such as relational databases, financial systems such as JD Edwards, customer relationship management (CRM) products such as Siebel, and enterprise resource planning (ERP) products such as SAP, or Baan.

For example, a transactional e-business application is deployed on a J2EE application server. Using the appropriate Java Connector Architecture connectors it can be quickly integrated with financial and mainframe manufacturing applications to provide dynamic processing of payments and accounts, and automation of order processing for product production. This process is depicted in Figure 6.6.

Figure 6.6 Enterprise integration using application server middleware solutions

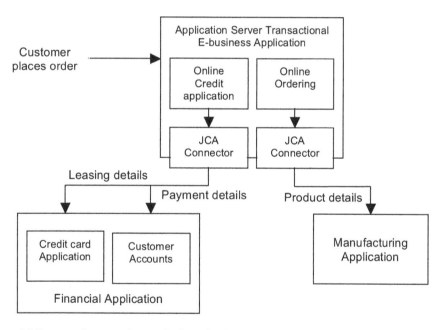

In the middleware integration solution depicted in Figure 6.6, a customer connects to a transactional e-business application to order a product. The application server includes JCA integration adapters to connect to the back-end manufacturing and finance applications. The e-business application has been modified to include business logic to utilize some of the additional functionality of these applications. It issues queries through the JCA adapters to tap into the additional credit functionality within the finance application, and to understand and process its responses. This in turn allows the company to expose this functionality for authorizing and issuing credit to select customers.

6.4.1 High-level design of application server middleware solutions

The transaction e-business application employs a standard n-tier application server based design to facilitate simplified application development and independent scaling of each tier.

The first tier receives requests from Internet or Intranet users through the web server, then passes them to the second tier application server for processing by the transactional e-business logic. This tier manages all business functions for customers, and includes integration code to access and return data from the enterprise applications. The second tier stores its configuration information and any transactional data in the database cluster in the third tier. This ensures the application server is not continually accessing the back-end data stores within the internal applications, thus maximizing performance by locating relevant data closer to Internet customers.

Application server EAI designs include a number of additional components necessary for integration and for reliable and scalable operation. Integration is provided through Java Connector Architecture-based connectors. The e-business application in the second tier accesses internal business applications on the fourth tier by sending messages from the e-business application via these adapters, using the Java Message Service. They reformat the messages into a form understood by the native applications, which then respond appropriately. Integration is therefore controlled by the e-business application logic residing on the application server.

The operational design of this solution includes reliability, scalability and availability features using multi-processor servers in all tiers. In addition, the two web servers in the first tier are arranged in a load balanced server farm for availability and scalability, with one server available if the other fails. This configuration can be expanded with additional servers as more customers use the system.

The transactional e-business application on the second tier is deployed in an application server cluster, with the e-business application software 'cloned' and distributed across multiple servers. The web servers in the first tier distribute user requests to these cloned applications, increasing the performance and availability of the complete solution. The e-business application in turn stores configuration information and interim data from the enterprise applications in a database cluster in the third tier, providing continual availability and increased performance. It also stores customer specific data used to authenticate and authorise customer access within an LDAP security server, which provides unified customer management and security. Critical information within this server is encrypted to provide high security.

Because this solution is accessing critical internal applications, the e-business application is segregated and regulated from the internal applications and corporate network by a firewall. All sensitive communication between each layer occurs via SSL certification to prevent interception by hackers/crackers. Other security mechanisms include encryption of sensitive financial and customer data in the application server database servers, and the use of multiple network level security systems including firewalls and intrusion detection systems.

This design is depicted in Figure 6.7.

Figure 6.7 High-level application server EAI design

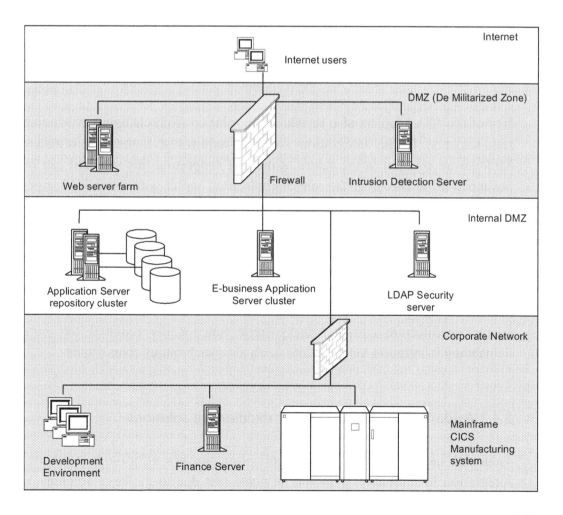

6.4.2 Benefits and limitations of application server middleware solutions

Application server middleware integration solutions offer an affordable and easily managed solution ideal for businesses requiring integration of enterprise applications.

Companies using this design will typically have a transactional e-business application developed using J2EE Enterprise JavaBeans, and deployed on an application server such as BEA WebLogic, IBM WebSphere or Sun iPlanet Application.

The use of a completely Java-based solution, including JavaBeans, JCA and JMS, removes unnecessary complexity and simplifies development around one programming language. This ensures developers need only understand Java, resulting in quicker, more tightly controlled projects. The use of Java also allows the solution to be moved to application servers from other vendors, reducing vendor dependence and hence project risk, and ensures the solution can be readily modified in the future to include new internal applications.

Use of the JCA adapters also insulates the solution from changing integration requirements. If the integration solution requires a higher performance Middleware solution in the future, a product supporting this standard can be 'swapped in' to take over the role of application server with minimal changes required in the e-business application.

However, this design may only be suited for small-scale integration initiatives due to potential scalability and performance problems. Typically, application servers have not been designed to handle large numbers of integrated applications or provide high performance in integration functionality. In addition, the JCA adapter architecture currently lacks some functionality required for more demanding integration requirements, such as asynchronous connections.

6.4.3 Vendors of application server middleware solutions

Table 6.1 lists vendors of J2EE Application Servers offering JCA adapter integration functionality. It should be noted that due to the large amounts of vendors and products available, this list is not exhaustive and should be used as a guide only before solution research is undertaken.

Table 6.1 Vendors of J2EE application servers

Vendor	J2EE application server
ATG	ATG Dynamo
BEA	BEA WebLogic Server
Hewlett Packard	HP Application Server
IBM	WebSphere Application Server
Iona	Orbix E2A Application Server
Jonas	Jonas Application Server (Open Source)
Lutris	Enterprise Application Server (Open Source)
Orion	Orion Application Server (Open Source)
Oracle	Oracle 9i Application Server
Pramati	Pramati Server
Sun Microsystems	Sun ONE Application Server
Sybase	EA Server

6.5 Hub and spoke middleware solutions

In contrast to application server designs, hub and spoke middleware solutions use a dedicated central Hub server connecting multiple 'spoke' applications together. Integration occurs via messages passed through the hub, which determines the appropriate message destination.

This design can provide businesses with an integration solution that can meet more demanding integration requirements than the previous designs. It is capable of scaling from modest requirements to demanding integration between multiple transactional e-business and enterprise applications, with moderate to high levels of messages passing.

Companies adopting this design will typically have several two – or three-tier transactional e-business applications offering customer-focused services. These applications may be written using many different Internet programming languages, and deployed on distributed stand-alone server systems or J2EE application servers. The solution will typically integrate these applications with several internal enterprise applications, such as financial, resource planning and legacy mainframe applications, and additionally provide integration between each application.

For example, a customer accesses a transactional e-business application to purchase a product and arrange online credit. The order passes through the integration hub, which in turn distributes the components of the order to the appropriate enterprise applications. When the manufacturing application needs to update the financial application with a request for new parts, it sends a message to the hub server as shown in Figure 6.8.

Figure 6.8 Enterprise integration using hub and spoke middleware solutions

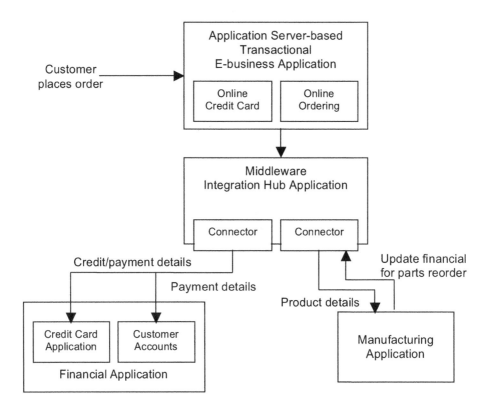

In the middleware integration solution depicted in Figure 6.8, the transactional e-business application issues an order request to the integration hub. This system in turn decomposes the order into constituent parts and sends them to

the finance and manufacturing applications through the integration connectors. Inbound messages from the applications are received by the connectors and re-formatted into the EAI server internal message structure for processing, transformation and routing to their final destination. This in turn allows the transactional e-business application to delegate some of these functions to the hub server so that it does not require detailed knowledge of the applications.

What to look for in a hub and spoke middleware solution

Hub and Spoke Middleware products should support a set of core architectural components to ensure the timely and accurate delivery of information between integrated applications and transactional e-business systems. These include performance, security, integration, message transport, routing, reformatting, transformation, and administration components.

Products should provide an integrated development environment (IDE) for developers to extend the functionality of the product and customize it to fit their specific integration requirements. Development tasks include creating new adapters for custom applications, tailoring routing and transformation rules to specific requirements, or integrating the solution with corporate security systems to enhance the security of transactional e-business applications.

Performance and reliability should be provided through support for multi-processor and clustered servers, and distribution of transformation and routing engines across multiple servers. However, due to their centralized nature, some hub and spoke systems may not readily scale performance using multiple servers. Performance assessment should be provided through systems management and monitoring tools.

Critical components should be deployed in fault tolerant configurations to ensure the solution continues to function if one component fails. Fault tolerance is achieved using redundant components to take over the work of failed components. For example, if an adapter fails, the product should restart the failed adapter or use an alternative adapter.

Security features should ensure application data is not sent to the wrong application or customer, and that customers cannot access applications for which they do not have access rights. This can be achieved through the use of security management infrastructures such as LDAP compliant directory services (e.g. Novell NDS, Microsoft Active Directory, IBM Secureway LDAP Directory Server), single sign on systems, and public key encryption infrastructures for very high security.

A wide range of intelligent adapters should be included with the products to provide immediate integration with packaged and custom-written internal enterprise applications. Adapters should offer performance monitoring, the ability to restart dynamically when failure is detected, logging, and data encryption. Advanced adapters may also offer the ability to perform reformatting and transformation of data within the adapter for highest performance.

Products should support multiple message transport functions to meet different application integration requirements. Asynchronous transport should be available for transactional e-business applications, as this allows them to send data and continue processing user requests without waiting for acknowledgement. Synchronous transport is more suited for real-time/near real-time closely coupled applications requiring transaction management, such as financial applications, as this requires the product to wait for acknowledgement from target applications. Synchronous transport is also used to emulate batch-processing systems in legacy environments.

Message transport functions should utilize industry-standard message communication protocols such as HTTP, the Java Messaging Service, or de facto standards such as the IBM MQSeries protocol. This simplifies the integration effort by allowing it to use a wide range of compatible products. This in turn lowers the total lifetime cost of the integration solution, and reduces dependence on proprietary vendor products. It also allows for the creation of a solution based on products from several vendors to create the best solution.

Routing of messages between applications is handled by a message broker component. This component uses rules to analyse message flows and re-route them according to predefined or dynamic criteria. Common forms of routing that should be supported include publish and subscribe, and request/reply routing. Publish and subscribe routing 'publishes' messages on certain topics from applications, to which other applications then 'subscribe'. This permits applications to issue messages without requiring direct connections or knowledge of receiving applications, and offers high scalability and a more robust integration solution. Request/reply routing requires an application receive a response before sending additional messages, and is used for closely coupled and real-time integration. Message brokers should also include the ability to reformat message source and destination information within the intelligent adapter, to relieve the workload on the central hub.

Message transport and routing/broker functions should together provide guaranteed message delivery capability. This ensures reliable message delivery and notification of message reception by the target application. If the message is not delivered, the sending application is notified and then can act accordingly. Messages should also be warehoused in a database for later analysis, and to preserve message integrity in case of failure of the message broker.

Transformation functionality is required to change message content between the source and destination applications. This allows the message broker to alter messages to an acceptable format for destination applications. As most applications understand data in a variety of incompatible formats, this feature ensures each application can successfully process the received message. Transformation engines should support XML, the de facto industry standard mechanism for data transformation, to ensure the product can support any application-specific data format. All transformation rules should be stored in a scalable and reliable storage repository to provide a centralized rule management mechanism.

Message transformation also requires transaction management to ensure alterations and updates to the messages execute successfully. This ensures data integrity is maintained between applications and the middleware product so that critical business transactions complete reliably. If a transaction cannot complete successfully, it is rolled back to ensure all messages are in a consistently known state. Transaction management also allows the product to execute a transaction and continue to process other messages. Once processing has completed it will then be informed if the message processed successfully or failed.

Finally, administration functions require the product to offer a graphical interface to manage the application. This should include the ability to create rule definitions, define transformation logic and conduct systems management functions such as tracking, logging, and notification of events. This allows the solution to determine the status of message flows between the applications and the middleware, and to provide reporting and analysis.

6.5.1 High-level design of hub and spoke middleware solutions

The hub and spoke integration design is intended for integrating several transactional e-business applications with a number of enterprise applications. It is also suited to moderate to high levels of message passing between enterprise applications.

The hub and spoke e-business integration design contains a number of operational and functional differences to the application server integration design to facilitate more demanding integration needs. Functional differences include using the hub server to analyse and route messages from applications, in contrast to the use of the application server in the previous design. This design also includes more sophisticated integration logic within the hub, such as message routing and transformation, providing higher performance and simplifying the e-business applications, as they no longer require integration control logic.

This functional separation in turn allows for optimization of the operational design components of the system. For example, integration hubs can be scaled independently from the transactional e-business application server for optimal performance. The hub server can also be placed closer to large groups of applications to reduce network latency times and therefore increase communication speeds.

Additional scalability can be implemented through deployment of hub and spoke 'federated' designs. This variation utilizes additional integration Hub servers configured as a hierarchy of integration servers, in a similar manner to the DNS system. This allows integration tasks to be distributed between local and remote sites, off-loading remote integration tasks from the central hub cluster and increasing availability, scalability and reliability. This design is depicted in Figure 6.9.

Figure 6.9 Federation of hub and spoke integration servers

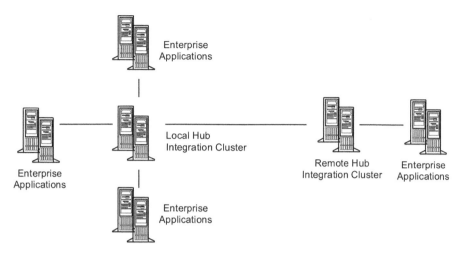

In contrast to the application server design, additional security systems are required due to the integration with greater numbers of internal applications. These include additional intrusion detection systems within the internal network, and centralized security management via integration with corporate directory servers such as Novell Netware NDS or Microsoft Active Directory, which are typically present in companies deploying this design. The hub integrates with directory servers via the LDAP protocol, providing simplified security control over access between enterprise applications and the e-business applications. As this directory server contains very sensitive internal information about employees and corporate applications, a two-tier LDAP directory system is used to prevent potential compromise of this information. The transactional e-business applications use a local LDAP security server containing information specific to external transactional customers. If it requires additional information, it checks the internal directory server that then regulates access to this information. Any retrieved information is never cached in the e-business LDAP server to preserve security.

Additional operational systems are required to manage the complete solution. These include the management and reporting station to manage the complete hub/spoke solution, and a development environment for design and proof-of-concept of changes and additions to the solution.

This design also includes the full set of features discussed in the section What to look for in a hub and spoke middleware solution. These include adapters to integrate packaged and custom enterprise applications with e-business systems and other enterprise applications, transaction management, security, multiple message transport, routing and transformation functions, and centralized administration.

The hub and spoke integration design is depicted in Figure 6.10.

Figure 6.10 Hub and spoke enterprise application integration design

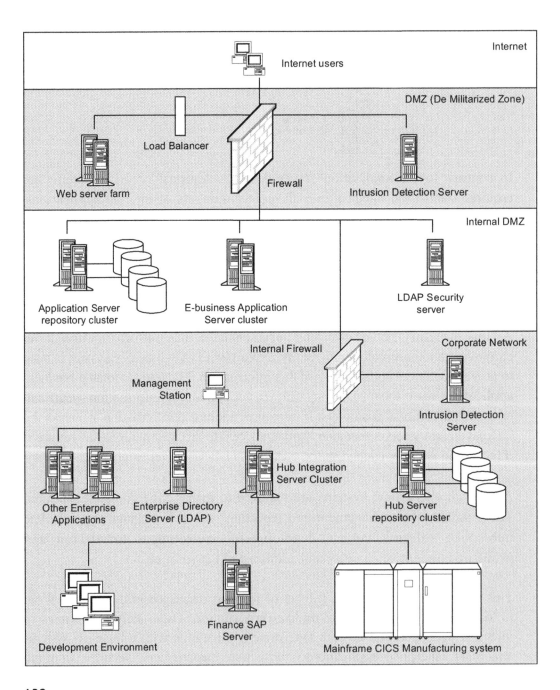

6.5.2 Benefits and limitations of hub and spoke middleware solutions

Hub and spoke EAI solutions represent an ideal solution for the majority of integration needs. They offer simple administration of the integration solution through their centralized design. Integration of additional applications is also simplified through the addition of appropriate adapters to 'plug' them into the hub, making them immediately available to other integrated applications. They also provide a wide range of sophisticated integration features and performance suitable for all but the most demanding integration initiatives.

However, for very large installations with many integrated applications or very high levels of message traffic, the central hub can become a bottleneck and suffer from poor performance. The hub can also form a central point of failure if it becomes unavailable, rendering the application integration solution non-functional.

Adopting federated and clustered solutions can alleviate some of these issues, but may result in increases in the management complexity of the solution. This may in turn suggest investigation of a message – bus solution to provide additional performance.

6.5.3 Vendors of hub and spoke middleware solutions

Table 6.2 lists vendors of hub and spoke-based middleware solutions. It should be noted that due to the large amounts of vendors and products available, this list is not exhaustive and should be used as a guide only before solution research is undertaken.

Table 6.2 Vendors of hub and spoke middelware solutions

Vendor	Hub and spoke middleware solution
BEA	WebLogic Integration
IBM	WebSphere MQ
Sun Microsystems	Sun ONE Integration Server EAI Edition
Peregrine	Business Integration Suite (also message bus design)
WebMethods	WebMethods Integration Platform
WRQ	WRQ Verastream
Open Source	OpenAdapter; Tambora

6.6 Message bus middleware solutions

Message bus middleware solutions integrate applications through a distributed and highly reliable message backbone or 'bus', in contrast to the central integration hub of the hub and spoke architecture which may provide a single point of failure (Sanchez, Patel and Fenner, 2001).

The message bus design is intended for companies expecting very high levels of message traffic between large numbers of internal enterprise applications distributed across multiple geographical locations, and multiple transactional e-business applications creating very high levels of message traffic. This design is also intended for companies expecting strong growth in their integration requirements, as it can be scaled up to support the most demanding performance requirements.

The integration bus is comprised of a highly distributed network of integration components, including distributed broker servers providing message data transformation and routing, integration servers with integration adapters and message queues for sending and receiving messages between applications, monitoring tools, and distributed repositories containing configuration information and message data. Applications are integrated through integration adapters and place messages onto message queues. The integration servers and brokers then send these messages to their intended destination. Receiving applications utilizes the same systems to receive messages from queues and process them according to their own internal systems and processes.

Each component in this design can be deployed in multiple configurations, depending on the requirements of the enterprise. Brokers and integration servers can be deployed on the same server, or alternatively separated into separate systems. Message queue management can also be distributed throughout the solution.

For example, a customer connects to a transactional e-business application to purchase a product. Manufacturing this product requires co-ordination between the corporate financial application for payment processing, the manufacturing application, and the logistics system for product shipment to the customer. The company supplying the product is spread across several offices in different parts of the country, and must integrate a wide range of internal applications, necessitating a distributed message bus design. This process is depicted in Figure 6.11.

Figure 6.11 Enterprise integration using message bus middleware solutions

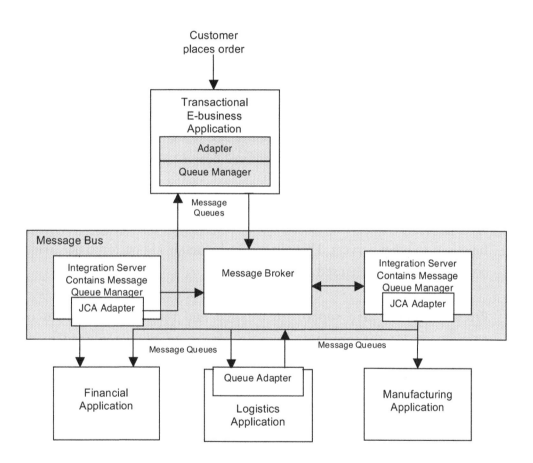

In the middleware integration solution depicted in Figure 6.11, the customer order is sent into the message bus by the transactional e-business application. The message bus uses a system of broker and integration servers to route this message to the financial system, which responds confirming successful payment. The e-business application then sends order messages to the legacy manufacturing system, which requires the message to be reformatted and transformed into different legacy data structures. The message is therefore routed through the message broker to transform it into the desired format. Once the customer's order is ready, the manufacturing application informs the logistics application that the order is ready for shipment to the customer via another message. This is routed to the message broker, which in turn communicates with the logistics application using a JCA adapter residing in the message broker.

What to look for in a message bus middleware solution

In addition to the functions and components required in hub and spoke products, message bus solutions require additional functional and operational components due to their highly distributed design.

Message transformation rules stored in a repository must be available to all message bus broker servers to allow for distribution of message transformation functions to other servers. This allows for reductions in performance loads and bottlenecks on heavily used broker servers.

Products should also support distributed and remote management of all components of the product. Remote management is required to allow integration servers, message queues and broker servers to be managed at remote locations to satisfy local integration requirements. However, all components of the solution should be capable of central administration to ensure continued cohesive functioning of the solution.

6.6.1 High level design of message bus middleware solutions

The message bus integration design employs a set of highly configurable, distributed components designed to offer very flexible deployments and very high performance, as shown in Figure 6.12.

In contrast to the previous design, applications do not communicate with a single central hub. Integration occurs via messages passed into queues, which may be installed locally on servers or hosted on integration servers. Queues communicate with nearby applications, and can access remote queues to integrate with applications in different divisions. Some applications may not be capable of running local message queues, and therefore integration is provided through integration servers acting in a similar manner to hub and spoke designs. If transformation and routing of messages is required, queues pass through message brokers.

The operational design of message bus solutions includes distributed integration servers and message broker servers spread across corporate organizational and geographical boundaries. Therefore, additional systems are deployed at sites requiring integration of many applications, or at geographically remote sites.

Clustering of brokers and integration servers is also provided for reliability, availability and scalability. As this design is highly distributed, repository database clusters should support federation throughout the integration solution, allowing distribution of required transformation and routing rules to remote locations.

Security systems include additional intrusion detection monitoring systems, and additional internal DMZ networks to support local and remote transactional e-business applications. Due to the large number of integrated applications, distributed LDAP directory servers are required to spread security information throughout the enterprise, and provide for higher performance and increase availability of security information. Secure message transport is also required between local and remote message bus components to ensure protection of sensitive data in transit.

Finally, additional management systems may be deployed at remote sites to facilitate administration of local integration resources.

This design is depicted in Figure 6.12.

Figure 6.12 Message bus enterprise application integration design

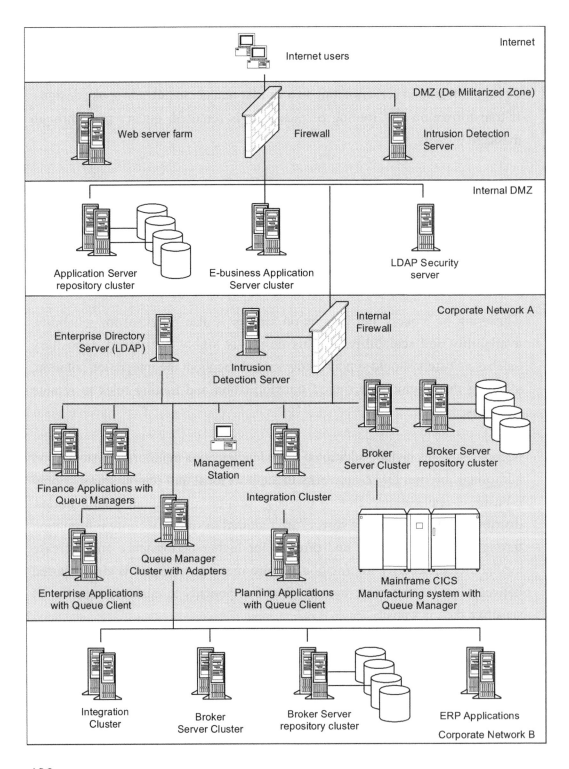

6.6.2 Benefits and limitations of message bus middleware solutions

Message bus EAI middleware solutions provide the greatest scalability and highest reliability of all enterprise application integration solutions. They are therefore recommended for companies intending to integrate large numbers of internal applications with considerable volumes of message traffic. Alternatively, they are recommended for companies expecting large increases in their integration requirements.

However, implementation and administration of this design can be more complicated than for hub and spoke designs as the number of interconnected systems and queues increases. Message bus EAI solutions also require more initial design and planning than hub and spoke or application server-based solutions, due to their potentially large numbers of components.

6.6.3 Vendors of message bus middleware solutions

Table 6.3 lists vendors of message bus middleware solutions and their products. It should be noted that this list is not exhaustive and should be used as a guide only before solution research is undertaken.

Table 6.3 Vendors of message bus middleware solutions

Vendor	Message bus middleware solution
BEA	WebLogic Integration
IBM	WebSphere MQ and WebSphere Integration
Peregrine	Business Integration Suite (also hub and spoke design)
SeeBeyond	Business Integration Suite
Tibco	ActiveEnterprise
Vitria Technology	BusinessWare Integration Platform
WebMethods	WebMethods Integration Platform
WRQ	WRQ Verastream

The fourth phase of e-business is external enterprise application integration, also known as business-to-business integration (B2B integration). This phase involves connecting internally integrated enterprise applications to the enterprise applications of external supplier and partner companies, in contrast to the internal focus of the EAI phase.

External enterprise application integration provides considerable benefits. These include real-time knowledge of product availability, real-time logistics for customer shipping status, increased efficiency through automation of existing manual processes when working with suppliers, and reducing time to market for new products and services.

Other benefits to external integration include improving communication between companies through the sharing of information and outsourcing parts of the business to highly valued partners, which enables all parties to function as an extended trading network with resulting economies of scale and specialization. This in turn supports gaining rapid competitive advantage, building closer partnerships with customers, partners and suppliers across all areas of business, reducing the business cost for procurement and production of goods, and reducing inventory levels. Finally, external integration also allows segregated business units to work together to integrate their processes with external partners and suppliers, and consolidate redundant processes, resulting in more efficiency and effectiveness and increased revenue and decreased business costs.

For example, a company sells products to customers online through an internally integrated transactional e-business system. If a product is in stock, the integrated internal applications determine if the item is available and an expected shipment time, and send these to the customer.

However, if the item is not in stock and requires parts or services from a supplier, the company systems determine the products and services required to fulfil the order, and request these from external partner and suppliers. The supplier systems determine the availability and shipment dates of the required products or services, and then informs the company manufacturing system. This information is then fed back to the customer, giving improved service and guaranteed availability. This process is depicted in Figure 7.1.

Figure 7.1 Order fulfilment process using EAI and external integration

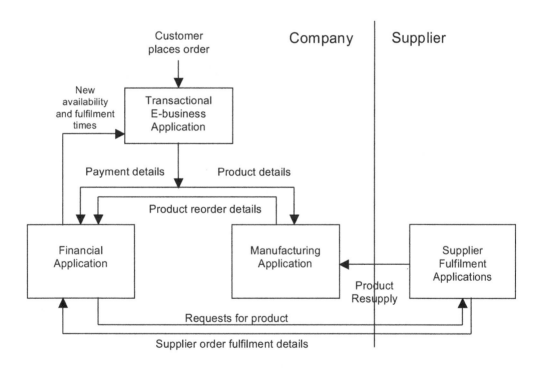

The transactional e-business application requests item availability from the manufacturing application. If this item is not in stock, the manufacturing system

sends a request for additional products to the financial application. This application then sends a request for new products to the external supplier systems, which respond with a quantity, price and logistics fulfilment schedule. The financial application updates the e-business application with this information, and the customer confirms the order and makes a payment. The financial application then approves the product resupply request from the supplier, and makes a payment if required. It then updates the manufacturing systems with the expected delivery time for the product. Once the item is in stock, it can be processed and shipped to the customer.

External enterprise application integration is used across the supply and demand chain areas of the business. The supply chain is the set of systems responsible for bringing a product to market, and includes internal and outsourced manufacturing, transportation, warehousing, procurement, and distribution. Typically procurement processes for goods and services are very inefficient, and involve manual effort from staff or alternatively use technology with minimal automation that may be prone to error, such as emailing or faxing orders to suppliers. Automation of procurement from external partners and suppliers can therefore achieve considerable productivity improvements and savings in staff time and business costs, and reduces the cost of the goods being procured.

Fulfilment of goods and services from external suppliers requires them to build a product, then use logistics companies to transport the finished goods from manufacturers to customers. Automation of fulfilment can provide real-time information on the current location and estimated delivery time for products. This can be used to provide customers with exact times for product delivery, and allows companies to optimize production schedules to reduce inventory levels, resulting in considerable savings.

The demand chain areas of the business involves processing sales orders from customers, taking direct payments or payment on account, and shipment of finished goods. Some of these areas may be outsourced to external partners or suppliers, such as using a payment provider for account settlement, and product shipping through logistics companies. Automation of these steps through external partner and supplier integration can therefore provide increased efficiencies, reduce errors in existing manual processing, and reduce processing times for customer orders. This improves customer service and satisfaction, and can increase customer loyalty and hence customer retention.

7.1 Key technologies used

External integration with partners and suppliers requires technology systems that can extend existing business processes used within the company to external partner and suppliers.

Business processes consist of a discrete set of steps that must be carried out to achieve a business outcome, such as producing products or services. Each step in a business process involves manipulating and moving information or physical goods. Typical business processes used in external integration initiatives cover supply and demand factors in a business, such as determining product availability and order status, processing payments, determining shipment times for goods and services, and transporting orders to customers.

For example, a supply chain replenishment process between company and supplier may include the following steps, as depicted in Figure 7.2.

Figure 7.2 Supply chain processing through an external supplier

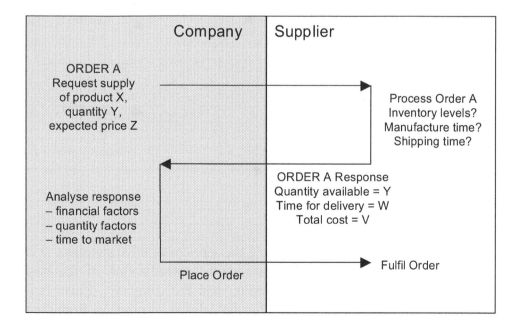

The initial order is specified by the company and then sent to their supplier. The supplier processes the order to determine if they can fulfil it. They then build a

response including the product quantities they can produce, their estimated time for delivery, and the total cost of the order. This is sent back to the company, who then analyse it to determine if the quantity of goods will be sufficient, and whether it will arrive in time and at the right cost. If these criteria are met satisfactorily, they will confirm and place the order.

With increased use of outsourcing, business processes are typically shared among multiple participants, such as a number of suppliers and logistics partners responsible for the delivery of finished goods. This extended process sharing is depicted in Figure 7.3.

Figure 7.3 Extended business process sharing

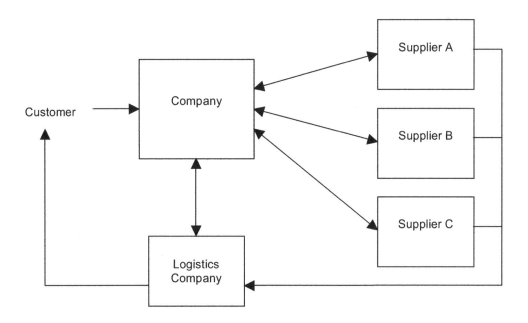

This diagram depicts a company using the services of three suppliers to create finished goods for customers. This requires co-ordination of the business processes shared between each supplier and the company. It also requires participation of a logistics supplier for the delivery of products from the three suppliers to the company, then delivery of the finished goods from the company to the customer.

Sharing processes with external suppliers and partners is complicated by the different technologies commonly used by each company. Such integration's are typically faced with either a wide range of diverse technologies used in loose networks of partners and suppliers (often small to medium sized companies). Alternatively, they may utilize tightly linked networks of suppliers with high degrees of integration between each company's processes and technologies. This form of integration is typically used for tightly integrated companies, such as subsidiaries of large conglomerates. Such companies typically have very homogeneous integration architectures with little variation in technology. Many companies will be faced with both extremes, as they are integrated with multiple suppliers.

Five forms of external integration solutions have evolved to share business processes between companies and their external partners and suppliers. These solutions can be categorized into customized solutions, supply chain solutions, extended EAI solutions, marketplace solutions, and business process integration (BPI) solutions. For most companies that are committed to using e-business for competitive advantage, business process integration solutions will be the best long-term solution. However, companies frequently utilize more than one of these integration solutions, as they may be involved in multiple trading relationships with different partners and suppliers and thus need to integrate with different systems.

7.2 Customized solutions

Before modern external integration solutions were developed, proprietary external integration solutions were often created to connect company applications to external partner and supplier systems. These solutions were developed in-house through customization of packaged software, or by writing completely new applications from scratch.

As each integration participant wrote different and incompatible software, this integration strategy relied on all trading partners agreeing on the data that they would use to encode the business transaction information they needed to exchange. Data exchange systems included custom HTML or text documents sent via automated FTP or email mechanisms, or Electronic Data Interchange (EDI) messages transmitted over closed proprietary networks. These include incompatible national and industry standards, such as ANSI X12 in North America and TRADACOMS in the United Kingdom and the international EDIFACT standard (Electronic Data Interchange for Administration,

Commerce and Transport). More recently, these solutions have begun using proprietary XML document formats to encode transaction information.

Data sent between participants was typically then integrated into internal applications via manual systems such as reading emails or files and manually re-entering data, or via automated systems such as low-level EAI data and platform integration technologies. This process is depicted in Figure 7.4.

Figure 7.4 External integration using proprietary solutions

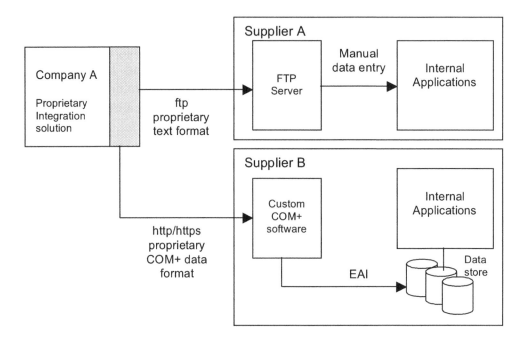

In this example, Company A has created a highly customized proprietary integration solution to cover very diverse integration requirements. This tool sends product orders to Supplier A via FTP using a proprietary text format agreed between the two companies. Supplier A receives these files at their FTP server, where they are read by staff members and manually input into existing internal applications. Supplier B has a proprietary integration solution written using Microsoft DCOM objects. This solution receives an object-level call from Company A, which passes the required information using a proprietary data format. Supplier B's software then uses ODBC to directly access the underlying databases of internal enterprise applications to enter the information received.

However, such proprietary solutions suffer from a considerable number of problems that render them generally unsuitable as external integration solutions. Because they are customized in-house, a company adopting such a solution requires design and development teams, and will thus have to manage potentially large-scale and time-consuming projects. The high levels of customization within such products also render them inflexible and unable to adapt to changes in technology and business processes. For example, if the technology used within internal and partner and supplier systems changes or a new partner is added, the solution will have to be rewritten. In addition, changes in the common data standards adopted will typically require substantial modifications to the systems of each participant.

Problems also arise from the need to develop proprietary common data standards to exchange information, which must be agreed by each integration participant. However, this is not always possible as one or more participants may be using an existing data standard that they refuse to change. This frequently results in the lowest common denominator data standard being employed, with resulting loss of potentially valuable trading information. Using EDI as the common data standard also suffers from a number of problems, as EDI standards are considered to be inflexible and thus only suitable for limited transactions (Varon, 2001), and frequently focused on direct material procurements and transportation of goods (Scala, 2001). EDI is also a costly and slow system to implement (Varon, 2001), relies on proprietary networks to connect trading partners, and lacks additional functionality beyond that offered in paper documents (Verbeck and Madda, 2001).

Customized external integration solutions may also use similar data and transport-level technologies to more advanced business process integration solutions, to exchange compatible information between companies. However, as customized solutions lack support for managing integration standards as part of a business process, any changes in data formats or shared business processes will require changes in the customized solution to accommodate these changes.

In addition, the reliance on exchange of common data to determine business process transactions does not address the issue of how to properly manage such interactions. Business process interactions require advanced functionality such as managing errors during data exchanges and compensating for errors through other processes, and determining how often data should be exchanged under different conditions.

Proprietary integration systems do provide some advantages, as they do not require complex integration infrastructure such as middleware brokers.

Therefore, such solutions may be appropriate to situations where trading relationships exist between a small number of companies with stable business models. Such companies will change their business processes infrequently, and seldom need to integrate new partners and suppliers. A cost-benefit analyses should be conducted to determine the value of adopting such a custom solution, compared to choosing a more open and flexible business process integration system from a well-known and stable vendor.

7.3 Extended EAI solutions

External integration using extended EAI allows companies to integrate with the enterprise applications of external partners and suppliers, using their existing EAI infrastructure.

This form of external integration uses the integration functionality included with an EAI product to connect to external partner and supplier application infrastructure, as depicted in Figure 7.5.

Figure 7.5 External integration using extended EAI products

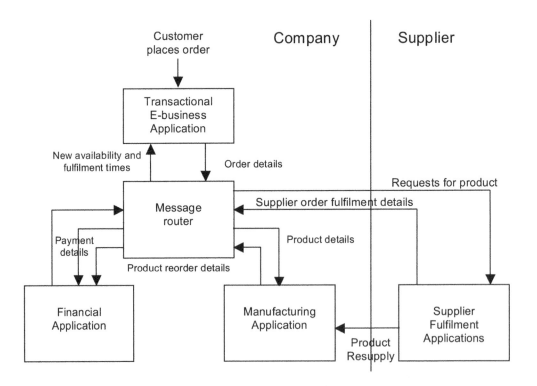

Figure 7.5 depicts a company routing internal messages between applications and a transactional e-business system via a message router, which consists of an EAI Middleware broker product. The message router breaks down the initial customer order into pieces destined for relevant internal applications. Product order details are sent to the manufacturing application, which responds with an out-of-stock message.

The router processes this message and sends a request to the external supplier requesting supply of additional product. This application responds with confirmation of quantity, delivery time and price. The router sends the response to the financial application, which then gives tentative approval to the order. The router then informs the client of the expected delivery time, and the client pays for their order, with payment details routed to the financial application for processing. Once the order payment is approved, the router responds to the supplier with confirmation to proceed with the new order, and sends confirmation that the order is being processed to the customer.

This form of external integration can be achieved through the EAI integration technologies discussed in the preceding chapter, such as JMS/JCA messaging and adapter technologies, or alternatively low-level direct access to application databases or software components.

High-level designs for extended EAI integration initiatives typically resemble internal enterprise application integration, and include modifications to firewall systems to establish virtual private networks (VPN) between partner and supplier company firewalls to secure messages travelling between participants. External integration with partner and supplier applications then becomes an extension of existing systems. Hub and spoke designs would therefore include external applications as another 'spoke', and message bus designs would deploy additional message queue definitions or queue brokers at the remote supplier site.

Extended EAI initiatives provide a means to reuse existing EAI infrastructure, potentially generating a higher return on investment. It also provides companies with current EAI systems a well-understood methodology for external integration.

However, such products may suffer a number of limitations that restrict their usefulness for external integration. They typically lack the ability to connect to external systems in a non-intrusive manner, thus requiring changes to be made to these external systems before integration can occur. Thus, changes in internal or shared business processes may require modification of the extended EAI solution, preventing rapid change necessary within the business.

In addition, external integration using such technology may not include all the functionality required to manage shared business processes, such as allowing for manual steps within processes, or manual intervention when errors occur (Hildreth, 2000). They are also frequently unable to handle the long duration required for many outsourced business processes.

These limitations also frequently lead to companies with strong, dominant relationships with suppliers mandating a common middleware infrastructure before participation in an external integration (Olsen, 2000). This results in a potentially inflexible integration solution that is incapable of extension to companies not using that product, thus excluding them from participating in the integration and restricting the companies' choice of partners and suppliers.

7.3.1 Vendors of extended EAI solutions

Table 7.1 lists vendors of extended EAI external integration solutions and their products. It should be noted that this list is not exhaustive and should be used as a guide only before solution research is undertaken.

Table 7.1 Vendors of extended EAI solutions

Vendor	Extended EAI solution
BEA Systems	BEA eLink Integration Server; BEA WebLogic Integration
IBM	IBM MQ/MQSI, CrossWorlds
Neon	NEON e-Biz Integrator
Peregrine	Business Integration Suite
SeeBeyond	E-Business Integration Suite
Sun Microsystems	iPlanet Integration Server, EAI Edition
Tibco	ActiveEnterprise
Vitria Technology	BusinessWare
WebMethods	WebMethods Enterprise
WRQ	WRQ Verastream
Open Source	OpenAdapter; Tambora

7.4 Supply chain management solutions

Supply chain management solutions are typically dedicated applications used to manage all aspects of the company's supply chain with external partners and suppliers, such as product planning and forecasting, product design collaboration with suppliers, outsourced manufacturing, and outsourced logistics management.

This form of external integration manages the company's supply chain through the functionality included in the supply chain management product, connecting to similar products within the external partner and supplier companies as depicted in Figure 7.6.

Figure 7.6 External integration using supply chain management products

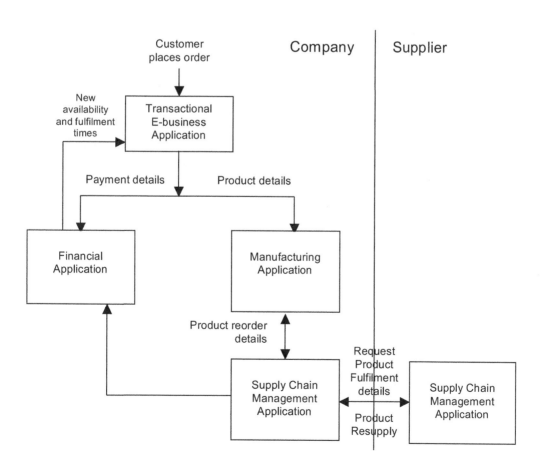

Figure 7.6 depicts a customer placing an order through a transactional e-business application. Product order details are received by the manufacturing application, which checks with the supply chain management application to determine stock availability. If the product is out of stock, this application will query the same application at the supplier to determine when new products can be supplied. Some financial functions may reside in the supply chain application, such as product costing and pricing, allowing it to approve orders automatically. It then responds to the manufacturing application with expected delivery times for the product, which is forwarded to the transactional e-business application. The customer approves the order, and their payment is processed and approved by the financial system. The product resupply is then approved by the supply chain management application.

Typical high-level designs for supply chain management external integration solutions resemble existing hub and spoke and message bus eai designs, with the addition of the supply chain management product as an additional integrated application. In a similar manner to the extended EAI external integration solution, a virtual private network is required to secure communications between participants.

Supply chain management solutions can provide a number of benefits to companies. These include very rigorous control over inventory and production levels, resulting in business cost savings and the ability to optimize their complete supply chain for increased automation and efficiency. They may also benefit from additional product features such as demand forecasting, allowing for prediction of customer demand and adjustment of production levels, and design collaboration to work on new product releases with suppliers.

However, supply chain management solutions have similar problems to those faced by the extended EAI solutions discussed above. Typically all participants must use the same solution and integrate it with their existing internal systems. This results in increased expense for participants, as they may require several different integration solutions for different customers.

In addition, not all participants will require all the functionality of such broad products, resulting in unnecessary expenditure. They may also find their own internal business processes are not catered for by such packaged applications. This may in turn force them to change their processes to suit the software. Finally, such products may lack the flexibility to change with ongoing changes in business processes within companies.

7.4.1 Vendors of supply chain management solutions

Table 7.2 lists vendors of supply chain management solutions for use in external integration initiatives with partners and suppliers. It should be noted that this list is not exhaustive and should be used as a guide only before solution research is undertaken.

Table 7.2 Vendors of supply chain management solutions

Vendor	Supply chain management solution
Ariba	Ariba Enterprise Sourcing and Spend Management
Commerce One	Commerce One Suite
Clarus	eProcurement
FreeMarkets	FullSource and QuickSource
Frictionless Commerce	Frictionless Sourcing and Enterprise Sourcing
InfoRay	InfoRay
i2 Technologies	i2
Manugistics	Manugistics Supply Chain Management
SageTree	SageTree Supply Chain Performance Suite
Moai	CompleteSource
Oracle	Oracle Supply Chain Intelligence/E-business Suite
PeopleSoft	PeopleSoft Supply Chain Management
SAP	mySAP Supply Chain Management
SAS	SAS Supplier Relationship Management
SeeCommerce	SeeChain
Syncra systems	Syncra Xt
Viewlocity	TradeSync

7.5 Marketplace solutions

Marketplace solutions (also known as net markets or exchanges) are designed to offer companies access to potentially hundreds of external suppliers and customers.

This model differs significantly from other forms of external integration, through centralized management of external suppliers through the Marketplace Broker. Brokers can also provide a range of added value services within the marketplace by managing and executing core business processes among participants, such as catalogue and pricing information, order management, transactions between participants, and shipping co-ordination.

For example, a company may wholesale certain products to customers. They require access to a wide variety of suppliers simultaneously to provide the best possible price to their customers, and therefore connect to a marketplace, as depicted in Figure 7.7.

Figure 7.7 External integration using marketplaces

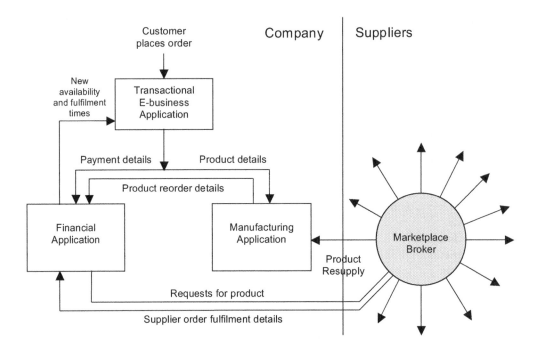

Using marketplace external integration, customers access the transactional e-business site to purchase products. If the item is not in stock, the financial application can access the marketplace and use the broker services to access multiple suppliers to source new products. The financial application validates the response from the marketplace to determine if the new supplier order meets the appropriate financial criteria, then updates the transactional e-business application with the new data. The customer can then approve the order and make a payment. Alternatively, the financial system can aggregate multiple orders from several suppliers to fulfil customer requirements.

High-level designs for marketplace external integration solutions resemble extended EAI solutions, as they require integration between internal enterprise application systems and the systems provided by the marketplace broker. Most marketplace solutions therefore typically feature an up-front integration cost before joining. Marketplaces are categorized into either public or private marketplaces according to membership status. Public marketplaces are often used to bring buyers and sellers together for trading in commodity products via auctions or catalogues, and may be used to identify new customers and sell excess inventory. Typically, independent investors or industry consortia own public marketplaces, which function as independent companies.

Individual companies often set up private marketplaces to transact with their existing customers, partners and suppliers, as this provides for a closer, more streamlined working relationship. They also offer participants greater security when trading sensitive information between participants, such as sales forecasts, and allow centralized control of supplier contracts.

Marketplaces are differentiated into four categories according to the specific industry segments they support, and the features they offer companies, including functional enablers, generic supplies, commodity products, and vertical marketplaces (Bolino and Conti, 2001; Frick and Hyrne, 2001). These four categories are depicted in Table 7.3.

Table 7.3 Common types of marketplaces

Type	Functional enablers	Generic supplies	Commodity products	Vertical
Services	Provides low cost services that are easily outsourced	Reduction in cost of transactions for low value, highly standardized products in most industries that can be easily compared	Provides marketplace for commodity products with 'market' pricing	Performs complex processes in vertical industries
Current status	Most recent, smallest	Fastest growing but most fragmented sector	Many commodity product marketplaces exist for most products	Hardest to create and least amount of progress
Possible future status	Will be transformed into service companies	Will consolidate into two or three dominant companies	Each commodity area will have one dominant company	Unknown
Examples	Hire.com PeopleSupport FinancialSettlement	Staples.com MRO.com Grainger	E-steel PlasticsNet	Transora Neoforma Chemdex

The functionality offered within these marketplace categories includes providing market information, facilitating trading relationships, supporting transactions, and providing integration (Tapellini, 2000). Market information is offered by all marketplaces, and includes providing information to participants in the marketplace in such areas as industry directories, databases of products, industry related articles, and discussion forums.

Facilitation is the ability of the exchange to match buyers to supplier product and service offerings through different mechanisms including product postings, request for proposals (RFPs), request for quotes (RFQs), auctions, and negotiation systems. Settlement of the resulting transaction may take place offline outside the marketplace via each company's current arrangements.

Marketplaces with support for transactions offer buyers and sellers the ability to complete the financial transaction online within the marketplace. This requires connections to external banks and to the internal financial systems of both participants.

Integration builds on the other areas of functionality, and offers participants the ability to share their data, business documents, and related business processes using systems supplied by the marketplace vendor.

Marketplaces provide an ideal opportunity to obtain access to a very wide range of customers and suppliers for diverse goods and services. They may offer compelling cost savings for many business transactions, with estimates of transaction cost savings range from $US 25 to $US 150 per transaction (Brox, 2001; Harrelson, 2001; Mehra, 2001). In addition, marketplaces present an opportunity for some companies to experiment with affordable external integration and business process automation without requiring sophisticated integration infrastructure.

However, this business model is currently undergoing considerable upheaval. Hundreds of online marketplaces have been launched in the past several years, with many vendors competing in each of the different industry segments available, such as forestry, automotive, and electronics manufacture. Some estimates report between 600 and 800 different marketplaces competing for customers.

Due to this intense competition, few marketplaces have been successful in obtaining members who will trade online. Suppliers are sceptical of the viability of marketplace business models, with high participation charges, limited levels of integration and automation offered by many marketplaces, and lack of custom catalogues restricting the amount of value-added information participants can publish. Other participant concerns include lack of sophistication in critical functions such as delivery times, quality of products and services, inventory levels and time to market.

Due to these problems, and the considerable competition among vendors in all industry segments, many commentators expect considerable consolidation will occur among marketplaces, with many public marketplaces ceasing trading resulting in consolidation in each vertical market segment to one or two primary marketplace vendors. It is also expected that in order to survive, many marketplaces will integrate with other marketplaces to provide additional services, and alter their business models to include fee-paying value-added services. This will in turn offer participants the greatest potential for sales to other businesses, and more opportunities for integration.

7.5.1 Vendors of marketplace solutions

Table 7.4 lists vendors of marketplace solutions for use in external integration initiatives with partners and suppliers. It should be noted that this list is not exhaustive and should be used as a guide only before solution research is undertaken.

Table 7.4 Vendors of marketplace solutions

Vendor	Solution
Ariba	Ariba Supplier Network
BroadVision	MarketMaker
Commerce One	Commerce One.net
Clarus	Clarus Sourcing
i2 Technologies	Network Services
Moai	LiveExchange
SAP	mySAP Exchanges

7.6 Business process integration solutions

Business Process Integration solutions are currently the most sophisticated external integration solutions available, and are becoming the predominant method to achieve external integration with partners and suppliers through their ability to optimize business processes to increase efficiencies and lower business costs. Business process integration (BPI) solutions achieve internal and external integration using a business-oriented approach, in contrast to the technical application-centric approach of other forms of external integration. This allows business users to rapidly create the integration solution without requiring programming knowledge or have a detailed understanding of internal and external applications and systems.

They are also designed to manage integrated internal enterprise applications and the external systems of partners and suppliers as elements of business processes used to run the company. This contrasts with the EAI approach of connecting applications together. However, BPI solutions also include all the application integration advantages of enterprise application integration systems.

Business process integration solutions are also typically highly responsive to changes in internal and shared external business processes, such as changes to manufacturing schedules and techniques, and can support short and long duration business transactions, such as purchasing commodity products from suppliers or managing negotiations. They can also support demanding integration with very large highly distributed corporate business structures and very high message loads between integrating companies, and can include human interactions and intervention within managed business processes.

A typical customer order process utilizing a business process integration solution is depicted in Figure 7.8.

Figure 7.8 External integration using business process integration

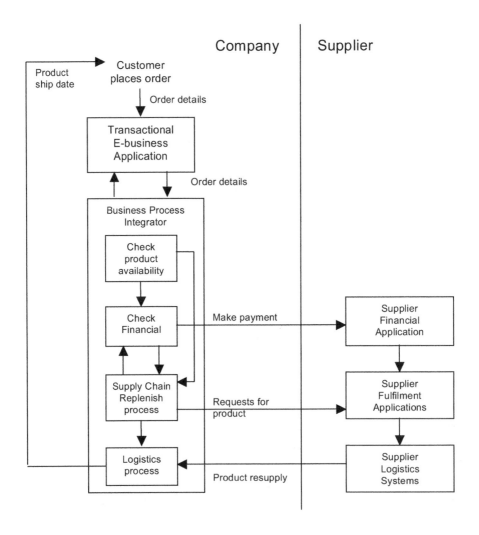

In Figure 7.8, a customer connects to a transactional e-business application to purchase a product. The business process integrator processes this request by analysing the request to determine what processes to use. As this is a transactional order, it runs it through the order process. Product availability is checked first, and because the item is out of stock, it triggers the supply chain replenish process. This process requests additional product from a supplier, who then responds with order quantity, expected delivery date, and price. This is fed to the financial process for checking, and when approved, payment is made to the supplier and approval given to make the new product. The ship date is fed to the logistics process, which estimates the delivery date for the customer. The order process then notifies the customer of the expected delivery date, and they confirm their purchase, which is processed and confirmed by the financial process.

What to look for in a process integration solution

External integration through business process integration solutions requires the solution provide a set of services consisting of process modelling, integration, monitoring and optimization (McDaniel, 2001), as depicted in Figure 7.9.

Figure 7.9 Process management services

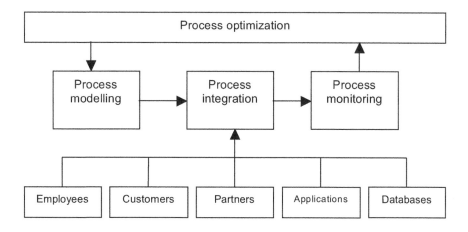

Process modelling is used to design internal and external shared business processes. These are then integrated by connecting corporate resources into the process integration solution, including internal staff, partners and customers, data sources, and internal enterprise applications. Process monitoring is then used to track the execution of process, and process optimization used to refine processes to increase corporate business efficiency and remove redundancy and waste.

Process management services are provided through a set of process management tools and their supporting connection mechanisms and data formats. These components are designed to isolate the process integration solution from dependencies on underlying technologies and data within the participating companies. This isolation in turn creates a flexible solution that can adapt to ongoing business change both within the business and between partners and suppliers.

These components of an external business process integration solution are depicted in Figure 7.10.

Figure 7.10 Functional components of a business process integration solution

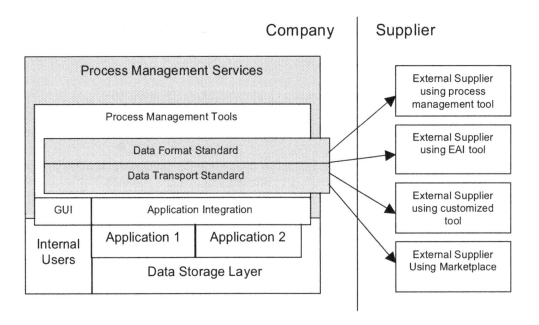

The following section discusses the different process management tools, connection mechanisms and data formats required in an external integration using business process integration solutions.

Process management tools

Process management tools provide the means to create and manage company business processes and data, including internal processes within the business, and processes shared across public and private networks with partners and suppliers.

Process management products include a set of tools to manage manual and automated business processes and data, including internal processes within the business, and processes shared across public and private networks with partners and suppliers. These tools typically include graphical process modelling tools, a development toolset, a process execution engine, a rules engine, an analysis tool set, administration and management tools, and a storage repository.

Graphical process modelling tools should define and modify the corporate business processes. They should be capable of generating integration code and include EAI features to interface with internal and external applications, such as integration adapters, brokers and messaging infrastructures. They should also offer visual GUI (Graphical User Interface) modelling of process flows for employees to manually action process work items and check process status, and the ability to modify processes as they are running.

Process modelling defines how information will flow through the different stages of each business process, with the physical integration implementation created from this. This approach is in contrast to EAI, which focuses on building a physical integration framework between applications. The modelling tool should support nested process models, where processes can be composed of subprocesses. This allows the solution to more closely model real-world business processes. This support should also include the ability to modify, add, remove, and manually invoke subprocesses within the currently running process model, with changes automatically incorporated into the running process.

The process engine (also known as the workflow engine or process broker) executes the processes defined with the modelling tool, manages the state of information flowing through each stage of the processes, and communicates with external process engines or integrated systems. The process engine should allow execution of multiple simultaneous processes, and support transaction control of processes where subprocesses must complete together successfully, or otherwise fail without affecting the state of the running process. It should also be capable of rapidly managing process exceptions, which are events that are not part of the process model. This permits the process engine to correct these events through another manual or automated step or process.

Modelling and process engine tools must support manual and automated steps within all processes. This is a critical feature, as most business process requires some human input when making high-level decisions, such as negotiation, or when an error occurs. It should also allow for manual changes to running processes. To accommodate manual intervention, processes should be accessible to users via web browsers, which also allows external suppliers with minimal automated systems to participate in the integration.

The development toolset is used to define the business processes' control rules. It also provides the mechanisms and tools to integrated processes with enterprise applications and resources such as databases.

A rules engine is used to evaluate executing processes against a set of business rules defined by the development tool. It modifies running processes according to these rules, and permits the setting of process exception criteria and responses.

The analysis tool is used to model the process flow and ensure it is valid before deployment. This tool uses business metrics stored in the repository to determine if the processes can be optimized by identifying bottlenecks, redundancies, waste, and inefficiencies in running processes.

Administration and management tools are used to re-route process flows and monitor the overall solution as a collection of integrated processes. They can also start, stop, suspend or resume the operation of processes. Management functionality should provide real-time process monitoring and reporting. This allows an organization to better react to changes in market conditions and improve efficiencies through monitoring and modifying processes, ending faulty processes, and optimizing existing processes. Monitoring can also provide a means to quantify service level agreements with trading partners, customer service levels, and guarantees made to partners.

The repository is used to store process data objects for use by the other tools. These include definitions of business processes, business rules, integrity constraints to control process execution, definitions of security objects and systems, policy definitions, and business metric definitions for performance analysis.

Connection mechanisms

Connection mechanisms are the systems required for communication between all participants of the external integration. These mechanisms include network transport technologies and data formats. Network transport technologies are used to send and receive information reliably across networks. Data formats are used to specify the form and meaning of the data being exchanged between companies so that all participants can understand the exchanged information.

Network and data transport technologies must support a variety of systems to ensure maximum ease of integration. Due to its pervasive use in business, low cost, and open design, the Internet is most commonly used as the network level transport mechanism for external integration.

Products should support standard Internet transport protocols including TCP/IP, HTTP, and various email standards. TCP/IP is the fundamental data transport protocol of the Internet. The HTTP (HyperText Transport Protocol) protocol runs on top of TCP/IP to transmit hypertext data such as HTML and XML. Email transport via the SMTP (Simple Mail Transport Protocol), POP/POP3 (Post Office Protocol) and IMAP (Internet Message Access Protocol) protocols provide an asynchronous mechanism for simple message transport, but lacks reliability features such as assured delivery.

In addition, products should also support older legacy transport standards such as value added networks used for EDI, asynchronous session protocols (e.g. X.Modem, Y.Modem and ANSI Clear) and synchronous session protocols (e.g. 3780 Remote Job Entry).

To integrate with a wide range of external suppliers, products should support multiple standards, as combinations of these standards are often used by a number of vertical segment industry groups who have defined specifications for data exchange between member companies. These include the Automotive Industry Action Group (AIAG) Advance Network Exchange standard using

TCP/IP, HTTPS and IPSEC, the Gas industry sending transactions via HTTP encrypted with the PGP (Pretty Good Privacy) standard, and the RosettaNet consortium using XML and the HTTPS protocol.

Products should also provide security of transport systems to prevent interception and compromise of sensitive corporate data. This is provided through the IPSEC protocol for encryption of IP packets over TCP, the HTTPS (HTTP Secure) protocol for encrypting hypertext data in transit, or the S/MIME (Secure MIME) standard for secure email transport.

Data integration formats

Data integration formats are used to describe common business processes and data used by each integration partner. These formats are routed and delivered between company and suppliers using the transport level technologies described above.

XML is the preferred data standard for data integration across most industries, and represents a very low risk solution for common data integration due to its unique properties. XML is a very simple, open, and extensible technology, providing a very low cost and easy to implement mechanism to describe the format and meaning of data. This has resulted in many industry consortia defining common business processes and data structures using freely available XML specifications. XML is also extensible, allowing companies to customize XML document standards for their own requirements and thus integrate with a very wide range of suppliers across different industries.

XML also offers several advantages over legacy EDI data formats previously used for limited external integration. EDI implementations suffer from limitations in the types of information they can convey between integration participants, and cannot easily be integrated with modern e-business development technologies such as Java and COM. In contrast, XML enables lower cost, rapid implementation with the ability to define any form of data or business process. However, due to the prevalence of legacy EDI solutions in many companies, it is expected that use of EDI and proprietary data formats will continue. Hence, an external process integration product must support multiple XML data formats as well as legacy EDI formats.

It is expected that the use of EDI will decline within business, as different industry segments agree and adopt common industry and global XML standards, and increasingly use Internet technologies for their integration initiatives. It is also expected that many companies will eventually replace their use of EDI with the XML-EDI standard, an emerging XML standard based on EDI and allowing connections to legacy EDI infrastructures.

7.6.1 High-level designs of business process integration solutions

The following section presents a generic design for process level integration of internal enterprise applications with external partner and supplier systems. This design supports direct sharing of business processes with external companies using similar process management systems, and indirect sharing of process-related data with companies via multiple data format standards.

This design is also intended to integrate internal enterprise applications within a company-wide business process framework to provide increased automation and optimization of corporate business processes.

Companies adopting this design will typically have several transactional e-business systems and a potentially wide range of internal applications. These may include applications located within a single geographical area, ranging up to large numbers of enterprise applications distributed across multiple regions and companies. They may be written using a very wide range of technologies, and be used in many internal and external business processes. They will also typically need to integrate with the systems of external partners and suppliers to support outsourced business processes.

Internal and external integration is achieved through the integration technology of the BPI product, including middleware brokers, intelligent adapters, and integration standards such as JMS. It should be noted that this design is also capable of integrating additional EAI systems within the process management solution in the event that companies acquire additional businesses with their own EAI solutions.

This design includes additional functional and operational components, compared to previous integration designs. The functional architecture emphasizes control of applications through the process management functions discussed above, including process modelling and analysis, process and business rules management and execution, and process repository. These functions initiate and control the data flow between applications as part of connected processes, in contrast to EAI solutions where applications initiate data flows.

Operational differences in this design include additional server nodes required to support the process management tools, and different availability, scalability, security, and manageability features.

Because the business process solution is controlling all corporate business processes, high scalability and reliability are required. To cope with potentially large numbers of external partners, applications, messages, and concurrently executing processes, cluster processing is used to distribute these functions across servers, with fail-over to redundant systems for increased availability. Vertical scalability is also achieved using multiprocessor servers.

Similar security mechanisms to previous designs are deployed, including encryption of sensitive data, secure data transport technologies such as HTTPS, SSL and IPSEC, and intrusion detection systems. Centralized security management is provided through corporate LDAP directory servers. Because the process management tools share only data with external parties and do not permit them to execute potentially insecure application code, the use of local LDAP servers for higher security is not required.

However, as the process management server cluster communicates with external parties through the firewall, it must be isolated into an internal DMZ network for additional security. To facilitate scalability in the design, an additional internal process management server cluster has been added to the internal corporate network.

It should be noted that other configurations of the process management tools are also permitted. For example, simplified deployments could be created for smaller sized companies through placement of the rules engine on the business process management server, and use of a shared repository server between the analysis server, rules engine and business process management server.

The external Business Process Integration design is depicted in Figure 7.11.

Figure 7.11 External business process integration design

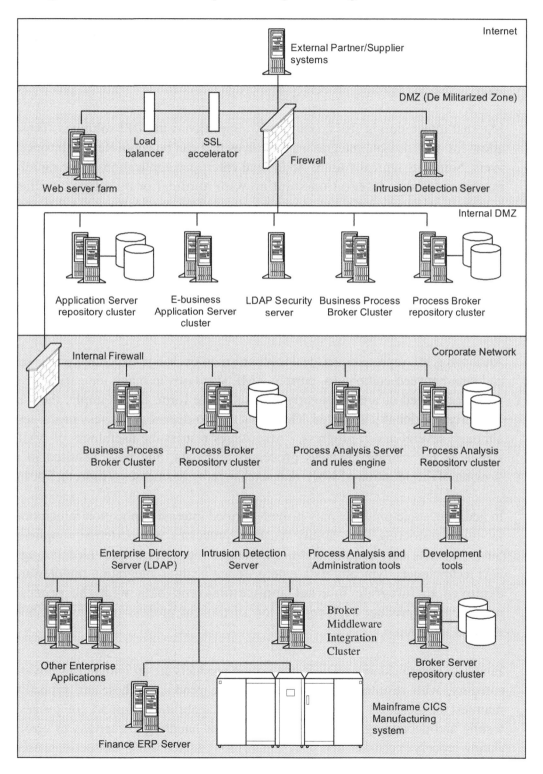

7.6.2 Benefits and limitations of business process integration solutions

Business process integration solutions provide considerable advantages to businesses by optimizing existing business processes to produce increased corporate efficiency. Efficiencies are achieved through reductions in the time taken to execute business processes, or through elimination of wasteful processes.

External integration is also considerably simplified using BPI solutions. These allow for very flexible integration initiatives that can be controlled by business users. Solutions typically allow additional enterprise applications to be rapidly incorporated into integration solution with minimal or no effect on other systems, or alternatively the swapping of existing applications for different versions or products. Multiple different external suppliers can also be rapidly integrated in the integration initiative.

However, current business process integration solutions have some limitations that currently restrict their usefulness, including immature standards and some limited integration functionality.

Although XML represents an ideal mechanism to exchange structured processes and data between companies, current XML standards in many industries have yet to be agreed or are in an early and immature form. For example, there is currently no globally accepted XML structure to describe business processes, although several are in progress. These issues restrict the usefulness of XML standards for sharing business processes and data, and have resulted in a slowing of the adoption of XML data exchange by businesses (Hildreth, 2001).

In addition, some products may provide limited internal application integration facilities, restricting their ability to share processes with external suppliers. Such products may require additional integration services provided through EAI technologies, typically with enterprise application integration middleware deployed to integrate internal applications and data with the process management product deployed on top of this for process management and external integration.

Finally, current business process integration products are an immature software category, with resulting weaknesses in some products. These are typically manifest in the areas of process modelling capabilities, support for process testing and debugging, inconsistent support for handling exceptions or errors during process execution, and poor support for compensating transactions, used to help processes complete when a part of a process fails. Product selection should therefore pay particular attention to these issues.

7.6.3 Vendors of business process integration products

Table 7.5 lists vendors and products used in business process integration initiatives. It should be noted that this list is not exhaustive and should be used as a guide only before solution research is undertaken.

Table 7.5 Vendors of business process integration solutions

Vendor	BPI Solution
Actional	Actional Control Broker
Attunity	Attunity BPI
BEA	WebLogic Integration
Bowstreet	Factory
FileNET	Brightspire
Fuegotech Inc.	Fuego4
Hewlett Packard	Process Manager
IBM	WebSphere MQ & MQ Workflow, IBM Crossworlds
Insession Technologies	WorkPoint
Iona	Orbix E2A Web Services Integration Platform
IPNet	EBizness Collaborate
Mercator	Process Integrator
Peregrine	Business Integration Suite
SeeBeyond	Business Integration Suite
Sterling	Integrator
Sun Microsystems	Sun ONE Integration Server, B2B Edition
Sybase	BPI Suite
Tibco	ActiveEnterprise
Vitria	BusinessWare
WebMethods	WebMethods Integration Platform
WRQ	WRQ Verastream

The fifth phase of e-business is dynamic e-business, which is used to integrate all internal and external corporate resources into a dynamic system. This level of integration allows a company to gain a real-time understanding of all areas of their business for purposes such as financial reporting or inventory management.

Dynamic e-business utilizes business process integration, with process management occurring in real time. This provides up-to-the-minute information on all aspects of the business both externally with customers and suppliers, and internally for staff and applications. Business managers can then use this information for dynamic business planning to respond to changing customer demands. This real-time view can extend across complete business to encompass areas such as financial performance, customer demand, staffing levels, manufacturing resources, inventory levels, and the status of suppliers.

Real-time analysis of the complete business can result in considerable savings through productivity improvements from optimization of all internal and external process, and reductions in resource wastage. It can also lead to dramatically increased responsiveness to customer demand, which in turn increases profits through improved customer loyalty and retention.

For example, a company seeks to increase productivity, decrease waste, and improve competitiveness in its industry segment through a corporate business process integration initiative. Using a real-time BPI solution, existing business processes for human resources, sales and marketing, manufacturing, distribution and financial reporting and management are mapped and encoded into the solution. Enterprise applications, databases, and roles and responsibilities for staff members are connected to the solution, along with external partner and supplier companies that contribute to many of the corporate processes.

Integration at this level therefore provides the company with detailed management of product inventory, real-time sales data, and dynamic assessment of the financial performance of the company. By understanding process flows across the company and its suppliers, business managers readily determine ways to optimise existing processes to increase efficiency. They also gain real-time assessment of the relative performance of external suppliers, which can be used to re-negotiate contracts to include performance penalties and incentives for production savings or reduced production times.

This example is depicted in Figure 8.1.

Figure 8.1 Dynamic e-business using BPI products

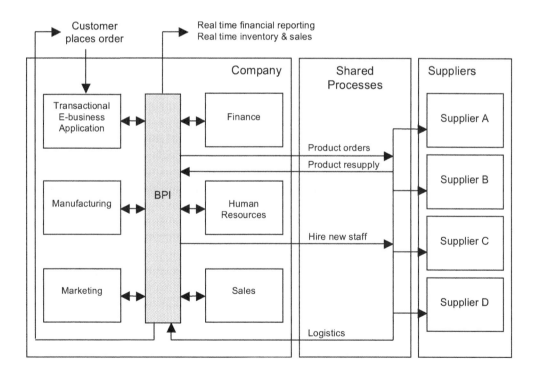

In this example, the corporate transactional e-business application is connected to a real-time BPI product. Product orders trigger processes to check inventory levels, and if these are low, to reorder new product from suppliers. Other processes check customer payments through financial applications to verify payment. Once received, production is started through the manufacturing applications. Large orders may require additional staff to meet required production levels, which is checked against the human resources applications. If additional staff members are required, these query external suppliers to see if qualified production staff members are available.

Sales and marketing applications are also involved in the process to match demand to marketing and sales initiatives. If these are proving successful staff are notified, allowing them to plan campaign extensions or new initiatives. Finally, the financial systems monitor all transactions in real time to provide dynamic financial reporting on the state of the company.

8.1 Key technologies used

Dynamic real-time business integration of internal and external business processes requires three sets of integrated technology components. These include real-time process integration systems for external partners and suppliers and internal systems, internal integration of applications and resources, and business intelligence systems for real-time processing of business information and customer demand and supply patterns.

The functional components of real-time internal and external integration solutions are depicted in Figure 8.2.

Figure 8.2 Functional components of a real-time business process integration solution

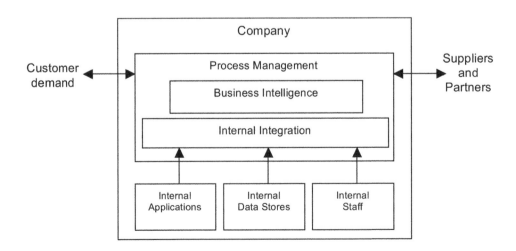

8.1.1 Process management and internal integration

Within the internal and external integration solution, the real-time process management function is provided by business process integration systems. Products offering BPI features must support real-time management of running processes, share and manage processes with external partners and suppliers, and integrate with all internal corporate resources. These include all sources of internal company information, such as internal human resources, CRM, ERP, and transactional e-business applications. They also include corporate data stores, and staff members who make manual contributions to business processes. The real-time BPI solution may also be required to integrate with existing EAI implementations within a company.

8.1.2 Business intelligence systems

In addition to the BPI and internal integration components, an internal and external integration solution must provide business intelligence systems for the real-time analysis of business activity across all integrated corporate and external resources. These systems analyse information flows within the integrated internal and external processes, and produce dynamic reports of sales and financial information. This analysis in turn allows a company to meet changing customer demand by modifying internal processes and shared external processes in real-time. It also provides a company with an up-to-the-minute understanding of its business.

Business intelligence systems typically provide analysis by building a dynamic model of customer behaviour in order to understand customer demand. This model is then matched to business supply functions required to meet customer demand, such as product supply, product design, or marketing and sales, across all company product and service offerings, as depicted in Figure 8.3.

Figure 8.3 Business intelligence modelling

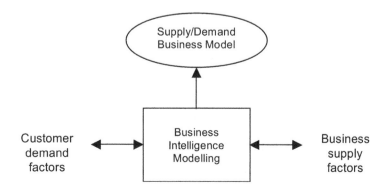

Customer demand is assessed by analysing information from all customer channels, such as shops, transactional e-business sites, catalogue and mail order initiatives, and direct sales. Data sources for these channels include transactional e-business logging and analysis systems, online publishing systems, CRM systems, and traditional data mining technologies used on recorded customer data.

Further customer data may be gathered via collaborative systems, such as email systems or online chat rooms. This data can provide valuable qualitative data to compare to the customer data analysis, allowing companies to better understand customer motivations or even determine up-and-coming trends to target.

As the customer data is gathered, the business intelligence system builds a dynamic model focusing on factors affecting demand for products and services. These typically include factors such as location, price, promotions, seasonal and weather effects, industry specific data, and market forecasts.

The business intelligence solution may also employ demand modelling functionality to build the model. This aims to predict the effect of changes in customer demand on the business, using customer data and factors such as seasonal trends or historical patterns. This allows the company to potentially avoid incorrect inventory levels, such as having low inventory in times of high demand or high inventory in times of low demand.

Supply factors are also included in to the business intelligence model. These include internal company and external partner and supplier factors such as current state of inventory levels, shipping times to customers, and lead times on new products and existing stock.

The model built by the business intelligence system then attempts to achieve efficiencies in production and logistics processes through a customer-centric view of the products and services the company needs to meet customer demand. In contrast, supply chain management solutions may focus on managing and optimizing supply chains from a less efficient planning perspective rather than being driven by customer demand (Langabeer, 2001).

Business intelligence systems typically consist of three functional units, including an integration hub, data warehouse and analysis system (White, 2001). Information is first gathered via an event-driven hub system, which receives information and places it into a data warehouse system. The analysis engine is then used to create and provide access to analyses from the data stored in the warehouse system. Finally, a decision engine is used to initiate actions based on the results of analyses of the data. These can either be through automated processes, or via manual triggering by staff. This process is depicted in Figure 8.4.

Figure 8.4 Functional components of a business intelligence system

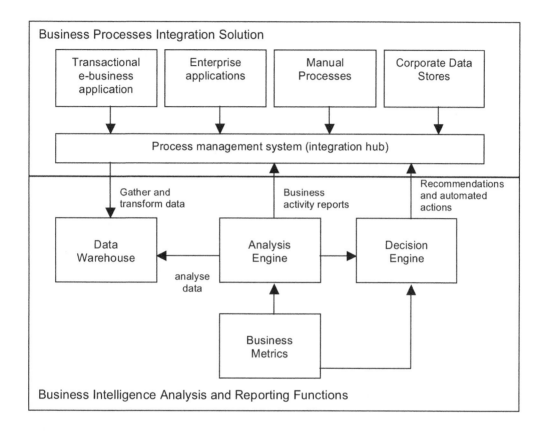

The BPI process engine usually fulfils the role of the integration hub, or alternatively an EAI messaging middleware solution managed by the process engine. All sources of demand and supply data used in the model are captured through this hub and fed directly into the data warehouse for storage and analysis.

The data warehouse provides storage for all demand and supply data received through the BPI process engine. It may also include predefined business analysis functions to calculate data summaries or important performance metrics for the business.

The analysis engine provides real-time analysis of supply and demand by processing data received by the data warehouse. Analysis may be initiated by analysis rules that evaluate the data as it is received through the integration hub. Alternatively, the analysis engine can periodically trigger the business analysis functions within the data warehouse to summarize and analyse business intelligence data. Once the data warehouse has processed the data, analysis reports can then be provided to business users via web-based front ends, such as portal systems.

The decision engine provides business processes and rules to determine what actions to take based on the analysis of the data. Decision engine functionality is sometimes embed in existing enterprise applications such as transactional e-business systems through rules-based marketing engines, or within application server personalization engines. However, for many business scenarios this function should reside in the process management layer, and be handled by the process rules engine. This allows different applications and services within the company to respond to business events in real time by calling on the services of the rules engine, without requiring separate engines in each application.

Business intelligence analysis and decision-making are guided by a set of business metrics that are specific to each company. Business metrics include industry-standard best practice, required performance factors unique to each company, and the functions such as quality, item and production cost, market share, real-time business performance, and customer satisfaction (Jain and Jain, 2001). Business metrics are used to guide both internal business processes and processes shared with partners and suppliers.

Once analysis of customer data is conducted against business metrics, it can be compared to current internal and shared processes across each e-business channel. This then allows companies to analyse and then comprehend the impact e-business collaboration will have on their own business, identify channel conflicts and inconsistencies, optimize collaborative processes that span multiple channels, and determine the costs of different channels.

8.1.3 High-level design of internal and external BPI solution

The following section presents a generic design for a corporate internal and external business process integration system between internal systems and external partners and suppliers. This design resembles the high-level business process integration systems design, but includes systems to provide the business intelligence functions discussed above. These include a data warehouse which receives information from the process management broker, a business intelligence analysis engine which creates the analysis model from data stored in the data warehouse, and the process rules engine, which provides business rules to act on the analysis model. These systems are depicted in Figure 8.5.

Figure 8.5 High level design of internal and external BPI solution

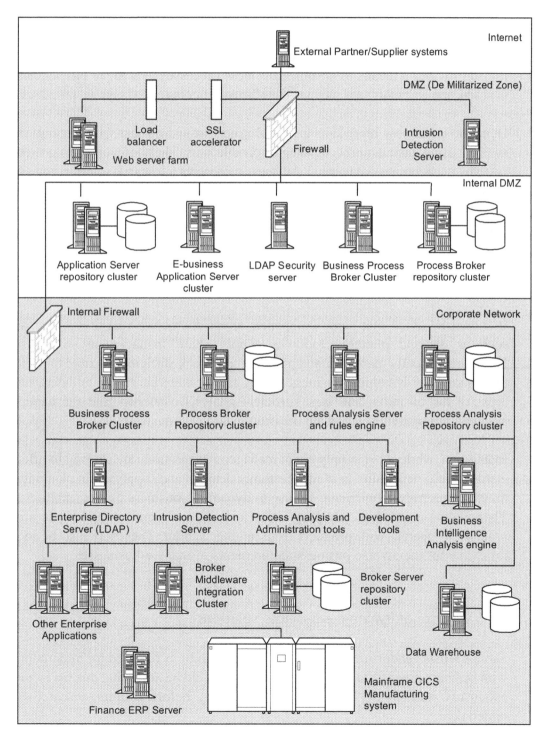

8.1.4 Benefits and limitations of dynamic e-business

Dynamic e-businesses provide companies with the ability to have real-time knowledge of the state of their business. This includes areas such as financial status, sales performance, and staffing levels. In addition, it provides a means for the company to respond to customer demand in real time to increase retention and sales. It also provides a means to optimize business processes to achieve efficiencies in production, inventory, and measure the efficiency of outsourced supplier processes.

Dynamic e-business represents a logical progression from external integration systems using business process integration solutions. Therefore, extending such systems to encompass dynamic e-business represents a low risk solution and an incremental change to existing infrastructure.

However, creating dynamic e-businesses is complicated due to the lack of off-the-shelf products. Such initiatives require some custom development, including construction of a data warehouse and integration with a business intelligence analysis engine.

It should be noted that some companies adopt alternative real-time systems, such as demand planning tools or supply chain management solutions. However, currently many demand planning tools lack sufficient flexible to meet the demands of dynamic e-business as they cannot integrate supply and demand areas of the business, and lack sufficient analysis capability and the expert automation required to automate decision making (Langabeer, 2001).

In addition, while some supply chain management solutions are starting to offer elements of functionality to model customer demand and supply chain planning, they are currently problematic for use in dynamic e-business implementations. These solutions are typically proprietary to individual vendors, and hence are unlikely to operate with products from another vendor. They may also be too inflexible for the diverse business requirements of many e-businesses.

8.1.5 Vendors of dynamic e-business solutions

Table 8.1 lists vendors of business intelligence solutions required for integration with business process integration solutions. It should be noted that this list is not exhaustive and should be used as a guide only before solution research is undertaken.

Table 8.1 Vendors of business intelligence solutions

Vendor	Business intelligence solution
Brio	Metrics Builder and Intelligence
BusinessObjects SA	Business Objects Intelligence and Analytics
Cognos Inc	Cognos Series 7
Crystal Decisions	Crystal Analysis
HNC	Critical Action
Hyperion Solutions Corp	Essbase XTD and Business Performance Management
IBM	DB2 Warehouse Manager
Informatica Corp	PowerCenter, PowerMart and Applications
Information Builders	WebFOCUS
Microsoft	SQL Server OLAP
MicroStrategy	MicroStrategy
OutlookSoft	EAP
Oracle	Business Intelligence Applications
SAP	mySAP Business Intelligence
SAS	SAS Business Intelligence and Analytic Intelligence
Siebel	Siebel Analytics
Sybase	Industry Warehouse Studio
Teradata	Teradata Warehouse
Viador	E-Business Intelligence
Visual Insights	eBizinsights

8.2 Web services

Dynamic e-business can also utilize the developing web services standards to automatically locate and outsource business processes in real time to support rapidly changing customer and business demands.

This real-time outsourcing contrasts with traditional external integration with suppliers that require an existing relationship before trading can commence. Establishing this relationship would typically take weeks or months, and involve considerable manual effort by company staff to locate suppliers then understand their business and negotiate outsourcing terms and conditions.

Dynamic outsourcing of e-business processes relies on web services technology, which is currently being developed by leading software vendors. It is therefore only available in limited form at present.

Dynamic outsourcing of e-business processes provides a company with another mechanism to satisfy customer demand, gain loyalty and increase customer retention by being able to immediately satisfy customers requirements. It also offers companies complete flexibility to outsource any business processes they do not have in-house, allowing them to rapidly optimize external processes for efficiency, levels of service, and operational business cost savings.

For example, a company receives a request for a customized product from a customer. Their current systems are unable to fulfil this order, as it would require considerable re-configuration of their production lines. However, this customer represents a valued account that the company wishes to retain.

Using automated web services technology, the company manufacturing and process integration systems create a product order incorporating the customized product specifications. They then query external directories to determine suppliers that may be capable of fulfilling the order. Once a sufficient number of suppliers have been located, the corporate systems issue the custom order to the external suppliers. They then receive automated responses from a number of suppliers containing contractual terms and conditions, expected delivery times, costs, and quality guarantees. The company business process integration systems then determine the optimum supplier and place the order.

This integration scenario would typically require transactional e-business systems with the ability to create custom product catalogues, or include customer collaboration systems such as online submissions to allow the customer to specify their custom product. Once their order is received, the internal process solution queries the internal manufacturing applications and finds this order cannot be created in-house. It then uses a business process and associated rules to determine if custom orders are worthwhile. This process queries the corporate financial applications to determine the customer spending patterns, then determines if they are a valued customer. The process then queries a web services directory to locate potential suppliers, and receives a list in return. It then queries each supplier with the custom order, and sends the responses to the process rules engine to evaluate the best match. Once this is determined, it issues approval to the supplier to manufacture the product, and makes the appropriate payment through the internal financial applications.

This process is depicted in Figure 8.6.

Figure 8.6 Automated integration of new partners and suppliers through web services

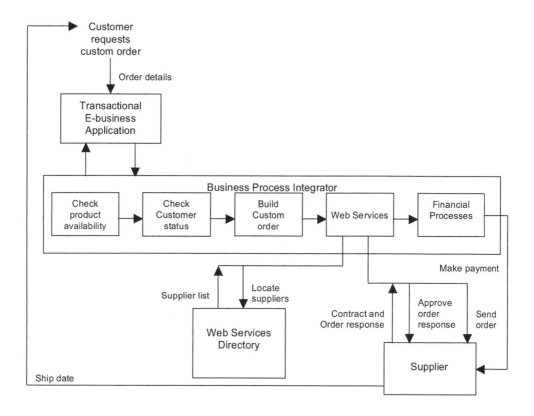

Companies in this phase of the e-business lifecycle therefore utilise dynamic web services e-business technology as their competitive edge to direct resources into creating new customer channels, increasing market share, and reducing the time taken to create and introduce new products and services (Schmidt, 2000; Seeley, 2001).

8.2.1 Key technologies used

Dynamic outsourcing of e-business relies on the emerging web services technology to provide rapid location and utilization of external supplier business processes. Web services arose from the desire of a number of information technology vendors to create an affordable services-based architecture for software development. The service based approach to software emphasizes the ability to sell software over networks, reducing the need for businesses and individuals to purchase, install and integrate separate software products.

This architecture in turn required a mechanism to allow for the integration of any technology in a rapid and very affordable manner. XML was chosen as this mechanism, due to its rapid adoption within business, and the ability of XML documents to be read by humans and automated software.

Web services technology consists of a simple set of XML based standards used to access and employ software developed by external parties. These include facilities for lookup services and discover their role, description of the requested inputs and resulting outputs generated by the web service, transport for messaging between services, the environment to develop and deploy a service within, and event notification to notify changes in the environment of the service.

Lookup, discovery and description processes utilize the facilities provided by products adhering to the UDDI (Universal Description, Discovery and Integration) specification. This describes businesses and the web services they offer using XML descriptions within public UDDI registry services.

Through a UDDI registry a company can discover services offered by another company, define how they can interact over the Internet, and share this information through the registry (Karpinski, 2001; www.uddi.org). The services offered through the UDDI registry are described via the Web Services Description Language (WSDL), which describes the XML messages the software uses as input and output.

Entries are classified within a UDDI directory as White Pages, Yellow Pages, or Green Pages. White Pages contain addresses, contact information, and known information about the company. Yellow Pages contain industrial categorizations using standard classification taxonomies, and Green Pages contain technical information about the services offered by each business, including reference and interface information about each service.

The Simple Object Access Protocol (SOAP) is used to provide XML-based messaging to connect application components together over the Internet. SOAP allows the exchange of structured information independently from the underlying systems or applications, and uses XML to encode messages.

Microsoft, IBM, and Dave Winer of UserLand Software Inc. initially proposed the SOAP standard. It is currently maintained by the World Wide Web Consortium, and consists of the SOAP envelope, which defines the framework for expressing what is contained within a message, who should handle it, and whether it is optional or mandatory (see http://www.w3.org/TR/SOAP). The encoding rules specify a serialization mechanism used to exchange application defined data. Finally, the SOAP RPC representation defines the convention used to represent remote procedure calls to other applications and their responses.

Application development using web services therefore emphasizes the creation of software as an interconnected set of software components, wrapped in WSDL, which provide discrete elements of the complete application functionality. Applications are then assembled from collections of components as required by issuing SOAP messages to UDDI directories. Because these components are small, they can be delivered over the Internet or corporate networks as required by users. Examples of application components may include functions such as credit card verification, mortgage approval, or travel reservation.

This approach is depicted in Figure 8.7. This diagram depicts an enterprise application assembled by a Business Process Integration tool using the SOAP protocol over HTTP. Application functions are typically provided by accessing components from external suppliers, which may be developed using a wide range of programming languages, including J2EE, COM and DCOM.

Figure 8.7 XML based web services model of applications

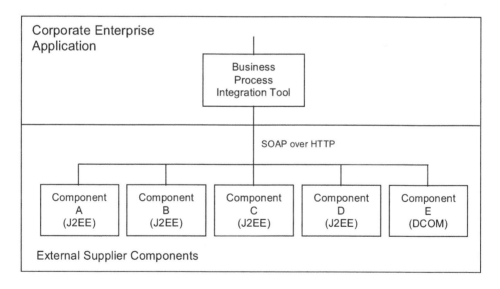

Components can be developed using any programming language, 'wrapped' in web services, and published to directories to become available online. Once wrapped, components exposed as web services can be used in more than one application simultaneously, and can incorporate processes and components encoded in remote web services for local use, and can be created on any platform using any object model.

Business process integration using web services components is depicted below in Figure 8.8.

Figure 8.8 Process integration via web services

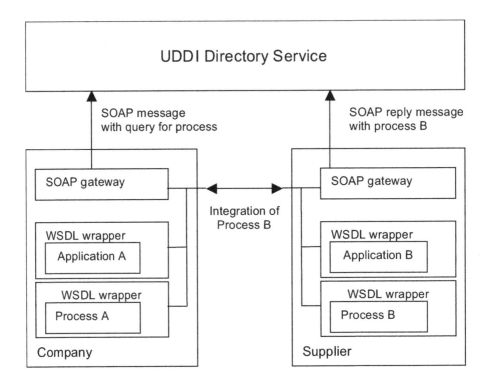

In this example, a supplier publishes their offered application and process functionality to a public UDDI registry. Company A urgently requires an additional process from an external supplier to help them meet demand for a new service that they have just launched. They issue a SOAP message requesting the new process to the UDDI directory, which responds listing Process B offered by Supplier A; both parties then directly integrate their processes via SOAP messages.

This model shifts process integration efforts to a service-based design. In contrast to more complicated technology-centric external integration initiatives, this service model focuses on finding and using publicly available business services from any vendor, allowing for very flexible real-time acquisition and use of business processes as required (Gisolfi, 2001).

8.2.2 Benefits and limitations of dynamic e-business using web services

Web services is an ideal set of technologies to develop and utilize applications within a business process integration framework. Processes and subprocesses can be encoded into web services software components using development languages such as Java, then published over the Internet to business partners, suppliers and customers on an ad-hoc basis as they are required (Colan, 2001). If internal or external processes change, the web services components used to execute the processes can be readily reconfigured to support this change, or alternatively additional external processes from suppliers and partners can be incorporated. This model is forecast by the Butler Group to become the predominant method of application development within five years (Jennings, 2001).

Web services also provide a means to preserve existing investment in information technology infrastructures. For example, existing e-business applications can be wrapped in web services and redeployed as a set of transactional e-business components, such as shopping carts for retail e-commerce. These can then be reused in different Internet initiatives requiring similar functionality, such as multiple corporate transactional sites, or sold as service to other companies requiring similar functionality.

In addition, as web services are being adopted by most software vendors and open source projects, the risk of developing software projects using web services will be considerably reduced due to the widespread availability of compatible tools and applications, and broad exposure of developers to this technology.

Web services are therefore an ideal tool for the creation of e-business applications across the five e-business phases discussed above. These include publishing online, transactional e-business applications, integration of applications within the enterprise, and integration initiatives with external partner and supplier systems. Web services also provide an ideal tool for the creation of a completely dynamic e-business enterprise able to respond to all customer requirements in real time.

However, web services suffer from a number of problems that preclude their widespread adoption at present. These include greater consumption of network bandwidth, lack of security mechanisms, and lack of support for complex transactions.

Web services consume greater bandwidth compared to other integration technologies, due to their use of 'verbose' XML text documents used by the SOAP protocol and enclosed WSDL content (Vaughn-Nichols, 2002).

Web services also currently lack required security measures. SOAP messages are sent as human readable clear text, with no security yet implemented within the SOAP specification. This necessitates securing SOAP messages via encryption, secure sockets layer transport, or virtual private networks between parties exchanging SOAP messages. However, more advanced security systems such as the Kerberos standard are required for authentication and authorization of web services components (Schwartz, 2002). In addition, the ability to dynamically locate and use software components exposes companies to security management issues, such as how to determine if the integrated components can be trusted.

In addition, the SOAP protocol cannot support complex features required for business transactions (Borck, 2001b; Sullivan, Scannell and Schwartz, 2002; Woods, 2002). These limitations include lack of support within WSDL specification for how web services can be used, and no means to provide for contractual agreements on the use of services such as trade-level agreements, support for interactions among multiple parties, and quality of service reliability.

Web services also lack agreed standards for describing shared business processes that are required for complex integration with partners and supplier systems. Currently three initiatives are under development to address this limitation. These include the WSFL (Web Services Flow Language) from IBM, the ebXML initiative from the OASIS group, and the OAGIS (Open Applications Group Interface Specifications) initiative.

8.2.3 Vendors of web services solutions

Table 8.2 lists vendors of web services products. It should be noted that this list is not exhaustive and should be used as a guide only before solution research is undertaken.

Table 8.2 Vendors of web services solutions

Vendor	Web services solution
BEA	WebLogic Enterprise Platform and WebLogic Workshop
Borland	jBuilder
Bowstreet	WebFactory
IBM	WebSphere products and Eclipse development tools
IONA	E2A Web Services Integration Platform
Microsoft	Microsoft .Net initiative; Visual Studio .Net development tools
Open Source	Eclipse development tools, XML development tools such as Xerces, SAX, Tomcat and Coccon
Oracle	JDeveloper development tools
Sun Microsystems	Java 2 Enterprise Edition; Forte Development tools; Sun ONE initiative, Java Web Services pack
Sybase	Web Services Integrator
WebMethods	WebMethods Integration Platform

Part Three

E-business supporting technologies

Successful implementation of e-business systems relies on the deployment and correct configuration of a set of critical underlying technologies. These technologies provide core foundation services utilized by all e-business systems and by existing corporate systems such as email and groupware servers, file and print servers, and legacy applications.

The e-business supporting technologies are deployed as a series of layers ranging from simple networking systems to complex e-business development languages, as depicted in Figure 9.1.

Figure 9.1 Dependence of e-business systems on core supporting technologies

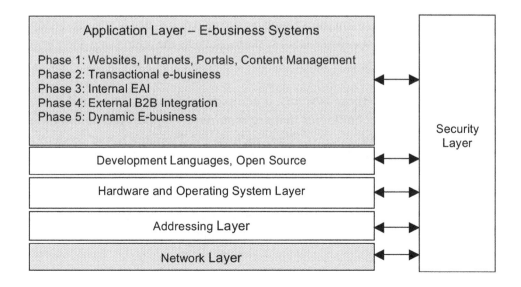

Each layer of core supporting technology relies on the services provided by the preceding layer. Technologies selected in lower layers therefore influence the subsequent choices available for deployment in successive higher levels.

The addressing and network layers are used to facilitate communicate between higher level systems and end users. The addressing layer translates communication requests from the application layer into a form that can be understood and routed by the network layer. The network layer takes translated requests and directs them to the user or other application system originating the request.

Hardware and operating system layers provide the operational deployment platform for all e-business systems. Selection of the correct hardware platform is critical to ensuring the appropriate levels of availability, scalability and reliability of the final e-business solution, and influences ongoing support and maintenance costs to the business.

The combination of these two layers in turn influences the choice of programming language and ancillary open source software components used to create the final form of the application layer. These have a strong influence on the viability, costs and strategic technology direction of the company, and hence of the functional design of the systems deployed across the five e-business phases.

Security systems are deployed to maintain the security of the complete solution. These are a fundamental element of the complete e-business solution, and enclose each preceding layer as well as the final e-business system.

Deployment of e-business systems using this layered structure permits higher-level systems such as e-business applications to be designed and deployed independently of the lower-level systems, such as the addressing and networking layers.

In order to deploy these systems, a company must understand and deploy two critical enabling technologies that are required to support the functioning of all Internet-based technologies. These include the Domain Name System (DNS) and TCP/IP-based networking. This dependence on DNS and TCP/IP is created because these two technologies are an essential foundation for the basic functioning of the Internet, and are used by all Internet-based systems. These include corporate Internet and Intranet systems, and advanced systems such as application server-based e-business, CRM and ERP systems.

E-business initiatives typically require some degree of customized development, either of commercial packaged applications, or of systems written in-house, in an attempt to achieve the desired levels of functionality.

Simple customizations typically require modifications to templates or small-scale changes to e-business application logic. For example, many packaged transactional e-business systems may require modification of store template files by page designers, usability experts and developers to provide a fully functional branded e-business presence. Alternatively, more complex customizations may be required, such as recoding application functionality within an external integration package to support specific industry specific data formats, or alternatively the creation of a custom integration adapter.

As such customization is an integral part of e-business, it is critical to the success of e-business projects to have an understanding of the development languages and technologies involved.

10.1 Key technologies used

Java and XML are the technologies most commonly used in the majority of enterprise class e-business developments, with the Microsoft .Net environment increasing in importance. Each technology is comprised of a set of components critical to successful e-business implementations, and to maintaining compatibility with emerging technologies such as web services.

10.2 Java

Java was designed by programmers within Sun Microsystems in the early 1990s to address many of the drawbacks of contemporary development languages, such as poor memory management, proprietary platform-specific implementations of technologies, and unnecessary complexity.

Originally conceived as a platform for networked consumer electronics, Java rapidly rose to prominence after incorporation into the Netscape Navigator web browser. Following this success, Java was retargeted at Internet-based development initiatives.

Java is now one of the most widely used programming languages for e-business, both for custom and packaged software development. For example, the Cutter Consortium reported in 2000 that more than 50 per cent of companies were using Java with another 12 per cent intending to use Java (Cutter Consortium, 2000). By late 2001 the momentum behind Java had increased to the point where more than three quarters of IT executives surveyed were prepared to adopt Java to develop emerging web services-based enterprise applications (Berger, 2001).

Sun Microsystems owns the Java language, and is responsible for ongoing development of the various Java standards through the Java Community Process. This process allows the participation of companies and individuals in the ongoing definition of Java standards, and was begun in response to calls for Sun to cede control of Java to standards bodies.

Java is divided into a set of technology blocks, offering specific sets of features required within different industry segments. The most recent version of these is the Java 2 standard. This standard incorporates the Java 2 Micro Edition (J2ME) for very small computing devices such as mobile phones, the Java 2 Standard Edition (J2SE) for client side desktop computing, and the Java 2 Enterprise Edition (J2EE), for enterprise-class scalable and reliable applications.

Java 2 Enterprise Edition provides many features to increase programmer productivity. These include programming interfaces for transaction management and security, and distributed programming suitable for the development of enterprise applications. It also separates design, development and deployment roles such as application developer, application deployer, application assembler and application server administrator.

The J2EE standard is composed of subsets of technology designed for e-business initiatives. Common J2EE technologies used in the five e-business phases include the Java Messaging Service, for integration projects connecting Java e-business applications and message-oriented middleware, and the Java Connector Architecture, used to create adapters to connect applications to a Java integration solution. Other standards include the emerging Java XML service architecture used to provide web services from Java components, and the Java portal integration standards, used in portal-based applications to provide standards-based integration with enterprise resources.

J2EE application servers

The development of the Java 2 Enterprise Edition (J2EE) standard for enterprise class computing has led to considerable industry support, including the rapid development of the application server product category.

These products provide highly reliable and scalable platforms to run applications written to comply with the J2EE industry standard. Their high degree of J2EE compliance allows J2EE software to run on application servers from different vendors. This in turn lowers the cost of ownership for companies and reduces the risk of being locked into technology from a single vendor. Therefore, if an application server vendor ceases business or does not provide sufficient functionality or performance, J2EE applications can be moved to a new application server from another vendor.

Application servers further benefit e-business development by bundling enterprise functionality into their core products, which developers can then use in their applications without additional effort. These include services such as transaction support for greater reliability, in-built security services, integral back-end database connection pooling for greater performance, enterprise application integration facilities, component and application level integration, and scalable clustering technologies.

Application vendors have in turn adopted the J2EE standard to increase the reach of their applications across multiple hardware and operating system platforms. For example, developing a portal solution using Java allows a vendor to sell the same product to customers with existing deployments of Windows,

Unix and OS/390 servers, without creating multiple platform-specific versions. In addition, the ability to leverage the underlying application server functions allows vendors to concentrate development resource on adding additional features to their products, resulting in increased competition.

Application servers also form the foundation for advanced development systems designed to allow non-programmers to create enterprise-class J2EE-based applications. Such systems incorporate visual design environments, allowing business users to create and customize corporate business logic for deployment within J2EE application servers. Examples include AltoWeb Application Platform, BEA Cajun, Bowstreet Web Factory, Versata Logic Suite, and Wakesoft Architecture Server.

Java Message Service

The Java Message Service (JMS) was designed to address problems experienced when integrating enterprise applications using message-oriented middleware solutions.

Current message-oriented middleware vendor products utilize different messaging systems, in turn restricting application integration initiatives to specific products from each vendor. Integration with another vendor EAI system, or the removal and replacement of an existing EAI product, is therefore complicated due to this dependence on vendor-specific technology.

The JMS standard was designed to address these limitations by providing a standard means for Java programs to create, send, receive and read messages from messaging systems. JMS provides developers with a standards-based mechanism to send, receive and read messages between their Java-based applications and vendor Middleware products, incorporating advanced messaging facilities such as asynchronous messaging.

This has in turn led to many vendors supporting JMS within their different message-oriented middleware products to ensure compatibility. It has also increased developer productivity and reduced the timeframes for integration initiatives, as developers are no longer required to understand the underlying programming technologies behind different vendor middleware products. This in turn lowers the total cost for implementing integration projects for businesses, and provides more choices of middleware products for integration.

Java Connector Architecture

The Java Connector Architecture (JCA) was designed to address the differences between different vendor implementations of application integration adapters, used to integrate enterprise applications through middleware solutions.

The JCA standard specifies a programming interface for Java applications to create and access application integration adapters. This allows integration projects to standardize on JCA for communicating between enterprise applications and Java-based software.

Currently, major EAI product vendors are shifting from their proprietary connector architectures to widespread adoption of the JCA standard. This will allow any JCA adapter to be 'plugged in' to JCA compatible integration middleware, resulting in the commoditization of the integration adapter marketplace and reduced costs. It should also lead to increases in integration project productivity, as developers will no longer be required to learn multiple, incompatible adapter integration methods for each project. This will in turn lead to reductions in integration project costs, reduced project delivery timeframes, and access to a wider pool of developers able to work across products from multiple vendors.

Java APIs for XML

The Java APIs for XML (JAX) provides a standard mechanism for Java applications to process XML documents.

The JAX API allows a Java application to represent and describe text as generated XML files for consumption by other software. The JAX interfaces also offer the ability to issue asynchronous and synchronous XML messages between applications, and the ability to publish available services to external registries, such as UDDI registries, and to consult such registries to find services.

These facilities allow Java applications to access and utilize web services from any source, which have been written using any development language. They also allow Java software to publish business logic components as web services for integration and use by other internal enterprise applications, and the applications of partner and supplier companies in dynamic e-business initiatives.

Java web services for remote portals and the Java portlet API

Two recent Java standards, the Java portlet and web services for remote portals APIs, have emerged in an effort to standardize and simplify the integration between portal servers and back-end application resources.

The Java portlet API defines a standard programming interface for writing 'portlets', the small-scale integration applications used for application aggregation functionality within portals. Portlets written to the Java Portlet standard can then be integrated into any portal product supporting this API, resulting in reduced development effort and making available a wider range of portlets for all portal product vendors.

The web services for remote portals API is designed to allow interoperability between portal products and any web services designed for visual display within portals. This allows compliant portal products to integrate internal or external content and applications published as web services.

Benefits and limitations of Java

The widespread adoption of Java has resulted from the extensive, well-developed set of Java programming interfaces that offer enterprise class functionality required in e-business projects. Developers are able to utilize this pre-existing functionality without the effort required in comparable languages lacking such features, resulting in enhanced productivity and reduced project implementation times.

In addition, adoption has been accelerated through utilisation of the reliability, availability and scalability services provided by the J2EE specification and compliant application servers.

Due to the widespread industry support for Java, developers have access to a huge range of Java tools and programming aids, and managers have access to a very broad base of available Java developers for projects. Such factors combine to ensure that Java-based projects are typically more productive and lower cost than those conducted with competing technologies.

However, the complexity of Java creates a steep initial learning curve for developers, who must learn the many application programming interfaces before becoming productive.

In addition, acceptance of additions and alterations to the Java standard through the Java Community Process can take considerable time. This in turn slows the adoption rate of emerging technologies such as web services.

10.3 XML

XML is a standards-based mechanism used to describe information in textual form. XML is becoming increasingly important due to its ability to support application and business process integration, without requiring alterations to existing applications, and its ability to repurpose one source of information into multiple target formats.

XML was first published as a standard in February 1998, and evolved from the earlier and more complex Standard Generalized Markup Language (SGML). SGML, first developed in 1969 and published as the international ISO standard ISO 8879 in 1986, was designed to separate document content from the form in which the document was presented. SGML is therefore frequently used in the creation of technical documents as it offers the ability to perform intelligent searches and queries for document content.

The less sophisticated HTML standard was also derived from SGML. However, in contrast to SGML, HTML encodes the presentation format into the data itself, with the data containing no inherent meaning.

HTML grew in popularity as it provided an open standard for the presentation of human-readable information across the Internet. However, although suited to human-readable information display, HTML lacks support for encoding meaning into data and has thus proved problematic for the automated exchange of business information between applications.

XML evolved to fill the gap between the complexity of SGML and simplicity of HTML, and to provide a facility to publish data to web browsers independently of participating systems.

The W3C XML Working Group, with the participation of many individuals and major companies, developed the XML specification, with the first version released in 1998.

Subsequently, XML was conceived as an ideal mechanism to exchange information between applications to address integration requirements. Numerous XML-based standards have therefore evolved to fulfil a diverse range of business uses across industry segments, typically focused around internal EAI integration and external integration between companies across industry sectors.

Key technologies

XML is comprised of a set of components for the encoding of document content, for interpreting the meaning of a document, and for transforming documents for reading by other applications.

Encoding data: the structure of xml documents

XML documents encode data using entities known as elements and attributes of these elements. Elements are comprised of data enclosed within a tag structure. These tags superficially resemble HTML documents in their use of the < > characters. However, in contrast to HTML, XML tags encode meaningful semantic information and metadata, not simply presentation information.

This difference can be illustrated by comparing a purchase order encoded in HTML with the equivalent encoded in XML. The HTML purchase order includes the purchase order date, number, and authorization as depicted in Table 10.1.

Table 10.1 HTML purchase order

HTML code	Browser display
<P><B>Purchase Order</B></P> <P>nbsp;</P> <P>Date:</P> <P>08/01/2002</P> <P>nbsp;</P> <P>PO Number:</P> <P>1287332</P> <P>nbsp;</P> <P>Name:</P> <P>John Smith</P>	Purchase Order Date: 08/01/2002 PO Number: 1287332 Name: John Smith

Within this HTML code, the purchase order has no intrinsic meaning. It is only recognizable as a purchase order once a browser has rendered it. Each HTML tag is designed to specify only rendering information for display purposes, such as the <B> </B> tags specifying bold text.

In contrast, encoding of the purchase order in XML provides meaning for the data through the enclosing tags, as depicted in Figure 10.1

Figure 10.1 XML Purchase purchase order

```
<ORDER:PODATE> 08/01/2002</ORDER:PODATE>
<ORDER:PONUMBER>1287332 </ORDER:PONUMBER>
<ORDER:AUTHORITY>John Smith</ORDER:PONUMBER>
```

This XML document includes both the purchase order data, and metadata in the form of the PODATE, PONUMBER and AUTHORITY elements. The meaning of each element is contained separately from the data within the enclosing tags. If this purchase order forms part of an information exchange in an EAI integration scenario, middleware brokers would reformat the tags to render this data readable for a target application without altering the underlying data.

For example, another software component may not recognize the <ORDER:AUTHORITY></ORDER:AUTHORITY> tag structure, instead using <ORDER:APPROVER></ORDER:APPROVER>. A middleware transformation engine would read the first set of tags and alter them to resemble the second set, without loss of data or meaning.

Interpreting XML documents: DTDs, schema and stylesheets

In order for different systems to read and interpret XML documents, they require a mechanism to interpret the syntax of the documents they receive and hence to understand the document elements.

This functionality is provided through a dedicated software system known as an XML parser. A parser reads an XML document and checks it for consistent structure against a document type definition (DTD) or XML Schema.

A DTD is used to define the structure of tags within the document, and to validate the document structure when it is read using checks based on the permissible document elements. These include types of data, structural aspects of the document such as repeating elements, and any mandatory and optional elements. The location of the DTD is described within the document header, or alternatively may be included within the document itself.

However, problems exist when using DTD to validate and understand XML documents. The use of a DTD is not compulsory for all XML documents, and they do not use XML syntax. These factors complicate parsing of XML documents. In addition, DTDs lack some crucial abilities to constrain and describe aspects of data.

XML Schema evolved to address the problems experienced using DTDs. Schemas are shared vocabularies that define the structure, content and semantics of XML documents. Schemas offer the advantages of including more capabilities than DTDs for richer document content. They offer more power for checking and validating XML documents through their ability to specify more in-depth definitions of the types of data held within the document.

Schema also provide the ability to specify relationships between elements and attributes of a document, including meaning, date type, elements, attributes, values, and usage and document component interrelationship (Editorial, IT-Director.com, 2001). For example, a DTD may specify that a purchase order contains a date, while a schema can specify the valid values of that date. Finally, schemas are extensible through their open content model, permitting custom schema creation from standard parts.

Although schemas provide more functionality than DTDs for parsing and interpreting XML documents, the widespread use of XML DTDs is likely to ensure their co-existence for some time.

Transforming XML documents

Transformation of XML documents is provided through the eXtensible Stylesheet Language Transformation (XSLT) system. XSLT provides the ability to transform XML documents and the schemas used to describe the document and its content, and are written in XML.

XSLT offers the ability to provide a standards-based mechanism to alter an XML document between source and destination applications within an integration solution. They can also alter the document to fit a final target presentation format, such as rendering a document into Wireless Mark-up Language for a mobile device, or HTML for a web browser.

The transformation abilities of XSLT allow it to be used in a variety of integration scenarios. It permits flexible transformations between source and destination applications through application of a style sheet to multiple documents, or alternatively multiple style sheets to a single document.

E-business and XML

Using DTDs, schema and XSLT permits the use of XML as a powerful means to automate the exchange and processing of business data between different e-business systems.

Using an integration engine incorporating an XSLT parser, different software systems can issue messages in XML format to the integration engine for parsing and transformation into XML formats understood by target applications, as depicted in Figbure 10.2.

Figure 10.2 XML-based e-business integration

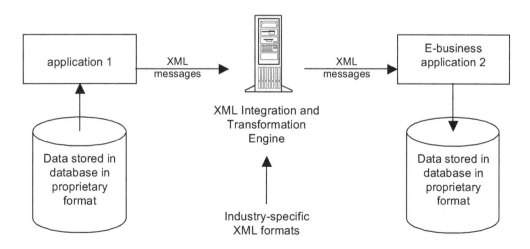

This process relies on common industry-specific data dictionaries to be used to mediate between the applications being integrated, which are discussed below.

Common XML standards

Due to the widespread adoption of XML and considerable industry momentum behind the use of XML for integration, vertical industry consortia began creating specific XML data structures for use in integration between their respective industries. For example, industries such as finance, banking, insurance, and healthcare began developing specialized XML dialects to describe the meaning of their business data; in order to facilitate standards-based information exchange between trading partners.

The initial lack of agreement on these standards led to multiple consortia developing competing standards in parallel, such as cXML from Ariba and xCBL from CommerceOne for transactional e-business data exchange. This proliferation of early XML standards in turn led to companies being required to learn multiple incompatible XML data structures.

For example, currently there are more than 400 such XML standards in use or in development, considerably complicating integration initiatives and requiring support for many different standards.

It is expected that the considerable diversity of XML standards will evolve to support core underlying XML infrastructure services (known as the W3C XML Protocol Stack) for the transport of XML documents, such as the SOAP transport standard. In addition to these services, industry specific add-ons will evolve to utilize these services.

The following section lists some of the common XML standards currently in development and deployment in the e-business industry. These standards are of particular use for transactional e-business, and internal and external integration initiatives.

RosettaNet

RosettaNet, created in 1998, is a consortium of companies in the information technology, semiconductor manufacturing and electronic components industries.

This consortium is defining a set of cohesive standards and practices for processes involving automation of the supply chain between manufacturers, distributors, and resellers across these industries. The objective of RosettaNet is to gain competitive advantages through lowering operational expenses and accelerating the pace of e-business.

In contrast to many initiatives focused on data driven information exchange, RosettaNet uses business process modelling to define common e-business processes. These include trading processes such as inventory, pricing, sales management, order handling, product configuration and shipping. Also included in these definitions are partners and product specifications.

RosettaNet is comprised of a set of components making the RosettaNet Implementation Framework, which is the specification of how trading messages will be constructed and exchanged between business partners. It includes partner interface processes (PIP), used to describe business process message flow and process interaction, and data dictionaries, defining a common data language including technical properties for describing product information, and business properties for describing information about catalogues, business entities and business transactions.

Technology components within RosettaNet include X12 EDI, the PKCS 7 digital signature specification, HTTP and SSL. In addition, XML is used as the mechanism to facilitate data exchange as part of the PIP business processes.

ebXML

ebXML (electronic business XML) is defined by the OASIS (the Organization for the Advancement of Structured Information Standards) group. OASIS have been working with the United Nations Centre for Trade Facilitation and Electronic Business (UN/CEFACT) since 1999 to define a global specification for XML-based e-business interoperability, known as ebXML.

This initiative seeks to lower trading entry barriers for e-business through the creation of a global, inclusive e-business standard suitable for all sizes of business. It is also designed to unify many emerging XML specifications, and extends traditional integration technologies including EDI.

Currently ebXML has industry support from diverse companies such as IBM,

Sun Microsystems, Cisco Systems, Ariba, CommerceOne, and the RosettaNet consortium, although it has not yet been adopted as a formal web services standard.

ebXML is comprised of profiles, agreements, and core components, which are used to build standardized document exchange mechanisms via XML. It includes support for emerging XML-based web services standards such as the SOAP protocol, with extensions including attachments for messaging transport, and can utilize the UDDI service registry to locate other ebXML services.

In addition, ebXML offers extended functionality beyond that offered within the UDDI specification. This includes key data standards for building partnerships and transactions, with roles, relationships and responsibilities during transactions. It also includes support for security, quality of service agreements, and business process modelling, allowing transaction scenarios to incorporate advanced functionality such as routing between services, sequencing and transactional non-repudiation for added security and reliability.

Process functions included within the standard include the ability to define collaboration protocol profiles (CPPs), which describe the processes of a business, and collaborative protocol agreements (CPAs), which standardize technical and business issues with trading partners. Using these standards, the CPP describes business processes, their interfaces, protocols for collaboration, and quality of service levels, with the CPA used to agree run-time parameters for their execution.

It is recommended that companies investigate the use of ebXML in their future trading and integration initiatives due to the strong industry support among vendors for the standard, support for emerging web services standards, and global reach. However, ebXML still requires additional work on the core components responsible for industry data-type translations such as EDI to XML.

tpaML

The tpaML is the Trading Partner Agreement Markup Language. This standard defines and implements electronic contracts between trading parties. The core component of tpaML is the Trading Partner Agreement (TPA). This component defines how different trading partners interact together, and includes information, which the trading partners must agree on to enable communication between their business processes and applications.

BizTalk

In contrast to the process-based use of XML in RosettaNet, the BizTalk project from Microsoft focuses on the use of XML in direct information exchanges. BizTalk provides a mechanism to integrate different XML schema to integrate enterprise applications and business processes for trading partners, exchanges or internal systems (Hildreth, 2001).

BizTalk consists of guidelines for the publishing of schemas in XML and the use of XML messages for application integration. In a similar manner to the OASIS ebXML standard, BizTalk emphasizes reuse of internal infrastructures and their adaptation through XML.

BizTalk supports its own XML standard, the BizTalk Framework, which consists of a set of BizTags specifying how XML documents are handled. This framework is implemented through the BizTalk server middleware broker. BizTalk also supports 'accelerators' or sets of development tools and parsers for popular XML formats, including RosettaNet, HIPAA for healthcare, FIX, SWIFT, and the EDI ANSI X12 and EDIFACT formats.

Integration through BizTalk focuses on translating different application data structures and meanings, the creation of a common XML message format, and a standard infrastructure for integration. Application integration requires participating applications create BizTalk compatible messages, which are transformed, formatted and routed by the BizTalk server.

The BizTalk.org site serves as a repository for tools supporting this framework, including publicly available schemas, and business process tools.

HIPAA

HIPAA specifies a set of standards for the exchange of healthcare information. This standard will become mandatory within the US in October 2002 for healthcare providers and hospitals.

Financial standards

Several different financial XML standards exist, including SWIFT (Society for

Worldwide Interbank Financial Telecommunication) for banking data interchange, FIX (Financial Information eXchange) for financial data, IFX (Interactive Financial Exchange) for financial transactions

OAGIS

The Open Applications Group Interface Specifications has defined a set of XML specifications and standards to ensure interoperability for enterprise applications, and between companies. This specification includes templates describing document specifications, and definitions of business transactions and business processes for several e-business scenarios.

BPML

The Business Process Modelling Language is used to describe business processes, defined by the Business Process Management Initiative.

XML and EDI

The Electronic Data Interchange (EDI) system utilizes different technology to XML. Initially EDI arose from attempts within vertical industries to define different standards for the exchange of data within supply chains. Subsequent development of EDI technology gave rise to common EDI document standards such as EDIFACT, ANSI X12 or TRADCOMS, supporting automated document exchange.

Integration via these EDI standards therefore required companies map their business documents, such as purchase orders, invoices or shipping notices, into the EDI document standards. Once these mappings were generated, specialist EDI-aware software automated the exchange process.

However, although EDI-based integration provides a common and mature standard, it suffers a number of limitations that typically render it unsuitable for ongoing development and use as an integration technology. These include the high levels of technical skill and cost required for managing EDI implementations, inflexibility in standards, and reliance on proprietary networks for the transport of EDI documents between participants.

It is likely that XML will eventually supplant EDI completely, subsuming EDI syntax within XML schema; however, XML still requires the ability to define processes, generate service level guarantees, and provide security and transactional efficiency (Borck, 2001).

Benefits and limitations of XML

XML represents an ideal mechanism to simplify different integration scenarios due to its ability to separate data content from final presentation format, very broad industry support, and inclusion in leading products from multiple vendors.

For example, stock reordering is dramatically simplified for a retail business if both parties use a single XML standard for retail transactions. Such a standard would include a common description of the product and the stock reordering process. External integration between these two parties would then consist of sending XML messages and receiving appropriate replies.

However, several problems exist with the use of XML for data exchange and integration. Integration requires agreement on the semantic meaning of business objects, such as what constitutes a stock item or business process such as ordering. Most industries already have multiple definitions for common business objects using different product specifications and descriptions, and different internal and external processes.

This diversity in industry sector semantics is reflected in the multiplication of different XML standards proposed for different industries, suggesting that the adoption of common XML business standards will be a complicated process.

In addition, integration products do not all support the same XML dictionaries. Some products utilize different XML specifications or specific vocabularies within specifications, which may then require human intervention to translate XML documents between companies. The addition of this step therefore removes the advantages of automated integration via XML.

Finally, although there is considerable interest in and promotion of XML standards for internal and external integration, XML does not form a complete EAI and B2B external integration solution by itself. Direct integration using XML document exchange requires participating applications support the creation, output and interpretation of XML documents. However, few enterprise applications currently support XML standards for integration.

It is expected that the adoption of XML-based technologies by enterprise applications over time will simplify integration initiatives from the adoption of common XML standards.

However, XML-based integration will still require mechanisms to transport, parse and reformat XML documents between applications and companies. This in turn requires the services of the message-oriented middleware and process integration technologies currently utilized in current integration initiatives. This has in turn led to the continued evolution of integration brokers and middleware solutions, with most products now incorporating XML-based document processing. Such products offer the ability to integrate non-XML compliant applications, while also providing routing and transformation services for XML messages between compliant systems and external companies.

10.4 Microsoft .NET

Microsoft .Net is a new initiative from Microsoft intended to replace the existing Microsoft development technologies such as Visual Basic, and the COM/COM+ object architectures.

Faced with the competitive success of Sun, IBM and Linux in enterprise computing (Yager, 2002), Microsoft designed .Net to provide an equivalent enterprise-class distributed networked environment, with similar features to the successful J2EE enterprise Java standard.

Although containing many similar features, the .Net initiative features two major differences to the J2EE standard, including support for multiple languages, with 25 languages currently available for coding .Net applications, and a single focus on the Windows platform. Unlike Java, which permits the same application to run on different operating systems, .Net is intended primarily as a Microsoft-only technology. However, Corel and Microsoft are currently porting the .Net project to the FreeBSD operating system, and the open source Mono project is currently porting .Net to Linux.

Key technologies

.Net provides a full set of object-oriented features, including services, programming languages, and libraries. In a similar manner to the Java technology components, these features are intended to increase programmer productivity by providing a broad set of functionality suited to the creation of networked Internet-aware applications.

.Net consists of four core technologies, including the Common Language Runtime, the .Net Class library, unifying components ASP.Net and Windows Forms, and Visual Studio.Net.

The Common Language Runtime is broadly similar to a J2EE-based application server, and provides advanced services including memory management, thread execution and management, configuration management, error handling, component lifetime management, and security services to all .Net applications, irrespective of the language they are developed with. All code is compiled into the Microsoft Intermediate Language (MSIL) for execution on the Common Language Runtime engine.

The .Net Class Library provides programming classes and objects for use in .Net applications. These are available to all languages, allowing a consistent and simple approach to using system provided services.

The ASP.Net and Windows Forms components provide web-based applications and 'traditional' Windows style applications, based on underlying .Net services. These compare to Java JSP/Servlet and client-side Java application front-ends.

Also part of the .Net initiative is a set of additional products based on mixed legacy COM/COM+ and .Net applications. These include the BizTalk 2000/2002 integration products, Microsoft Commerce 2000/2002 Server for sell-side commerce, and SQL Server 2000/2002. Although not directly part of the .Net technologies, these products provide components recommended by Microsoft for the creation and maintenance of .Net-based products and services.

Benefits and limitations of Microsoft .Net

Microsoft .Net provides much needed stability and reliability to Windows-based development, and simplifies development using many Microsoft technologies (Yager, 2002). For example, although still in beta, pre-production release, .Net is proving to be relatively stable and reliable. It also offers integral support for current web services standards, and the .Net development tool set provides for simple creation of web services code for

.Net projects.

However, a number of limitations exist with the .Net initiative. Current Windows-based developers will require extensive retraining in the new .Net technologies to utilize the improvements it offers. In addition, core .Net servers required to support many .Net services have yet to be released from Microsoft, holding back implementation of this technology (English, 2001).

Due to its newness and unproven reliability, availability and scalability, implementation of projects using .Net represents some business risk. Therefore, many commentators believe .Net will obtain no more than 35 per cent of the enterprise software development marketplace from Java, centred around smaller companies due to this immaturity, lack of production level stability, and lack of cross-platform flexibility (Arnott, 2001). In addition, a recent informal market survey of IT executives by the Giga Information Group suggested that more than three quarters of executives surveyed viewed J2EE server software as the most effective platform to create web services (Berger, 2001).

However, .Net represents a solid upgrade path for companies with existing investments in Microsoft COM/COM+-based Internet and Intranet projects. It is therefore recommended that companies intending to create Windows-based e-business initiatives evaluate the emerging .Net technologies with a view towards eventual migration of current projects.

11　Hardware platforms and operating systems

The hardware platform selected for an e-business project provides the fundamental underlying operational infrastructure supporting an e-business system. Hardware platforms are used to run e-business software, and are comprised of servers and their associated operating systems, and ancillary support systems such as hard disk storage, memory systems, and clustering systems.

E-business hardware platforms are frequently chosen using a minimal set of simple criteria, such as an existing relationship with a vendor or compatibility with existing infrastructure. They are also frequently selected by default through the selection of an application or development technology supported by a specific operating system.

However, selection based on such criteria may often result in the creation of a solution that is unable to support the current or future needs of the e-business. It is therefore critical to the success of an e-business implementation to conduct an informed hardware platform selection to suit project requirements.

Hardware platform selection should include a focus on the ability of the platform to achieve appropriate levels of performance. This allows the e-business solution to scale performance to meet increased user and system demand.

Minimal downtime is also a critical element of hardware platform selection. Lack of system availability may result in the customer dissatisfaction, and hence the loss of customers who may turn elsewhere for products and services. In addition, the failure of a critical system, such as a broker in an EAI system, can result in considerable lost revenue if the business is unable to continue functioning.

11.1 Key technologies used

E-business hardware platforms consist of different categories of hardware, their associated operating systems, and the reliability, availability and scalability features (RAS) they provide. In addition, hardware platforms are distinguished by their degree of support for e-business technologies and applications.

11.2 Types of hardware platforms

The information technology industry is divided into four major hardware platforms, with each platform providing different features that govern their suitability for e-business. These platforms include Unix servers from multiple vendors, two enterprise-class IBM platforms, and the Intel server platform.

Each platform was developed to meet the requirements of different industry sectors, and has since evolved to share many common features. However, this initial platform differentiation strongly influences their current feature sets, and hence their suitability for e-business.

The Unix operating system and hardware originated in the 1970s academic and scientific computing environments, and focused on the creation of powerful multi-user systems supporting portable applications that could be readily moved among different Unix platforms. Most of the early Internet systems and standards were developed on Unix systems.

Modern Unix systems offer modular and highly stable operating systems, and are available in different versions from a range of vendors. Currently three primary vendors are responsible for the majority of sales of Unix systems, including the Solaris operating system running on SPARC hardware from Sun, the HP-UX operating system running on PA-RISC hardware from Hewlett Packard, and the AIX operating system running on the pSeries hardware from IBM. These Unix versions feature highly efficient utilization of their hardware platform to provide very high levels of performance. They are also available in a very broad range of solutions from low-end desktop and small-company solutions competitive with Intel servers, to high-level mainframe alternatives. These Unix systems provide an ideal foundation for e-business solutions, as they provide high performance, native support for all Internet technologies and have a very broad portfolio of available e-business and enterprise applications.

The two enterprise-class IBM platforms include the iSeries and the zSeries. The iSeries servers (formerly known as the AS/400) and associated OS/400 operating system originated in the 1980s from IBM. These systems offered companies in a diverse range of industries a reliable and secure computing platform, capable of running many enterprise-class manufacturing and business applications. The iSeries includes many advanced concepts such as a virtualized operating system similar to a Java virtual machine, and single system storage with no distinction between memory and disk storage. It also offers highly scalable levels of performance, and high levels of reliability. Although initially constrained by their use of proprietary technologies, iSeries systems have recently adopted many standard e-business technologies, such as Java, LDAP and J2EE application servers, rendering them suitable for integration into e-business initiatives.

The zSeries servers (formerly known as OS/390) and zOS operating system evolved from earlier mainframe enterprise computing platforms within IBM. These systems are designed to provide very high performance, reliability, availability and security for demanding back-end functions in many critical industries, such as banking, billing, insurance, and finance. They also offer support for thousands of simultaneous users. Currently the zSeries provides the highest level of availability of any computing platform, and has begun adopting standards-based technologies suited to e-business in a similar manner to the iSeries.

The Intel server platform, running Microsoft Windows or the Open Source Linux operating systems, evolved from the early IBM PC design of 1981, and still shares many aspects of this architecture. Although offering the advantage of low cost commodity components shared throughout the PC industry, this platform typically lacks high-end architectural features found in the other platforms, restricting their availability and scalability. All e-business technologies are available on Intel servers, making them ideal platforms suitable for low to mid-range e-business initiatives.

What to look for in a hardware platform

Selection of an appropriate hardware platform and operating system for an e-business initiative requires an understanding of how well these platforms support the project's operational and functional requirements.

Operational requirements are comprised of the physical factors specific to implementing a particular e-business solution. These include factors such as the levels of reliability, scalability and availability of the proposed solution, and include the ongoing maintenance and support requirements they incur within the business.

Operational decisions on hardware platforms are frequently made based on two decision criteria, including existing corporate support policies and corporate purchasing policies. Pre-existing internal support resources often dictate purchasing specific hardware solutions with compatible support requirements in an effort to minimize investment in new support resources. Corporate purchasing policies may also dictate the vendor and type of hardware platform in an effort to lower costs and create well-known 'standard' environments.

However, reliability, availability and scalability should be the primary basis for hardware platform decisions, as these directly influence the ongoing business value of the e-business initiative. Customers demand reliable and continually available, high performance e-business systems to service their needs. If an unstable technology platform is purchased to satisfy support or purchasing requirements, considerable downtime may result, with a corresponding loss of customers. This will in turn negate any perceived savings to the business from adoption of a 'standard' corporate platform.

Reliability is measured by the length of time the hardware solution can continue to function without suffering failure. This is typically measured in terms of the 'mean time between failure' (MTBF) statistic for different system components such as hard disks or power supplies. Thus, a hard disk with an MTBF of 50 000 hours would be considered a less reliable solution than a disk offering an MTBF of 100 000 hours. The more components a solution has, and the shorter their MTBF, the less reliable the total solution will be. High reliability is desired as this ensures the solution can perform useful work for a longer period before requiring replacement parts.

Availability is defined as the ability of the complete hardware solution to continue functioning in the event that one or more of its components fail. Availability can be achieved through several mechanisms, depending on the number of servers involved. Availability within a single server is typically achieved by using multiple redundant components operating simultaneously. Low-end single server hardware solutions often provide availability for common system components, such as RAID (redundant array of inexpensive disks) solutions for hard disk storage, grouped network adapters to support failure of a single adapter, multiple power supplies, and error checking memory.

Additional availability can be achieved through high-end mainframe class techniques such as dynamic hardware reconfiguration, which supports the ability to detect failing components and remove them from operation without affecting running systems. Other availability solutions include the ability to partition servers into multiple virtual servers, allowing resources and running applications to be moved between partitions for maintenance and upgrading of server components.

Availability can also be provided using multiple servers in a clustered configuration. This form of availability distributes applications across additional servers, either in an active/passive 'hot standby' configuration with a standby server ready to take over from a failed server, or alternatively in an active/active configuration with additional active servers participating in simultaneous workload management. Thus, failure of one server will not compromise the total e-business solution. Clustered availability is dependent on the type of network hardware deployed and the level of cluster support offered by the hardware, operating system and applications.

Scalability is the degree to which the hardware solution can increase performance, using horizontal or vertical techniques. Vertical scalability requires the hardware and associated operating system utilize additional resources within a single server, such as memory, internal bus bandwidth, and multiple processors in symmetric multi-processor (SMP) designs.

Horizontal scalability can also utilize clustering to improve performance, with multiple servers grouped into a single cluster image. Clustering can be provided through operating system facilities, or via modern e-business applications clustered across multiple servers using application server software. However, the performance and management of horizontal scalability is often problematic due to poor operating system or application support, or due to limited hardware support for multiple cluster members.

Manageability and support of the platform will also influence hardware choices. Multiple servers are typically more complex to manage than single servers. Therefore, consolidating multiple e-business functions within a single server provides a more manageable system than distributing that function across many servers. This requires a hardware and operating system platform to support high performance and availability, and the ability to dynamically allocate system resources to different computing tasks. Such sophisticated features typically then require fewer, more highly trained support resources.

11.3 Hardware platform performance

The different hardware platforms can be classified into low-end solutions, mid-range solutions, and high-end solutions, depending on their support for the operational requirements of reliability, availability and scalability within an e-business initiative. This categorization is depicted in Figure 11.1.

Figure 11.1 Hardware platform suitability

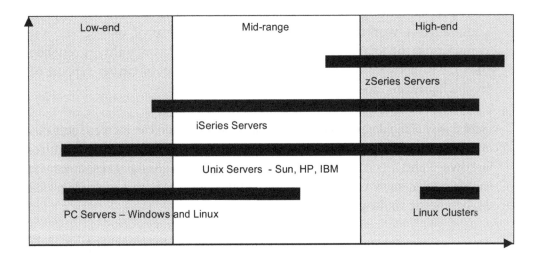

Low-end solutions are suited to e-business initiatives requiring low levels of functionality. Such solutions typically require less complex application logic, low to moderate levels of performance, and are typically not critical to the functioning of a business and may therefore require low to moderate levels of availability. Examples of such initiatives include simple Internet and Intranet online publishing sites and low or moderately utilized portals and content management systems.

Mid-range solutions are suited to e-business initiatives with moderate to high levels of functionality and more complex application logic. Such initiatives are typically more demanding and critical to the functioning of the business, and therefore require moderate to high levels of performance and availability. Examples of such initiatives include transactional e-business systems, internal and external integration solutions, high-use portals, high-use content management solutions, and enterprise applications such as ERP and CRM systems.

High-end solutions are suited to traditional back-end processing functions within sectors such as manufacturing and finance, which generate very large volumes of information and may have thousands of simultaneous users. These solutions are often used to provide added functionality to front-end e-business systems, such as additional business logic processing functions for finance products, or to provide access to legacy data. Such solutions typically require very high levels of performance and availability, and are critical to the functioning of a business.

Low to mid-range solutions

The Intel server hardware platform is typically employed in low to mid-range solutions for workgroup computing within companies and provides simple e-business functionality such as Internet-based publishing. Intel server hardware is commonly offered with the Windows operating system and can also run with the Linux operating system.

Although the Intel server platform utilizes symmetric multi-processor (SMP) systems for vertical scalability, Windows is currently limited to supporting a maximum of 32 processors through a special version of Windows, the Windows Datacentre Server edition. Datacentre Server is only available for Microsoft-certified customized hardware solutions direct from select vendors, and provides proprietary extensions to Windows 2000 to support additional system memory beyond the standard Windows 4 GB limit. These proprietary extensions may in turn require software developers recode and retest their applications to ensure compatibility.

Other versions of Windows provide support for more limited levels of scalability, suited to low-end and mid-range solutions. Windows 2000 Server supports up to 4GB of memory and four processors, with Windows 2000 Advanced Server supporting up to 8 GB of memory and eight processors.

Horizontal scalability and availability through Windows-based clustering is also limited to low-end to mid-range solutions. Currently, Windows supports clustering of two servers with Windows Advanced Server and four servers with Windows Datacentre Server. These solutions offer services for clustering network connections, DCOM application components and fail-over support for critical applications in case of server failure. Currently Windows Intel Servers lack high-end availability features found in Unix, iSeries and zSeries systems such as dynamic reconfiguration and dynamic pathing.

This limited support for scalability, availability and reliability features restricts the use of Windows to workgroup-based computing tasks, such as file and print sharing, and e-business application and database tasks where a moderate degree of system downtime is permissible.

The open-source Linux operating system is also available for Intel server hardware. The Unix-like design of Linux allows it to offer many of the advantages of Unix operating systems, including high levels of reliability and scalability. For example, Linux-based systems support vertical scalability with up to 32 processor SMP systems through the version 2.4-release kernel.

Linux systems also offer horizontal scalability through a number of cluster solutions supporting a broad range of SMP servers. They also offer advanced super-computer clustering solutions such as the 'Beowolf' cluster system, supporting the connection of hundreds of servers into a single system image for extremely high levels of performance suited for supercomputing-class applications.

The sophistication of Linux-based servers and the growing availability of large numbers of enterprise and e-business applications have led to growing acceptance of Linux within companies and their deployment for e-business implementations. For example, Linux shipments have come to represent more than 27 per cent of all servers sold during 2000 (Connolly, 2001), with various versions of Unix taking almost 14 per cent. The widespread uptake of Linux within business has also resulted in greater availability of support staff with experience of Unix-type systems.

Mid to high-end solutions

The three major Unix server platforms, Sun SPARC running the Sun Solaris operating system, IBM pSeries running the AIX operating system and

Hewlett-Packard PA-RISC systems running the HP-UX operating system, provide an ideal solution for mid to high-end e-business solutions. These platforms offer high levels of reliability as well as supporting scalable deployment of applications across hardware systems ranging from affordable personal desktop systems to mainframe-class enterprise systems without requiring different application versions.

Vertical scalability for Unix systems is typically higher than other hardware platforms, with the largest systems supporting up to 256 processors in a single system. Due to its long development history, Unix operating systems are also more efficient at utilizing such high performance multi-processor systems, when compared to Windows– and Linux-based systems.

Horizontal scalability of Unix systems is provided through advanced cluster solutions. These typically provide a number of advantages compared to Windows – and Linux-based systems, including support for a wide range of off-the-shelf cluster-aware applications, increased cluster scalability, and the ability to consolidate cluster resources into a single virtual server for simplified manageability.

Unix-based systems provide additional scalability through support for 64-bit operating systems and hardware architectures, which allow for computation on very large quantities of information. For example, Sun Solaris and SPARC servers currently support up to a half-terabyte of system memory. Sixty-four-bit architectures also allow Unix hardware and operating system platforms to support very large storage volumes for applications such as large databases, compared to 32-bit systems.

Sun Solaris and the SPARC hardware architecture were the first major Unix vendor systems to offer 64-bit support in 1995, and all major versions of Unix now provide 64-bit hardware and operating systems. They also provide transparent concurrent support for older 32-bit software.

In addition to support for scalability through SMP designs, clustering and high levels of reliability, Unix systems offer mainframe-class management features such as multiple system partitions and dynamic resource management. System partitioning allows a single SMP Unix server to host multiple copies of an operating system and applications, saving hardware and management costs compared to multiple separate servers. This server consolidation in turn simplifies administration, support and management. Dynamic resource management enables Unix servers to respond to changes in hardware configuration in real time without affecting currently operating applications. For example, if a system component such as system memory or processors fails during operation, the server continues to function.

The ability of Unix systems to provide very high levels of reliability, availability, and scalability, a broad range of hardware options, and the availability of thousands of enterprise and e-business applications render them ideal for all forms of e-business. These include workgroup functions and enterprise class e-business applications such as portals, content management, database servers, transactional e-business, CRM, ERP, and EAI.

High-end solutions

The zSeries (OS/390) and iSeries (AS/400) platforms provide very high levels of reliability, scalability and availability for mid-range to very high-end e-business applications. Scalability in these platforms is provided through multi-processor hardware, with support for up to 32 processors and additional dedicated hardware to off-load common tasks from these processors. Support is provided for 64-bit hardware and operating systems, and for similar levels of clustering to other IBM systems. In addition, the zSeries is specifically designed for multi-user application processing, providing access for thousands of concurrent users to applications on a single zSeries system.

The recent adoption of Internet technologies such as Java has allowed the iSeries and zSeries platforms to provide additional e-business functionality. However, the expense of these systems and the limited levels of third-party experience in deploying e-business systems into such environments restrict their widespread use within e-business. This has typically led to the use of iSeries and zSeries systems being deployed as mission-critical back-end providers of data and enterprise and legacy applications, integrated with Unix, Windows or Linux e-business systems using technologies such as EAI.

11.4 High-level designs of hardware platform architectures

Due to the different levels of reliability, availability, scalability and manageability provided by the different hardware platforms, each platform can be utilized to perform different services within common e-business architectures.

Due to their low cost and widespread availability, Windows – and Linux-based systems are frequently utilized in e-business web server farms in the presentation tier. Linux systems are typically recommended when availability and reliability are critical elements of the e-business solution. Alternatively, if high availability considerations are less important, Windows-based solutions are often utilized.

Business logic and back-end storage tiers typically utilize highly available Unix systems to provide high levels of performance and availability, and support for a very broad range of applications. Alternatively, Linux – or Windows-based systems can be utilized when high performance and availability are of lower importance.

An additional integration tier may access iSeries and zSeries systems to provide very high performance business logic and data storage from enterprise applications.

Two-tier e-business architectures

E-business solutions utilizing a two-tier e-business architecture employ hardware and software systems deployed across two layers. This design provides for low to moderate performance and availability, and has lower management requirements compared to the three-tier architecture.

Within this design, the first-tier utilises a combined presentation and business logic layer. The second-tier data storage layer incorporates database storage servers and their attached storage devices. This design may be extended using additional business logic located in the second tier as high performance database stored procedures.

Typically, this design utilizes different classes of hardware platform distributed across these two tiers. The first tier may include a smaller number of moderate performance web and application servers, with the second tier employing a small number of high performance database servers.

The two-tier e-business architecture is depicted in Figure 11.2.

Figure 11.2 Two-tier e-business architecture

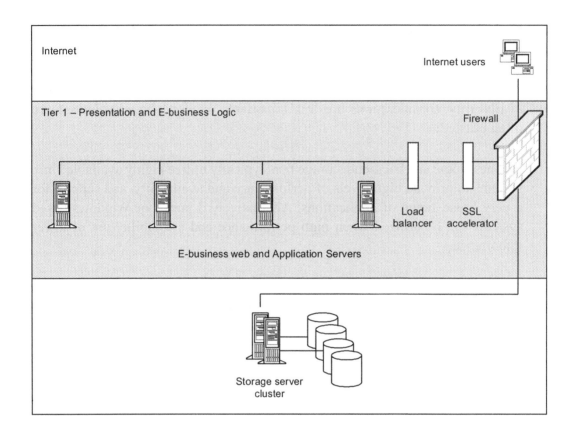

Within this architecture, additional scalability can be achieved through the inclusion of additional load-balanced servers in the first tier, and database clustering in the second tier. Parallel database products offering active/active cluster configurations (where all servers are active), such as Oracle 9i or IBM DB2, allow for higher performance compared to active/passive cluster solutions (where one or more standby servers are employed). Both tiers should support the expansion of servers to accommodate more processors, memory and storage.

Management requirements for this architecture can be minimized by deploying a smaller number of higher performance servers, thus simplifying administration. In addition, having fewer web servers in the first tier allows simpler mechanisms to synchronize content between these servers.

Typical deployments of this architecture utilize hardware platforms with varying levels of availability and performance, as depicted in Table 11.1.

Table 11.1 Common hardware platform solutions for two-tier e-business architectures

	Medium availability **Medium performance**	**High availability** **High performance**
Tier 1	Linux Windows	Windows (load balanced) Linux Unix
Tier 2	Linux Windows Unix	Unix iSeries zSeries

Three-tier and n-tier e-business architectures

Three-tier e-business architectures offer a number of advantages over two-tier architectures. The separation of presentation, business logic and data functionality into separate tiers in this architecture reduces dependencies between layers and simplifies the programming model of the solution. Changes in one layer therefore minimize changes in other layers, increasing system reliability and maintainability. In addition, servers within the individual tiers can be scaled separately from other tiers, allowing a more efficient use of hardware.

Typically, this design utilizes multiple low to medium performance web servers in the first-tier presentation layer. Specialist small and inexpensive servers are employed in this role, providing functionality dedicated to single tasks such as web page serving, mail serving, or DNS serving. Most Unix and Intel server vendors provide such appliance servers, with some vendors increasingly offering servers based on emerging server Blade technology, featuring multiple highly compact servers within a single chassis.

The second-tier business logic layer employs multiple medium or high performance servers to manage the performance demands of e-business transaction processing. E-business applications are typically clustered across these servers through the workload-management services provided by technologies such as DCOM, or Java application server products. This permits the deployment of applications into high availability and high performance configurations.

The third-tier data layer incorporates one or more high performance database server clusters, based on the requirements of the e-business application. For example, an application may require a separate management database and separate application content database. In addition, multiple applications may be deployed on the second tier, requiring separately scaled back-end databases. N-tier architectures extend three-tier architectures to include additional services on four or more tiers. These may include other e-business systems such as portals, publishing systems, or internal and external integration systems interfacing to enterprise applications and partner and supplier systems. Many of the functions in this tier are typically provided by iSeries and zSeries systems. These systems provide access to enterprise applications and data stores through enterprise application integration with e-business systems and other internal applications.

Typical three tier and n-tier architectures are depicted in Figure 11.3.

Figure 11.3 Three and n-tier e-business architectures

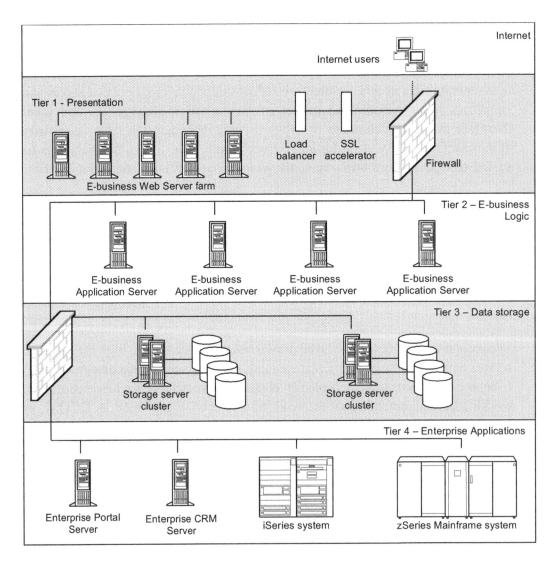

Typical deployments of this architecture utilize hardware platforms as depicted in Table 11.2.

Table 11.2 Hardware products suitable for three and n-tier architectures

	Medium availability **Medium performance**	**High availability** **High performance**
Tier 1	Linux Windows Unix	Windows (load balanced) Linux Unix
Tier 2	Linux Windows Unix	Linux Unix
Tier 3	Linux Windows Unix	Unix iSeries
Tier n	Linux Windows Unix iSeries zSeries	Unix iSeries zSeries

Consolidated tiers

In addition to 2-n-tier architectures, recent developments in Unix and zSeries operating systems have led to vendors promoting 'server consolidation' strategies. These consolidation strategies utilize operating system partitioning, where multiple virtual servers are created within a single hardware server. This allows the solution to consolidate multiple discrete servers into a single large physical server, as depicted in Figure 11.4.

Figure 11.4 Consolidated virtual servers

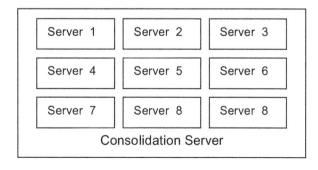

225

Server consolidation represents an efficient strategy for many companies to reduce the proliferation of e-business servers running enterprise e-business applications such as DNS serving, portal and content management, EAI, and enterprise functions such as CRM and ERP.

However, adopting this strategy requires reliable and high-speed internal networks capable of deploying centralized applications to internal users. It also requires very reliable, high performance hardware and operating system solutions.

Currently a range of vendors offers consolidation solutions. For example, in February 2002 IBM released a new class of zSeries mainframe servers exclusively dedicated to hosting multiple copies of the Linux operating system. This allows a single zSeries server to run hundreds of concurrent Linux servers, with considerable reductions in management and support of the complete solution when compared to managing discrete servers. Sun Microsystems also offer a similar partitioning strategy for high-end and mid-range SPARC servers, allowing the creation of 18 separate partitions per server, each running a discrete copy of the Solaris operating system. Similarly, Hewlett-Packard also offer partitioning within their Unix servers.

However, although ideal for internal application consolidation, this model of hardware deployment leads to increased levels of risk when centralizing public Internet-facing e-business applications into one server. For example, compromise of a publicly accessible Linux partition within a consolidated server could potentially lead to compromise of all partitioned resources. In contrast, compromise of separate servers hosted within a DMZ network would not directly compromise other DMZ or internal systems.

Security is a critical aspect of all e-business initiatives due to the need to observe regulatory requirements on the use of personal information, the need to maintain the trust of customers, and the need to ensure the continued, secure and reliable operation of all corporate systems.

Regulatory requirements for security differ between countries, but will typically include three core principles governing the storage and handling of customer data. First, companies must use customer information only for the purposes for which it was gathered. For example, this requirement stipulates that customer data should not be on-sold to external companies without user permission, and that all customer identifiers be removed if it is to be used for testing purposes outside the company. It also dictates that mechanisms be put in place to regulate access to data to approved individuals.

Second, customer information must be stored within a secured environment to prevent it being compromised and put to unintended use. For example, customer data must not be stored in a manner that will allow it to be read by unauthorizsed users, such as an online bank allowing access to a customer's account details by other customers. This dictates that all customer data be stored in a secure manner, and be accessible only by its owner or by authorized personnel within the company.

The third requirement is that customer data should only be stored for as long as required for the operation of the business. Examples of this requirement include telecommunications companies storing lists of phone numbers of calls made by customers to generate billing information. This dictates companies maintain mechanisms to securely store, manage and dispose of customer information.

In addition to regulatory requirements for the secure use of information, maintaining security of customer information is vital to retaining customer trust. High profile security breaches have resulted in reduced uptake of online e-businesses initiatives due to the fear by customers that their information is not being treated in a secure manner. In addition to the issue of trust, security breaches also expose a company to the threat of legal action from customers for the mishandling of their information.

Finally, security is critical to ensuring the continued, efficient operation of corporate computing resources. Weak security typically leads to company security being breached, resulting in expensive investigative and remedial repair efforts. Security breaches also have the potential for intruders to utilize company resources to launch attacks on other systems within and outside a company, therefore using these resources for unintended and potentially illegal destructive purposes.

For example, a company may provide a transactional e-business system for online financial services to its customers. Weak security may result in compromise of this system, and the release of critical personal information such as billing details, credit card numbers, and account numbers, as depicted in Figure 12.1.

Figure 12.1 Customer data compromise through security breaches

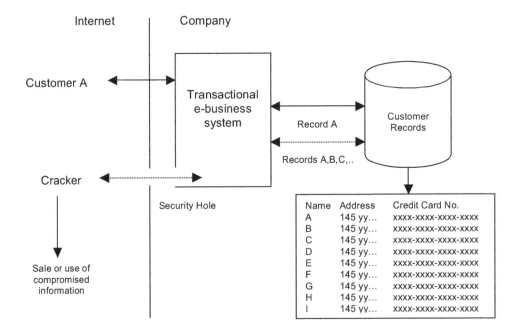

Security breaches can be categorized into three common forms of security incident. These include unauthorized compromise of secure information through the release or modification of information such as customer and corporate data, modifying such corporate resources without permission, stealing corporate computing resources, and denying service from corporate resources.

Unauthorized compromise of customer and corporate data is one of the most serious categories of security incident, and involves the theft or modification of customer and corporate data. Typical high profile thefts of customer information include stealing credit card and banking details, and the more recent trend towards 'identity theft'. This involves an attacker stealing enough information about an individual to impersonate them. This then allows the attacker to use this information for personal financial gain, or psychological gratification through online and offline stalking. Unauthorized modification of secure information involves an attacker intentionally changing corporate or customer data such as changing a credit history for personal gain, or changing corporate information in an attempt to damage a company.

Stealing corporate resources involves an attacker compromising internal systems within a company and using them for their own aims. Examples of this form of compromise may include launching attacks on other systems within the company, launching attacks on systems outside the company, or using computing resourcse for the attacker's own purposes, such as storing stolen software or data.

Denial-of-service of corporate resources occurs when an attacker commandeers corporate systems to prevent them being used. Denial-of-service may involve an attacker overwhelming corporate systems with huge volumes of network traffic, or through propagation of viruses within corporate systems. Distributed denial-of-service attacks are another variation on denial-of-service attacks, and utilize automated software agents to attack resources from multiple external systems. Typically, the originator of these attacks cannot be easily traced due to their use of other compromised systems to launch their attacks.

Although considerable publicity is given to external attacks on systems by 'hackers' or 'crackers', the majority of security breaches of the three types discussed above originate from internal users within the business. Therefore, it is imperative to deploy secure systems within the business to ensure employees cannot compromise corporate resources, in addition to securing business systems from external attack.

12.1 Corporate information technology security policies

Corporate security policies form the foundation of how an enterprise conducts business in a secure manner. Security policies are designed to ensure that all corporate activity is assessed against this policy, in order to identify security weaknesses within the business and respond accordingly.

The most widely accepted security policy standard is BS 7799 (versions 1 and 2) from the British Standards Institute. Version 2 of this standard has recently been incorporated as the ISO standard ISO 17799, guaranteeing worldwide acceptance.

ISO 17799 details a set of security assurance controls created and maintained by management within an organization. It identifies ten detailed security controls designed to ensure the implementation of a successful information security initiative. These include business continuity planning, system access control, system development and maintenance practices, physical and environmental security, compliance, personnel security, security organization, computer and network management, asset classification and control, and a documented security policy.

Business continuity planning is designed to minimize interruptions to ongoing business and processes that may result from major failures or disasters. This ranges from the provision of standard availability and reliability features within infrastructure and systems, to sophisticated disaster recovery facilities such as duplicate data centres.

System access control is designed to provide controlled access to information. It governs the prevention of unauthorized access to information systems, ensures network systems are protected, prevents unauthorized access to computer systems and detects such access, and ensures security is applied across mobile and remote working facilities.

System development and maintenance practices are designed to ensure security is built into corporate information technology systems. This ensures systems are developed and maintained to prevent loss, modification or misuse of data, and protect the confidentiality, authenticity and integrity of information. It also requires all projects and support be conducted securely to maintain the security of application system software and data.

Physical and environmental security is designed to prevent unauthorized access, damage and interference to business premises and information, to prevent the loss, damage or compromise of corporate assets and resulting interruptions to business, and to prevent the theft or compromise of corporate systems.

Compliance measures are designed to ensure all relevant laws, contracts and security requirements are complied with. This ensures systems comply with organizational security policies and standards, and maximizes the effectiveness of and minimizes the interference with the systems audit process.

Personnel security is designed to ensure risks from human error, theft, fraud and resource misuse are minimized. Users must be made aware of security threats, and trained to support the corporate security policy in their work. They must also minimize damage resulting from security incidents and learn from these when they occur.

Security organization is designed to create structures to manage information security within the company, to maintain security of information processing facilities and assets accessed by third parties, and to maintain security of information when the information processing has been outsourced to external organizations.

Computer and network management is designed to ensure that facilities operate securely and correctly. The risk of failures within systems should be minimized, and all software and information protected. The integrity and availability of information processing and communication must be maintained, information in networks safeguarded, and supporting infrastructure protected. Interruptions to business and the loss, modification or misuse of information exchanged between organizations must also be prevented.

Asset classification and control is designed to maintain the protection of corporate assets and to ensure that they have appropriate levels of protection. This typically requires deployment and use of asset management systems, policies, and procedures for asset maintenance.

Finally, a documented corporate security policy forms the basis of all security within the organization, and provides management direction and support to ensure consistent company-wide information security.

Once an organization has adopted an information security policy such as ISO 17799, it is imperative that ongoing compliance with the system is assessed on a periodic basis. This should include a minimum of yearly audits to ensure compliance with the policy, and more frequent tests of corporate security systems, depending on the degree to which corporate infrastructure and application systems change.

12.2 Key technologies used

Security systems must be capable of coping with a wide range of requirements, including exposure to security threats from deployment of internal and external e-business systems and integration with external partners and suppliers, and the increasing levels of attacks on corporate systems.

Security technologies must now protect internal resources from internal and external attack while providing controlled access to critical resources. They must also cope with the dramatic increase in automated software viruses and worms, such as Code Red and Nimda, and denial of service attacks. In addition, corporate security must keep abreast of the constantly changing nature and volume of attacks being employed.

These requirements dictate that security systems be designed using a series of overlapping technologies to secure all corporate systems. Security is therefore typically provided through layered security systems and access control systems.

Layered security systems are comprised of overlapping sets of security technologies designed to provide security services to all corporate systems. As multiple overlapping technologies are deployed, the compromise of an individual layer does not result in total compromise of the complete e-business solution. The layered security model also utilizes the services of corporate access control systems to restrict all activities crossing security system boundaries.

Access control systems are security technologies that regulate access to corporate resources based on predefined criteria. These may include the origin of a connection and request, the type of request, and the identity of the requestor. These systems provide detailed and fine-grained control over access to valuable corporate resources.

12.3 Layered security systems

Many of the security implementation goals of ISO 17799 can be achieved through the adoption of layered security systems. Layered security systems are designed to ensure that the compromise of individual security layers does not result in the complete loss of corporate security, as additional layers remain intact and continue to secure corporate resources.

Layered security systems typically employ four distinct layers and associated access control and auditing and monitoring mechanisms. These include the network layer, operating system layer, data layer and application layer, as depicted in Figure 12.2.

Figure 12.2 The layered security system

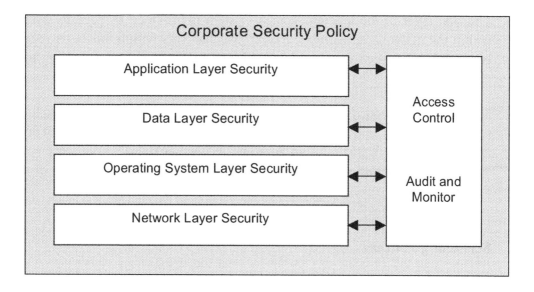

Each layer is governed by the constraints of the corporate security policy to ensure continued compliance with security directives. Each layer must also incorporate access control systems and audit and monitoring systems to provide controlled access to resources and ensure any suspicious activity that may compromise security is notified to the appropriate authorities.

This system can be configured to support deployment of additional components to compensate for weaknesses in components within individual layers. For example, if an application has been deployed with known security weaknesses, additional security systems within other layers, such as input-checking proxy servers in the network layer, can be interposed in front of the application to isolate it from potential threats.

The layered security system also permits extension of different layers into external partner and supplier systems connecting to the enterprise. For example, before permitting such external connections, additional network and application level security mechanisms can be mandated for the external party, such as the addition of firewalls, screening routers, and use of digital certificates. A corporate security policy should therefore specify that the layered security model be extended to all third parties wishing to establish connections into a business.

12.3.1 Network layer security

The first layer of the layered security system is provided by security systems within the network infrastructure layer. Mechanisms within this layer regulate connectivity between the outside world and internal systems according to the security policy.

Network layer security is governed by the networking hardware, including screening routers and firewall devices. These devices allow the network to respond to network traffic in an appropriate manner by identifying the source and intended destination of requests for corporate resources, and permit or deny the requests.

Screening routers

The first point of network security is provided through the deployment of screening routers. Routers control network traffic flows between internal corporate networks and the Internet, and within the corporate network between network segments with different address schemes.

Screening routers employ access-control filtering lists to monitor the source and destination IP addresses, and the content of the network traffic. This restricts access to users across network boundaries by ensuring connections originate from the appropriate network. It is also designed to prevent so-called trusted systems forgery attacks, where an external user impersonates an internal system in an attempt to utilize incorrectly configured internal resources.

Users originating from external networks with internal addresses are blocked, thus preventing the user from gaining potentially privileged access to internal systems. Such attacks are depicted in Figure 12.3.

Figure 12.3 Network level trusted system forgery

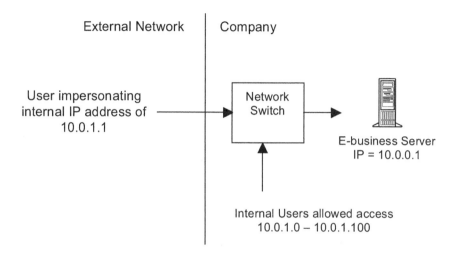

The network layer can also be configured to restrict denial-of-service and distributed denial-of-service attacks. These attacks utilize very high numbers of simultaneous connections to e-business systems in an attempt to overwhelm their resources and prevent them from being used. Distributed denial-of-service attack utilizes multiple external sources for the attack, in contrast to denial-of-service attacks that originate from a single source.

Router changes to prevent distributed denial-of-service attacks include disabling IP broadcasts to prevent their use in attacks, and implementing egress filtering. This ensures only traffic originating from within the network is allowed external access to the Internet, preventing the use of internal systems to attack external systems (see http://www.sans.org/y2k/egress.htm). The network should also be continually monitored for signs of denial-of-service activity via network management tools and intrusion detection software.

Denial-of-service attacks can be mitigated using automated tools and network devices that monitor network traffic and instruct routers to drop connection attempts from IP addresses with a signature matching such attacks. A detailed description of such network layer protections can be found on the www.securityfocus.com and www.sans.org security sites.

Firewalls

Firewalls inspect all network traffic according to predefined rules, and permit or deny connections to e-business resources based on these rules. Connection attempts that fail this inspection are then rejected. This allows firewalls be interposed between internal and external networks to control access to network, data, and application layer resources.

For example, firewalls are typically deployed between corporate e-business networks and the Internet and allow standard HTTP and HTTPS traffic to an e-commerce server. Insecure protocols, such as telnet or ftp, are then denied between internal and all external networks to preserve security.

Firewalls allow for filtering of traffic to potentially insecure internal systems and services, and can therefore be used to stop a wide variety of attacks targeting commonly used and insecure network services, or services that may reveal too much internal information to intruders, such as DNS zone transfers.

Firewalls should therefore be configured to deny connection attempts to common network services. These typically include the time service (37/tcp and 37/udp), TFTP (69/udp), finger (79/tcp), NNTP (119/tcp), NTP (123/tcp), LPD (515/tcp), syslog (514/udp), SNMP (161/tcp and 161/udp, 162/tcp and 162/udp), BGP (179/tcp), and SOCKS (1080/tcp).

Potentially 'revealing' network traffic that should be blocked includes incoming echo request ICMP traffic and outgoing echo replies, time exceeded, and destination unreachable messages except for packet too big messages. All UDP packets sent to non-required UDP ports should be blocked, and all traffic arriving from external networks with private address space addresses (RFC 1918) should also be dropped.

Insecure network services should be blocked by the firewall, as these may have exploitable security holes. These typically include login services such as telnet (23/tcp), SSH (22/tcp), FTP (21/tcp), NetBIOS (139/tcp), rlogin (512/tcp through 514/tcp); RPC and NFS services, NFS (2049/tcp and 2049/udp), and lockd (4045/tcp and 4045/udp). Windows specific network systems are also affected, including NetBIOS in Windows NT and 2000 (tcp and udp 135,

137/UDP, 138/UDP, and 139/tcp, and Windows 2000 445/tcp and udp). X Windows traffic should be blocked (6000/tcp to 6255/tcp), and DNS naming services (53/udp) restricted to all machines which are not DNS servers, with DNS zone transfers (53/tcp) disallowed except to external secondary DNS servers.

Other e-business-related services that should be restricted include Lightweight Directory Access Protocol (LDAP) directory services (389/tcp and 389/udp), email services to all systems that are not external mail relays, including SMTP (25/tcp), POP (109/tcp and 110/tcp), and IMAP (143/tcp). Web traffic to public web servers should be allowed but denied to all other servers including HTTP (80/tcp) and SSL (443/tcp) traffic.

Firewalls constitute a mission critical element of a company's network and security infrastructure, and should therefore be subject to strict change control. The firewall rule sets should not be changed on an ad-hoc basis before going through change control procedures to ensure business continuity.

In addition, firewalls should be deployed in a high availability configuration to provide guaranteed availability. This can be provided through the deployment of firewalls in a dual redundant firewall cluster configuration, incorporating two firewalls running in parallel, with each cluster member sharing network traffic information. Failure of a single firewall will therefore not compromise the screening of network traffic as the remaining cluster members will continue to operate.

Firewall clusters should be deployed in an active/active mode, with each cluster member participating in simultaneous traffic filtering. This provides twice the performance of a single firewall or of an active/passive standby cluster configuration, which utilizes a passive standby firewall ready to take over from the failed active firewall. In addition, a high availability deployment configuration should be utilized to eliminate all points of failure within the cluster.

Additional corporate security can be achieved through deployment of firewalls on desktop and laptop computers used by roaming and remote users. This provides protection for mobile computers or home workers when outside the company, in the event that an individual attempts to compromise such systems to obtain access to corporate data.

Remote firewall products should include the ability to be managed remotely through a firewall policy defined by a central management station. This should permit propagation of the policy to all remote computers, and the ability to manage applications on the remote computers to prevent leakage of unintended information.

In addition, it is recommended that roaming and roving users be issued with virtual private network software. This permits such users to establish a secure encrypted connection to their office when they need to access office resources such as file servers. This encrypted connection prevents outsiders from deciphering their communications and potentially gaining access to critical information.

Although frequently deployed as the primary defence mechanism for company security, firewalls cannot protect networks and systems against many modern attack methods, such as email viruses or application level vulnerabilities. Such firewall-transparent attacks exploit known and newly discovered flaws in applications, and are not picked up by firewalls as they employ firewall-approved channels to gain access to systems such as HTTP web traffic or legitimate inbound email traffic. Therefore, additional security layers are required to protect affected systems.

DMZ networks

Additional security is provided by the creation of secured de militarized zone (DMZ) networks. A DMZ is a separate network connected to a corporate firewall used to host systems requiring external communication such as an e-business server or email gateway.

DMZ network designs are required due to the inability to fully trust e-business infrastructure with external access to insecure networks, such as the Internet. These systems will be in contact with unknown and untrusted users, who may compromise the e-business infrastructure. The DMZ therefore restricts the opportunity for such compromised servers to be used to compromise other internal systems.

Wireless network security

Although increasingly popular, wireless networks based on the new 802.11b standard currently have considerable security holes in the WEP security protocol employed to secure the connection.

It is therefore not recommended that such devices be attached to corporate networks, as these may result in attackers gaining complete access to internal corporate networks, and potentially compromising internal systems. Once wireless security standards improve, all wireless network access points should employ advanced encryption systems to secure network traffic.

12.3.2 Operating system layer security

The second layer in the layered security system is the operating system layer, which consists of a secure deployment of a server and its associated operating system. This requires the 'hardening' of all servers within the organization, which removes known security holes in the operating system thus preventing these being used to compromise the system.

Hardening occurs before a server is first connected to a network and before application software is installed. It requires that a server operating system be installed with a minimal set of critical components and utilities to reduce the likelihood of installing non-essential components with potential security weaknesses.

Vendor operating system security patches should then be installed to bring the system up to date with all known security holes. Patches should be scanned for viruses then provided on removable media such as CD-ROM for installation on the server. This ensures the server is not connected to a network and potentially compromised until hardening is complete. Application software can then be installed following security patching.

As new security holes are discovered in operating systems almost daily, it is recommended that security patching of previously hardened production servers be conducted on a periodic basis. This minimizes the risk of compromise to live servers arising from new security holes discovered since the server was patched. To minimize potential disruption to live systems, it is recommended that new security patches be tested on development servers prior to deployment on hardened live production servers.

12.3.3 Data layer security

The third layer in the layered security system is the data layer security, which consists of the secure storage of data within databases and secure networks, and the secure transmission of critical corporate data between networked systems.

Encryption mechanisms utilize software algorithms to scramble human-readable data into an unreadable form. Encryption is employed to protect sensitive information stored in externally accessible areas, such as credit card information stored within a transactional e-business server in a DMZ network. This ensures that in the case of the server being compromised, the information is unreadable.

Encryption is also used to secure data in transit over insecure networks, such as the Internet. This is typically provided through the Secure Sockets Layer (SSL) data transport technology. SSL employs an encryption module within the e-business infrastructure, typically on web servers, which is used to encrypt communication with a user's browser. This ensures data in transit between the user and the e-business system cannot be intercepted.

Data layer security is also provided by the deployment of database servers behind additional firewalls within DMZ networks. This provides an added layer of security in the event that preceding security layers are compromised.

12.3.4 Application layer security

The fourth layer of the layered security system is the application layer security. This layer consists of the creation, deployment and maintenance of applications using security best practices to minimize the potential for the creation of security holes.

This layer is critically important to e-business security, as the majority of security breaches now occur within applications behind firewalls. These exploits utilize flaws in poorly configured or poorly written applications to send invalid input designed to exploit known or suspected weaknesses in the application. This typically results in an intruder gaining control over the server hosting the application, and either changing corporate content such as defacing a public website, or using the server to stage attacks on other systems.

Creation of secure applications requires correct security procedures be designed into all applications. This typically requires the design of applications to check input such as validating user input to prevent the sending of information capable of compromising the application, and designing the application to respect operating system security settings. It also requires periodic security audits by developers during the development of the application to ensure security weaknesses are caught before applications are deployed into live environments.

Secure application development can also be enhanced using development languages such as Enterprise Java and Microsoft C++ for .Net. These languages enforce strict controls on application code, preventing many security issues from arising within applications, such as memory buffer overruns.

Application deployment requires applications be installed and configured on servers using operating system accounts with minimal privileges. In addition, deployment of packaged applications requires installation of vendor-supplied security patches to address known security issues.

Deployed applications can be further secured using operating system security mechanisms such as Windows Security Policies for Microsoft Windows systems, or through high security Unix policy-control systems, such as Trusted Solaris. These systems enforce strict controls on the server resources each application is permitted to access, thus ensuring attackers cannot use flaws in one application to compromise other applications or the underlying operating system.

DNS security

Corporate DNS systems form a critical application within all e-business initiatives, and necessitate special security measures to ensure continued name resolution service.

Deploying DNS servers typically opens a company to two potentially serious security risks, including the 'hijacking' of DNS information, and compromise of publicly accessible DNS servers.

Compromises of publicly accessible DNS servers occur through insecure configuration of operating systems, and through flaws in DNS software. Hackers/crackers utilize these security weaknesses to compromise the server. Once compromised, a DNS server can be used to launch subsequent attacks on internal systems, or used to stage attacks on other external systems.

To prevent compromises of DNS servers, the operating system should be configured in a secure manner. In addition, for very high security configurations DNS server software should be deployed on Unix systems in a chroot environment, where access is restricted to a virtual 'sandbox', protecting the underlying operating system in case of compromise of the DNS software. This deployment can be found in the BIND v9 Administrator Reference Manual for a discussion of this option.

Hijacking of DNS information occurs through a hacker/cracker gaining access to DNS information and altering it to point to other resources. This constitutes a form of denial-of-service attack, as it denies access to corporate resources for internal and external users. This may result in lost business and considerable time spent rectifying the hijacking. Hijacking of DNS systems typically occurs if a cracker is able to exploit flaws in DNS server configuration, such as allowing dynamic updates from untrusted sources, to redirect DNS requests to another DNS server.

Hijacking of DNS systems can be mitigated through the deployment of split-level DNS designs to reduce the availability of critical DNS information of use to a cracker. Split-level DNS partitions a corporate name space into public and private sections, hiding sensitive internal DNS information from external users. A subset of public DNS information is then provided to external users through separate, externally visible DNS servers within the DMZ network, and changes to the DNS server configuration files (see the section 'DNS server configuration'), as depicted in Figure 12.4.

Figure 12.4 Split-level DNS

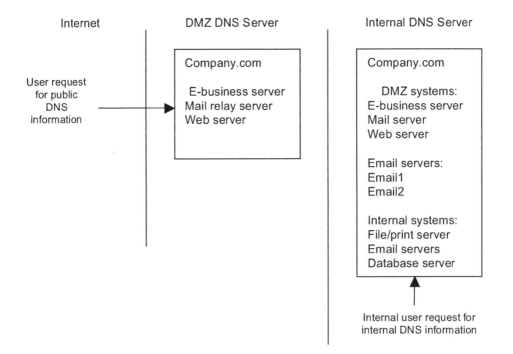

242

Provision of email delivery from the Internet to internal email systems also requires the use of split-level DNS to provide DNS security. Email is typically delivered to a central email relay server on the DMZ network, and then routed to different internal email delivery servers. If the public DMZ DNS servers contained entries for these internal email servers, this sensitive information could potentially be exposed to untrusted external individuals.

Additional security precautions for DNS systems include restricting zone transfers, to prevent the widespread release of important information, as it may be used in subsequent attacks, and to deploy access control lists. In addition, dynamic updating of DNS information should not be permitted for critical systems using static addresses, such as e-business servers. All dynamic updates should be secured with digital certificate signing of all update requests, and external access should be disallowed for updates to records.

Access control lists (ACLs) are used to regulate access to specific DNS records, allowing for fine-grained control over the security of records. Typical options include the ability to restrict access to individual records based on the network of the originating request, or even specific IP addresses. This feature is critical for supporting split-level DNS configurations utilized in high security DNS and DMZ designs. Support for ACLs should also include the ability to restrict zone transfers, which are used to update zone files held by secondary DNS servers.

12.3.5 Access control mechanisms

In addition to the four layers described above, all security systems should implement industry standard directory-service mechanisms for access control. Access control is the process of validating the identity of users against a directory service before granting them access to regulated resources. This reduces security risks by ensuring only approved users can utilize corporate e-business resources.

The current standard for user directory services for e-business systems is the Lightweight Directory Access Protocol (LDAP). LDAP directory systems store user credentials in a high performance server, and accept and respond to standard LDAP queries issued by e-business applications. This provides a company with a centralized, standards-based user authentication system. Corporate e-business applications can then query this system to determine the identity of users requesting connections to resources. Approved users are granted access by the e-business application, and unapproved users denied access.

Due to widespread adoption of the LDAP protocol, many packaged applications and development environments support LDAP directory server queries. This in turn allows companies to adopt the LDAP directory service as the single access control system for internal and external e-business initiatives, such as corporate portals and transactional e-business systems, and integration initiatives with external partners and suppliers.

Although offering support for the LDAP protocol, Active Directory and NDS are not recommended for external accessed deployment in e-business as they typically contain sensitive internal information about corporate users and business systems, in addition to management systems for these resources. Therefore, compromise of these directories would give intruders access to highly sensitive information and potentially widespread control over corporate systems.

It is therefore recommended that a two-tier directory service model be adopted for the provision of access control to e-business and internal corporate resources. This model allows applications to obtain security information for external users, such as customers or suppliers, independently of internal security information on corporate staff. This architecture is depicted in Figure 12.5.

Figure 12.5 E-business directory services model

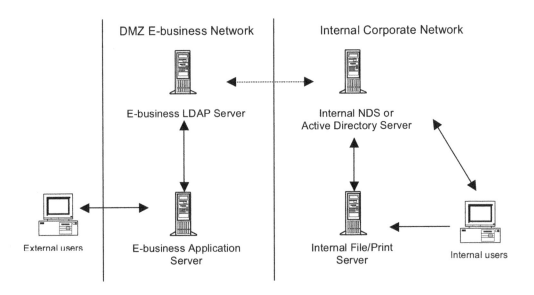

In this model, an internal user attempts to access a document stored within a file and print server. When they first log on to their computer the NDS or Active Directory Server validates their credentials and returns them a security token appropriate to their level of access. They are then free to access the desired resource, being validated using this token each time they access other resources. In contrast, an external user connects to the e-business application in the DMZ network. When they connect to the secured resource the application queries them for their security credentials, then validates these against the user database held in the LDAP server. Access to resources appropriate to their privileges is then granted.

In addition to providing access control to external users, this model can also be extended to provide access control for partners and suppliers in external integration initiatives. For example, integration of a business process integration broker system with an LDAP directory server would provide a centralized repository of user information allowing the broker to regulate external supplier access to internal corporate systems participating in the integration initiative.

Finally, this model may also be deployed to enhance other security layers. Network-level firewall security can utilize LDAP directory services to validate the identity of corporate users accessing internal networks and resources via virtual private network connections while roaming outside the company. Data level security can also be enhanced through LDAP. Database servers can be configured to query LDAP directory servers to obtain user credentials before granting controlled access to secure data.

Public key infrastructures

A public key infrastructure (PKI) provides a highly secure form of access control through the issuing of digital certificates to participating users, which contain encrypted information unique to each user. This allows the PKI system to validate user identity with a very high level of certainty.

The security provided by a PKI system exceeds that of other user authentication and verification schemes, and is typically utilized in situations where it is critical to validate identity with a high degree of certainty. For example, PKI may be deployed to provide secure access to a valued trading partner in a dynamic e-business initiative, and ensure the correct entity is accessing business-critical internal systems such as enterprise resource planning applications.

The PKI architecture consists of three core components designed to control the issue, management and destruction of digital certificates. These components include the certificate authority (CA) for creating and digitally signing certificates, the registration authority (RA) for issuing certificates requested by users (to be signed by the CA), and the validation authority (VA) for verification of certificates presented by users. The VA also revokes certificates if they are no longer valid.

A certificate authority is considered the 'root authority' for a company, which is the single originating source of authority for the creation and signing of certificates within the corporate PKI system. The CA is typically maintained within a highly secured environment, and delegates the right to issue individual certificates to the registration authority.

The registration authority receives requests for digital certificates from users and applications, and then grants or denies these according to specific policies deployed within the server. Registration authority policies may also include the option of manual intervention for a staff member to perform identity checks on the user requesting the certificate, such as checks on credit criminal records.

The registration authority can issue digital certificates to a user's browser or via email software to customers and suppliers, permitting the use of highly secure email and Internet access to e-business applications. When these users subsequently send email, or connect to secured web pages, the certificate they present guarantees their identity and thus validates their email as originating from them or permits them access to secured web pages or resources.

The validation authority is responsible for verifying a certificate presented by a user or application. In the event that the CA has revoked the certificate, the VA will reject it. Expiry of a certificate can occur via a manual process, or automatically, for example by specifying a total lifetime for the certificate.

Although providing the highest security for authentication and authorization of customers, partners and suppliers connecting to corporate e-business systems, PKI implementations suffer from a number of problems. These include high expense, poor support for client systems, and lack of interoperability between different PKI vendors. This typically restricts PKI implementations to specific vertical uses, such as integration between well-established trading partners or providing secure document audit trails within regulated industries such as the pharmaceutical industry.

12.3.6 Security auditing and monitoring

Corporate security systems must also implement continual auditing of all systems to determine if they remain secure. Security auditing is an ongoing process, and involves deployment and use of intrusion detection, server auditing, and monitoring systems across the four security layers.

Typically, intrusion detection systems consist of servers and network sensors running software providing network and host-level protection. Network protection consists of a server listening to network traffic for activity that matches known patterns representing a security threat. In the event that a threat is detected the intrusion detection system notifies the appropriate staff member via email or pager, and may block the suspicious activity. Host-level protection incorporates software agents installed onto servers to monitor attempts to modify and compromise the server.

However, the detection of attacks using network and host-level intrusion detection products is currently limited due to their tendency to frequently report security threats that do not exist. Such 'false positives' may consume considerable resources as staff attempt to respond to each perceived threat. This can be partially alleviated through deployment and extensive tuning of multiple intrusion detection systems, permitting cross-correlation of false positives. In addition, many intrusion detection tools are frequently overwhelmed by large volumes of network traffic, and suffer from poor reporting and management features.

The design of network and host-level intrusion detection products also often renders them unable to respond to newly emerged threats. Such products typically incorporate a database of security threats, and respond by matching network traffic to these 'signatures'. Therefore, vendors must continually update their products as new security threats are discovered, which lag the latest attacks. This in turn requires companies dedicate resources to tracking the latest security threats on a daily basis to respond accordingly to preserve corporate security.

Emerging forms of intrusion detection systems are now addressing these limitations, through mechanisms such as anomaly detection and security event aggregation and correlation tools. Anomaly detection tools construct a baseline of network behaviour, and compare current activity to this baseline to determine if an attack is in progress. However, this system depends on having a predictable and well-understood network, which may not be possible. Security event aggregation tools rely on real-time data and log analysis correlated to network level events to determine the status of network and resource accesses.

Static auditing employs tools either installed on each server or running across a network, to periodically scan all servers for newly discovered operating system security holes. Such products run tests based on an internal database of all known security holes. If a security hole is detected, the operating system vendor can be contacted to supply the required security patch.

A variation on static auditing utilizes software such as the Tripwire product to ensure that the operating system of each server is maintained in a known state. Following installation and hardening of the server operating system and application software, the static auditing tool is run on the server, producing a baseline configuration that can be compared to later runs to determine if the server has been modified. Signature files generated by such tools should be securely stored off-site, and periodically compared to the actual configuration of the server. This ensures that if an intruder has altered the operating system to compromise the server, their changes can be detected.

Security monitoring requires security staff analyse log files output by the systems within each security layer to determine if users of applications have violated corporate security policies. This requires monitoring of firewall logs, application access control logs, and intrusion detection and auditing system logs. In addition, all security policies and procedures should be continually reassessing to cope with changes within the business.

Monitoring also requires attention to vendor security notifications and subscription to online security notification sites, to ensure awareness of current security threats. For example, the Security Focus website (www.securityfocus.com) provides an online database of current and past security exploits, with the option to subscribe to regular security alert updates. The SANS website (www.sans.org) also provides a list of the top 20 security vulnerabilities, based on the most commonly reported security exploits.

In the event that a security threat is discovered, responses should follow the policies and procedures detailed in the security policy. Typically, responses to security alerts will follow six phases, including Preparation, Identification, Containment, Eradication, Recovery and Follow-up, and these should be documented in the corporate security policy. In addition, companies may provide an emergency action checklist for staff, with a simple set of steps to follow in case of security alerts.

Such checklists typically suggest noting the nature of an attack then notifying the correct staff members, using alternative and non-compromised communication methods such as telephone or fax. The problem should then be contained through steps such as disconnecting affected systems from the network, and the affected systems backed-up. The cause of the problem should be removed if possible, such as a removing viruses or Trojans, and affected systems restored to bring the business back up as soon as possible.

12.4 High-level designs of security systems

Two sets of high-level designs for e-business security systems are depicted in Figure 12.6, covering secure DMZ network design issues, and a comprehensive design featuring the systems and services offered within the layered security system.

High-level design for secure dmz networks

High-level designs of secure DMZ e-business networks provide secured networks for e-business systems separated from the Internet and corporate networks by firewalls and screening routers.

A typical secured DMZ network design is depicted in Figure 12.6.

Figure 12.6 DMZ network design

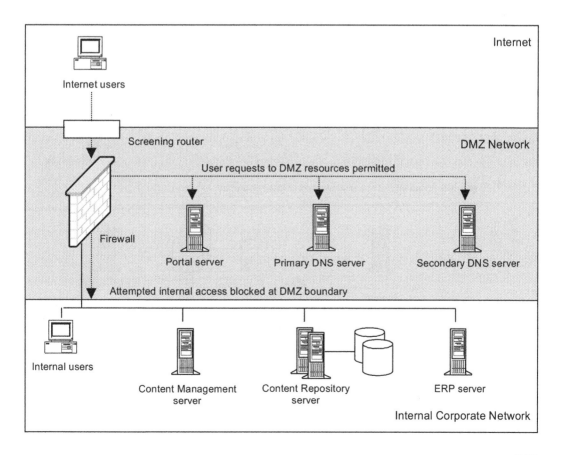

In this design, the screening router and firewall restrict user requests originating from the Internet, and ensure they are only granted access to the e-business servers located within the DMZ network. Servers on the DMZ are in turn physically separated from other servers and users on the internal corporate network. All user requests to critical internal resources are blocked at the DMZ network boundary.

Corporate networks frequently deploy more than one DMZ in order to provide enhanced security for critical internal systems, as depicted in Figure 12.7.

Figure 12.7 Additional DMZ network configuration

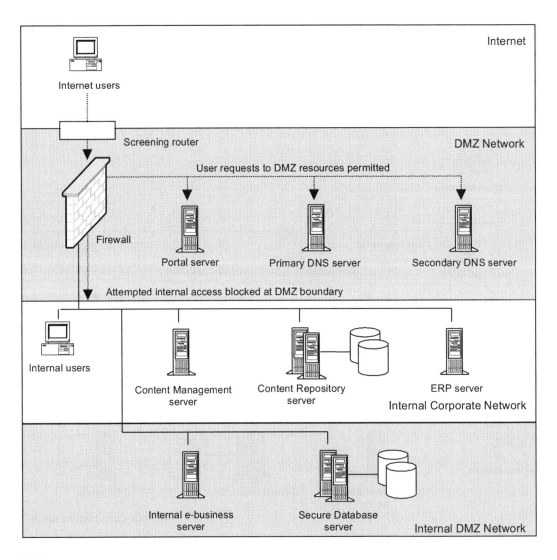

In this configuration, an additional internal DMZ network has been created to host a secure e-business server and database used for internal purposes. As the information on these systems is highly sensitive, these servers are isolated from internal access from unauthorized users.

Additional DMZ networks are also frequently required for connections to external partner and supplier networks for purposes such as external e-business systems integration initiatives.

Although partners and suppliers are frequently trusted entities, and may have long-term trading relationships, it is often not possible to ensure complete security with such external parties. For example, it may not be possible to conduct a complete audit of the partner and supplier security systems to determine levels of potential security risk. These risks may include having unprotected external connections, insecure connections to other unknown third parties, or having been breached by hackers/crackers and potential compromises such as Trojan software installed without the knowledge of the partner or supplier.

It is therefore necessary to minimize the risk associated with connecting to partners and suppliers by restricting the possible access they have to internal corporate systems, as depicted in Figure 12.8.

Figure 12.8 External partner and supplier DMZ

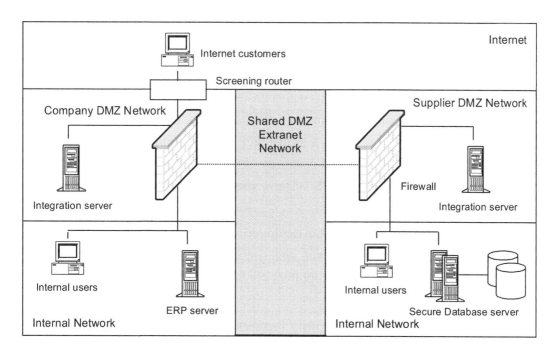

In this example, an integration server located in the DMZ network of a supplier connects to the integration server located within the company's DMZ. Both servers are connected through a common shared DMZ Extranet network dedicated to secured, private connections for partner and supplier companies.

Comprehensive high-level security design

Comprehensive high-level security designs should employ the full range of layered security systems described above. These include the use of secured DMZ network zones, deployment of network access control devices between networks, deployment of network monitoring devices at strategic points, use of access control mechanisms, use of hardened servers, and data and application-level security systems.

The following high-level security design depicts a transactional e-business system consisting of an e-business web server farm in a secured DMZ with an SSL accelerator and load-balancing switch.

Additional DMZ networks are provided for VPN connections to external third parties, an internal DMZ for e-business application and LDAP directory servers, a database server DMZ for secure data storage, and a corporate PKI DMZ for secured control of a Certificate Authority.

Additional security features include the use of multiple intrusion detection servers and network sensors, a split-level DNS system, a two-tier directory service design with an internal corporate directory server and an internal DMZ LDAP server, a split-level DNS system, and hardening of all servers.

An internal PKI system is also deployed to supply certificates used by the LDAP server, application server and firewalls to authenticate and authorize external trading partners and suppliers connected across the VPN connection.

The use of these combined security features is depicted in Figure 12.9.

Figure 12.9 High-level design of security systems

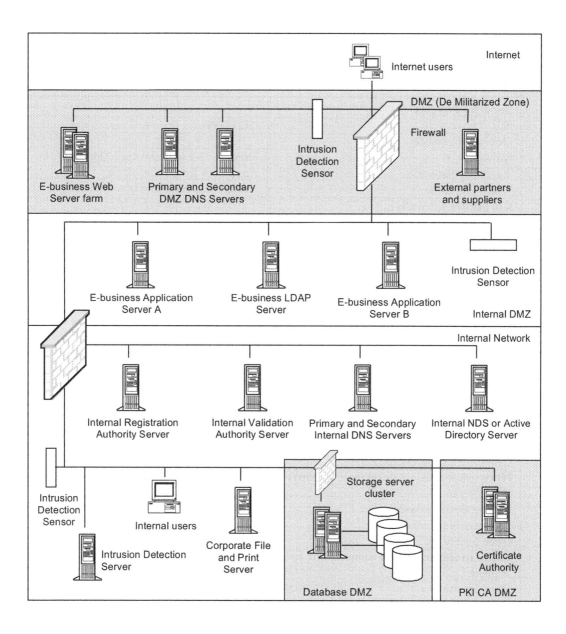

12.5 Vendors of security solutions

Table 12.1 lists vendors of products used in enterprise security systems. It should be noted that this list is not exhaustive and should be used as a guide only before solution research is undertaken.

Table12.1 Vendors of security solutions

Vendor	Security solution
Security Policies	
ISO	ISO17799
Denial-of-service	
Radware	Fireproof 2.2 with SynApps software
Top Layer Networks	AppSwitch & AppSafe
Mazu Networks	TrafficMaster Enforcer
Corporate firewalls	
Cisco	PIX range (e.g. PIX 535)
CheckPoint	Firewall 1 and CheckPoint NG
Eagle Systems	Raptor
Lucent Technologies	VPN Firewall Brick
NetScreen Technologies	NetScreen-1000
Nokia	IP 51-740 range
Nortel	Contivity 600 and Optivity NCS
SonicWall	SonicWall Pro-VX
Watchguard Technologies	Firebox 1000
Roaming/roving firewalls	
InfoExpress	CyberArmor Suite
Sygate Technologies	Secure Enterprise and Management Server
Host intrusion detection systems	
Symantec Corporation	Intruder Alert
Internet Security Systems (ISS)	RealSecure
CyberSafe Corporations	Centrax
Network intrusion detection systems	
Cisco Systems	Secure IDS
Internet Security Systems	BlackICE
Enterasys Networks	Dragon
Open Source	SNORT
Static monitoring and assessment tools	
Tripwire	TripWire
Open Source	Nessus Security Scanner
Open Source	Whisker
Open Source	Snort
Internet Security Systems	Real Secure

Networking systems consist of physical connections between systems, and network hardware devices designed to interpret and route information between systems. They provide standard mechanisms to connect users within a company to e-business systems such as online publishing or transactional systems, and to other users over the Internet. These are also used to provide connections to partner and supplier companies participating in e-business integration initiatives.

In addition to simple connectivity, networking systems provide critical security services necessary for secure e-business, and can assist in providing high availability and reliability services to e-business infrastructure.

For example, a company provides Internet access between internal systems and users, and the Internet. This in turn allows for connection to users and systems within partner and supplier companies, and necessitates systems to transmit and receive data and ensure security of internal systems, as depicted in Figure 13.1.

Figure 13.1 Internet and partner and supplier connectivity through networking systems

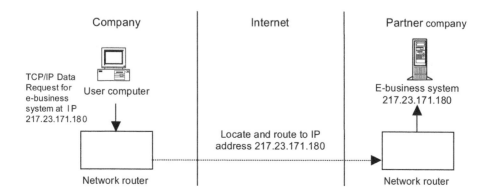

In this example, a user sends a request for a resource located on an e-business system in a partner company with the IP address of 217.23.171.180. The request is conveyed to the company router, a device dedicated to sending such requests to the correct destination. The router forwards the request across the Internet to nearby routers that are physically closer to the destination. Eventually the information is at the partner company router, which then forwards the request to the e-business system.

13.1 Key technologies used

The Network layer utilizes three core technologies to transport data, including transport protocols to encode and transport data, addressing schemes built using these protocols for identification of systems, and specialist hardware devices to route data between source and destination addresses.

The information technology industry has standardized around the TCP/IP protocol to provide data transport functionality for networking systems. TCP/IP provides for reliable delivery of data across Intranets and the public Internet, and utilizes the IP protocol to assign unique addresses to each connecting system.

Each networked system is identified through a unique IP address and subnet mask. These are allocated by an external Internet connectivity provider, and both IP address and subnet mask consist of a group of four numbers between 0 and 255 separated by full stops, such as 198.45.78.3. The IP address is used to identify servers and clients across the Internet, while the subnet mask is used to identify the network the server or client is located on.

To further simplify routing, networks are divided into classes according to the subnet mask. These classes include Class A, B and C, with the subnet mask in turn determining the number of available IP addresses within the block. The Class A address block is denoted by a subnet mask of 255.0.0.0 and permits 126 networks with 16, 777, 214 addresses. The Class B address block is denoted by a subnet mask of 255.255.0.0 and permits 16, 383 networks of 65, 534 addresses. A Class C address block is denoted by a subnet mask of 255.255.255.0 and permits 2, 097, 150 networks of 255 addresses. Example addresses are depicted in Table 13.1.

Table 13.1 IP address classes

Class	IP address	Subnet mask
A	10.10.34.5	255.0.0.0
B	157.23.70.200	255.255.0.0
C	217.23.171.80	255.255.255.0

However, as the total number of available IP addresses is constrained, IP addresses are often allocated in blocks smaller than the Class C group with subnet masks such as 255.255.255.240. This ensures wastage of IP addresses is minimized by only giving companies the addresses they need.

13.2 The corporate IP address allocation scheme

IP addresses are issued to networked systems through Dynamic Host Configuration Protocol (DHCP) servers, or manually by modifying operating system network properties. However, before allocating addresses companies must determine how their address space will be used for different corporate systems, users and office locations.

An IP address allocation scheme is designed to allow a company to efficiently allocate the finite number of addresses they have been issued between resources, users and locations. This allows a company to conserve available IP addresses and ensure that systems are allocated unique addresses to prevent network address conflicts.

A corporate IP Address Allocation Scheme consists of static and dynamic addresses. Static addresses are used for commonly accessed resources such as servers and printers, which will typically not change location. Dynamic addresses are used for transient systems, such as desktop client systems and notebooks, which do not typically provide networked services to other systems or users such as serving web pages.

Dynamic addresses are allocated to conserve addresses and simplify IP address management. For example, desktop systems are constantly being added and removed within companies as employees shift department or building, move jobs, or are absent on business. If such systems used fixed addresses, a company would incur a considerable management overhead tracking addresses in use and allocating unused addresses to other systems.

An allocation scheme can use either public Class A, B or C addresses, or the private addresses, known as the RFC 1918 private address scheme. This scheme, a special form of Class A address, was designed for use within companies and is therefore not routed across the Internet. IP addresses within the private address space run from 10.0.0.0 to 10.255.255.255, providing 16, 777, 214 available addresses.

Although recommended for internal use, the RFC 1918 private address space is not routed across the Internet, and therefore cannot be used for systems directly accessible from the Internet, such as e-business servers.

Use of private addresses on such public systems therefore requires a company to deploy either network address translation, to 'translate' internal addresses into public addresses (typically via a firewall or router), or use separate private internal and public DMZ networks, as depicted in Figure 13.2.

Figure 13.2 Public and private address schemes

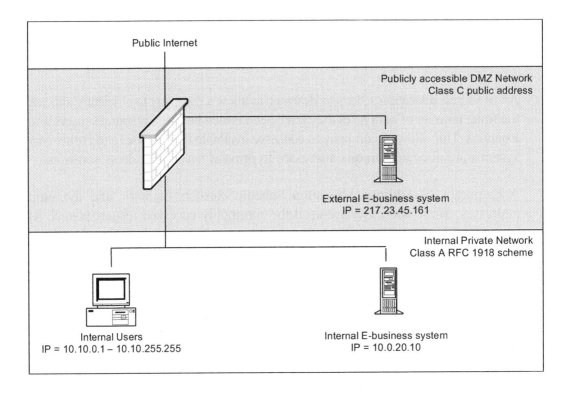

In this example, a Class C IP address has been allocated to the DMZ e-business system. Alternatively, a large organization such as a university or global corporation may utilize a Class B address for this system.

An allocation scheme based on the RFC 1918 private address space allows for the creation of a very large and flexible scheme by providing a single network (10.x.x.x) consisting of 16, 777, 214 (256*256*256 minus 2 reserved addresses) possible addresses, ranging from 10.0.0.1 to 10.255.255.254.

The flexibility of this scheme arises from the ability to partition this range according to the requirements of the company. Using a different subnet mask allows for the creation of more networks with fewer addresses per network. For example, using a Class B subnet mask of 255.255.0.0 divides the RFC 1918 space into 256 different networks each containing 65, 534 addresses. Similarly, a Class C subnet mask of 255.255.255.0 allows for 65, 536 networks consisting of 254 hosts in each network. This division of addresses is depicted in Table 13.2.

Table 13.2 Possible class B and C subnet masks

Item	Class B subnet	Class C subnet
IP address	10.x.0.0	10.x.x.0
Networks available	10.1.0.0– 10.255.0.0	10.0.1.0– 10.255.0.0
Hosts available per network	10.1.0.1– 10.1.255.254	10.0.1.1– 10.0.1.254
Note: X denotes an arbitrary number from 0 to 255.		

Creating an IP address allocation scheme requires determination of the number of fixed and dynamic resources and their distribution across physical locations such as buildings, floors, or cities. The number of physical locations will determine the number of networks, and the required numbers of addresses determined by the number of resources in each location.

For example, Table 13.3 depicts a medium sized company with four divisions spread across four physical locations, with different numbers of static and dynamic resources in each area.

Table 13.3 IP allocation example of company resources

Division	Marketing	Sales	Manufacturing	Head office
Dynamic resources				
Number of users	20	100	3000	200
Total	20	100	3000	200
Static resources				
Number of servers	1	5	30	10
Number of printers	2	2	10	5
Other systems	1	2	20	1
Total	4	9	60	16

In this example, the company has four locations with between 20 and 3000 dynamic resources, and between 4 and 60 static resources. Possible address allocation schemes include a Class C scheme, with 254 hosts per network and 65,536 networks, or a Class B scheme with 65,534 hosts per network and 256 networks.

The 3000 dynamic resources in the manufacturing office exceed the limits of a single Class C network of 255 devices. Selection of a Class B scheme allows for the allocation of 65,534 possible addresses, sufficient to meet the current number of users and any foreseeable future growth. If additional branches or divisions within existing offices are created, a further 252 networks are available for growth.

Once the allocation scheme address class has been determined, available addresses must be allocated between dynamic and static hosts. This ensures that addresses reserved for static hosts will not be issued to dynamic hosts via DHCP servers.

In this example, each Class B address has 65,534 available addresses, of which 60 static addresses and 3000 dynamic addresses are required in the manufacturing plant. Allocating 1024 fixed addresses (4*256) would permit substantial future growth in fixed addresses for this network while still preserving more than 64,000 addresses for growth in dynamic hosts.

The allocation scheme would therefore resemble that depicted in Table 13.4.

Table 13.4 Example IP addresses allocation scheme

Division	Static range	Dynamic
Marketing	10.0.0.1-10.0.3.255	10.0.4.0-10.0.255.255
Sales	10.10.0.1-10.10.3.255	10.10.4.0-10.10.255.255
Manufacturing	10.20.0.1-10.10.3.255	10.20.4.0-10.20.255.255
Head office	10.30.0.1-10.10.3.255	10.30.4.0-10.30.255.255

13.3 Network hardware

Specialized hardware devices are used to route TCP/IP data, or packets, between source and destination systems. The most common devices include routers, switches and hubs.

Routers consist of intelligent devices used to connect networks of systems with different addresses together. Routers utilize sophisticated algorithms to determine the optimal path for TCP/IP packets to reach their destination based on knowledge of the addresses in use within adjacent connected networks.

Switches are used internally within corporate networks to transfer packets point to point between local systems at very high speed through dedicated channels. In contrast, hubs employ a shared local connection between multiple systems. This may result in congestion due to the shared nature of all connections.

Other network devices include firewall systems and DMZ networks to provide network security, and specialist e-business devices such as load balancers and SSL accelerators to provide enhanced e-business facilities.

Firewalls provide a mechanism to tightly regulate the flow of information within a company, while DMZ networks are subnetworks separated from main corporate networks for the purposes of isolating systems exposed to external contact. This ensures that compromises to such systems do not result in direct access to critical internal resources.

Load balancers are used to aggregate multiple servers into a single virtual server by distributing requests to a 'virtual' address to multiple back-end servers. This allows a group of servers to provide increased levels of performance and availability, as failure of one or more servers will not affect the total functioning of the solution.

SSL accelerators are utilized to increase the performance of SSL encryption and decryption for sites with high volumes of secured traffic.

13.4 High-level designs for networking systems

Companies employing e-business systems typically require specialist network designs to ensure the security and high scalability and availability of their e-business applications. These designs are discussed below.

SSL accelerated networks

Specialist network devices are frequently deployed to enhance the performance of e-business security systems. For example, network devices can be used to increase the speed of secure services running over the network, such as SSL encryption for communications between users and e-business servers.

Such network devices are known as hardware SSL accelerators. These devices off-load processing of SSL connection encryption and decryption from e-business web servers. SSL accelerators use custom designed hardware optimized for SSL calculations and offer performance several orders of magnitude faster than web server processes SSL. This in turn frees the web server hardware for more efficient processing of user requests.

Hardware SSL accelerators are available as network devices (sometimes incorporated into switches) or as hardware accelerator cards added to servers. Network switches provide an excellent mechanism suitable for offloading SSL processing from multiple servers. However, network switch-based SSL accelerators render the decrypted traffic visible within internal DMZ network, and thus subject potentially sensitive information to interception if the internal network has been compromised. In contrast, hardware accelerator cards within servers can provide additional performance, as well as offering greater security, as all decrypted information is retained within the server.

When utilizing hardware SSL accelerators, the resulting network infrastructure may resemble that depicted in Figure 13.3.

Figure 13.3 Hardware SSL accelerated network design

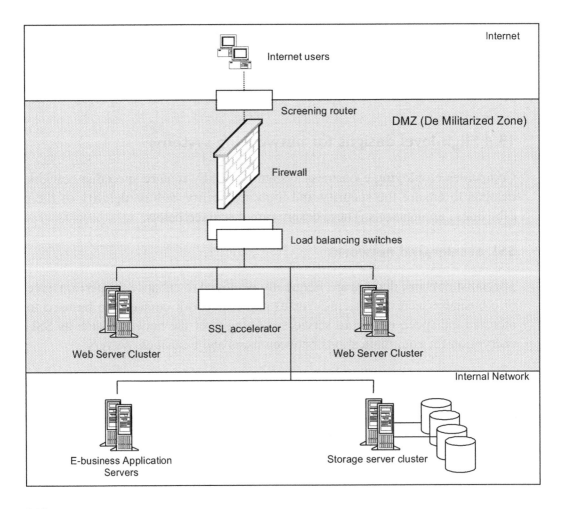

High availability network design

Network systems provide business critical connectivity to e-business applications. Failure of individual components within the network can therefore render the e-business infrastructure unable to serve customers or internal users and systems. It is therefore recommended that a corporate e-business network be configured to support continual availability for e-business systems.

Standard techniques for e-business network high availability focus on the elimination of all single points of failure. These can occur through failures in cabling, failure of network devices such as switches and routers, failure of network cards within servers, and failure of complete servers.

The diagram depicted in Figure 13.4 depicts a design with no single points of failure.

Figure 13.4 High-availability e-business infrastructure design

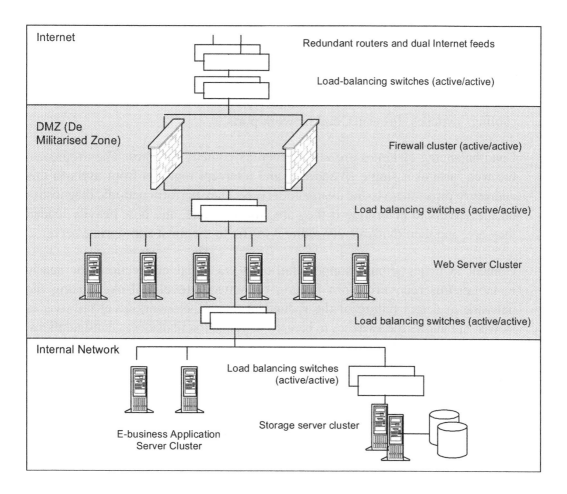

Using this design, single points of failure are eliminated using multiple redundant systems within each network layer. The network connections into the infrastructure are deployed in a redundant configuration using two routers and a second connection to the Internet. Each router has two connections into the telecommunications provider to allow for failure of a cable. If either router fails, the remaining router reconfigures the network routes through its connections to provide continual availability of connectivity.

The routers are in turn connected to an active/active load-balancing switch cluster, which is connected to the firewall cluster. Each router and firewall has two connections to each active/active switch. Thus, if a cable or network port fails on one switch, the connection to the other switch will continue to function. Both switches are linked together, and in the event that a switch fails, the remaining switch will still function and continue to switch the traffic of the failed switch.

Behind the firewalls are a set of load-balancing switches designed to direct network requests to an array of web servers, called a server farm or web cluster. These switches also function in active/active mode to eliminate failures as discussed above. This configuration provides higher performance by balancing traffic among the web cluster member servers, preventing the failure of an individual server from affecting the complete e-business service. In addition, cross-connecting systems in this manner eliminate failures of network cards, cabling, switches, firewalls, and network ports.

Load-balancing switches are also known as content switches. They represent the web-farm as a single IP address, and intercept requests from users to this address to direct them to the available servers. They perform periodic diagnostics on the servers to determine if they are still available, and how heavily loaded they are, and then dynamically redirect traffic to the most appropriate server.

Content switches should support fail-over via serial connection, for nearly instantaneous recovery from failure, or network-level fail-over, using the network to detect failure of the redundant switch. Network-level fail-over is slower, but allows the switches to be used in global load-balancing configurations. Switches should also offer fail-over support for user connections, so that connection information is not lost as the backup switch assumes control.

It should be noted that the functions provided by switches positioned on each side of the firewall can be amalgamated into one layer using VLAN technology (virtual LANs). This feature allows each switch to segment traffic into two or more virtual LANs, providing multiple virtual switches in one physical device.

Behind the web server farm layer, another two active/active switches provide connectivity to two or more e-business application servers, which are themselves connected by active/active switches to the database cluster at the back-end. Similarly, if VLAN capable switches are used, this additional switching layer can be amalgamated into one set of devices. Load-balancing switches may not be required in these layers if the application servers are configured as a single cluster image. This feature, present in many J2EE application server implementations, deploys Java components across multiple application servers. Requests to these components are dynamically load balanced by application server code, removing the need for front-end load-balancing switches.

The database cluster in the back-end utilizes database and operating system clustering to present the multiple cluster servers as a single system image with very high availability. Additional storage options such as storage area networks (SANs) should be investigated for very high levels of storage.

Global load balancing

Although eliminating points of failure within the e-business infrastructure in Figure 13.4, this design retains the geographical location of the infrastructure as a single point of failure. Loss of connectivity at that location through a catastrophic event such as bomb damage, or accidents such as the severing of a major telecommunications cable, can render e-business sites unavailable for prolonged periods.

Full uptime requires the deployment of global load balancing configurations. These designs use an additional copy of the e-business infrastructure, physically located at a different site, often in another country. If one site fails, the site at the other location will continue to function, preserving e-business continuity.

Global server load-balancing configurations can also be deployed across countries for enhanced performance. Using this option, an e-business site may be duplicated at datacentres in the US and the UK. Connections to the site from Europe would be routed to the UK site, and requests from the Pacific Rim and Americas would be routed to the US site. Load balancing in this fashion ensures that e-business resources are located closer to users within broad geographical areas, ensuring connections do not have to pass through congested long-distance Internet links.

This design utilizes intelligent content-aware switches, known as Layer 4 – 7 switches, to achieve global load balancing. Redundant switches located at each infrastructure location are configured to act as primary and secondary DNS servers for their e-business sites.

As each switch receives user requests for the IP address of an e-commerce resource, the switch determines their original location by reading their IP address and comparing it to global IP address allocations. If the address is closer to that set of infrastructure it will return the local IP address for the resource. However, if the request originated closer to the other set of infrastructure, the switch will respond with the remote site IP address, thus diverting the user to the closer resources. Each site monitors the other so that if one becomes unavailable, the opposite site will handle all requests.

High-level remote access designs

Remote access to corporate resources as well as the Internet may be required for users who work from home, or alternatively for users who travel with their computer. This presents additional security issues with corporate network designs, which must be addressed in order to ensure security for e-business systems.

Remote access technologies use dial-up access to networked modems located within the corporate network, virtual private networks over the Internet, or dedicated private networks supplied by third-party providers such as telecommunications providers. These forms of connections are typically restricted to authenticated users via firewall technology or access control systems such as Secure ID, which require users to present an electronic token to authenticate before being given access.

When designing networks for remote access, similar principles for connections to external partner and supplier networks must be used, as it is not always possible to guarantee the integrity and security of such remote connections.

Therefore, it is recommended that connections to these remote workers be secured via virtual private network (VPN) technology. A VPN encrypts communications between parties to ensure the security of information in transit, and can utilize hardware or software VPN solutions.

Software VPN solutions utilize encryption and decryption services provided through an application deployed on a server. This typically takes the form of firewall-based software VPNs, for simplified management. Software VPN solutions are typically deployed for small numbers of remote users, as these provide a low cost entry into VPN technology.

In contrast, hardware VPNs may be used in place of software solutions for large numbers of remote users, as many simultaneous connections can overwhelm software VPNs. These solutions utilize dedicated network devices to process encryption and decryption of network traffic to remote users. Hardware VPN solutions are typically placed within a separately managed DMZ network for added security.

It is also recommended that the VPN products adopted should be compliant with the IPSEC standard. This standard is designed to ensure interoperability between different vendor VPN products, and is currently undergoing advanced development to include more sophisticated authentication systems to validate the identity of VPN participants.

Alternatively, managed VPN solutions from telecommunications providers can provide cost-effective VPN solutions. As these utilize the services of a third party, connections to the provider network should be regulated through a DMZ network for added security.

All forms of remote access solutions should employ user authentication systems such as Secure ID tokens, RADIUS username and password authentication, and advanced systems such as PKI-based authentication. These allow a company to validate the identity of the user connecting through the remote access entry point.

High-level designs for external hosting/co-location

As an alternative to internal deployment of e-business infrastructure, external hosting, or co-location, within third-party facilities is often utilized.

Co-location offers advantages such as full-time monitoring and management of infrastructure provided as a complete managed service. This typically includes in-house security teams, very high availability network infrastructure providing guaranteed network uptime, and physical security control of hosted systems. In addition, such arrangements can frequently provide considerably more available bandwidth to the hosted infrastructure that many companies could afford themselves.

Hosting providers should be selected based on their ability to provide a full range of hosting services. These include physical security and network management services provided through a 24 by 7 dedicated network management team. Physical security services are typically comprised of protection from fire, bomb damage, and earthquakes in the hosting building, with video and physical security of the hosting premises to ensure only authorized personnel are permitted access.

Network management services typically include highly available and redundant internal and external network connections to multiple bandwidth providers. Connections to providers should include major international telecommunications carriers, and utilize multiple connections into peering facilities.

Peering facilities provide network entry points for multiple carriers to exchange private connections with each other. This permits traffic to flow efficiently between network providers without their having to use public Internet connections. For example, if a user on Network A sends data to Network B and they have a peering arrangement it will be directly transmitted between the two private networks without using the public Internet. This in turn allows such companies to provide more bandwidth between the Internet and their own networks for use by their customers.

High-level designs for hosted e-business systems require full access between existing corporate networks and the equipment located within the hosting provider premises. This should be provided through VPN connections between firewalls to encrypt traffic in transit between the two networks.

To ensure network traffic will route correctly between these two locations, the IP address allocation scheme at the remote site should be compatible with the corporate scheme. It is recommended that the RFC 1918 private addressing scheme be used as this allows for simplified removal and resiting of equipment in the event that another co-location provider is required. In contrast, utilizing addresses supplied by the hosting provider binds the e-business infrastructure to that provider. This in turn complicates resiting of equipment due to the necessity for reassigning IP addresses to all servers and their dependent application services when moving equipment.

The Domain Name System (DNS) is the industry-standard technology used to locate e-business systems over the Internet or within corporate Intranets. DNS employs specialist servers to translate human-readable requests for e-business resources into computer-readable IP address for routing to their destination by the network layer. Correct implementation of the DNS system is therefore required to successfully deploy and utilize all e-business systems.

DNS functions in a transparent manner, with users and systems requiring no understanding of the mechanisms and operation of the system. This allows access to resources irrespective of the underlying network or resource location. For example, a user within a company in Los Angeles can access Intranet and e-business servers located in their UK office without knowing their location.

DNS is a core component of the Internet, and is therefore required for all businesses to utilize Internet and Intranet systems. It provides a very robust design capable of scaling to accommodate huge numbers of users and servers through distribution of multiple copies of DNS information among different locations.

The process of locating and accessing of resources through DNS is known as Name Resolution. Name Resolution translates the names of e-business resources such as the website address http://www.company.com/ into IP addresses such as 145.45.34.2, which are used by network hardware to communicate with the resource. The process of name resolution is depicted in Figure 14.1.

Figure 14.1 DNS name resolution process

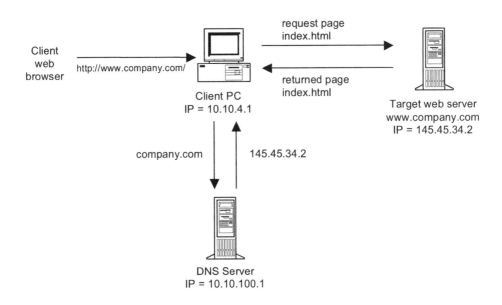

In the example depicted in Figure 14.1, a user clicks a link to the website www.company.com in their web browser. This sends a request to their computer to locate this resource, which their computer does not know the location for. It therefore sends a request to the corporate DNS server for the resource. The DNS server in turn looks up the IP address that corresponds to this request, and returns it to the user's computer. This computer now has the correct destination IP address and issues network packets with this address, and the request for the homepage at www.company.com, to be routed to the destination server. The destination server reads the originating IP address of the user's computer and responds with the requested web page, allowing the user to view the homepage at http://www.company.com/index.html.

14.1 Key technologies used

The DNS system locates names for e-business resource and their corresponding IP addresses as elements within a structured tree. This tree structure is in turn physically deployed within DNS servers distributed in a global federated architecture consisting of multiple redundant DNS systems.

The tree structure consists of a root, top-level domains, subdomains, and zones, as depicted in Figure 14.2.

Figure 14.2 Functional view of DNS tree structure

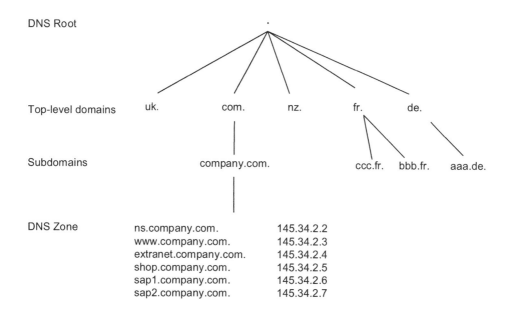

In the example in Figure 14.2, Company owns the 'company.com' domain name, which lists six publicly accessible e-business servers. The domain name of each of these resources is therefore the total collection of all subdomains, top-level domain and root, such as 'www.ebusiness.company.com.' for the company.com web server.

All e-business resources are therefore located within a hierarchy of names built beneath the root level. These include top-level domains, corresponding to countries such as .uk. or .nz., and organizational entities such as .com. (company), .org. (organization), or .biz. (business); subdomains, corresponding to names owned by entities such as businesses; and zones, containing the DNS records of individual e-business servers and websites. This structure allows extension of names through the addition of multiple subdomains and corresponding zone files for companies with many e-business resources. All DNS records are stored as text files within servers running software dedicated to servicing DNS requests.

DNS requests are propagated through this hierarchical tree structure until the correct server is reached, starting with the 'root' of the tree structure designated by a full stop '.' and maintained on 13 root servers. For example, a query for www.company.com is received by a root DNS server and passed to a server managing the 'com.' top-level domain. This server in turn forwards the query to the 'company.com' server, which then responds with the IP address for www.company.com.

The complete DNS name space, corresponding to all domain names and IP addresses, is therefore distributed among top-level and subdomain DNS servers, with each server managing a sub-branch of the total name space. This distributed design provides considerable redundancy, ensuring that failure of one or more DNS servers will not impact the ability of the total system to service DNS requests. For example, if the 'com.' servers fail, other branches of the name space continue functioning.

Multiple primary and secondary DNS servers are also deployed for each top level and subdomain, providing additional redundancy. Secondary DNS servers are designed to support the primary servers by replicating their information. This provides redundant backup copies of zones in case of failure of a primary DNS server, and allows secondary servers to service DNS requests.

Secondary DNS servers can also distribute the name space within a company, so that local clients query local secondary DNS server. This reduces the load on the primary server. It also provides for a more robust configuration in case of server failure, as clients can be configured to still know of the existence of the primary.

What to look for in a DNS system

Successful e-business implementations require the design and deployment of a corporate-wide DNS system. Such systems are comprised of a corporate DNS name space, e-business resource zone files, and correctly configured DNS servers deployed using an appropriate design.

The corporate DNS name space

A corporate DNS name space is comprised of a hierarchical structure of domains and subdomains corresponding to the distribution, logical function and name of company e-business resources. Typically, this structure is created using organizational naming according to the business group owning the resources, functional naming describing the functions provided by the e-business resources, or geographical naming using the geographical location of the resources.

Organizational naming utilizes the names of different business groups to create the name space. This in turn binds resource names directly to the company organizational structure. For example, an organizational structure may include domains for 'sales.company.com.' and 'marketing.company.com.', corresponding to sales and marketing departments.

However, this strategy is sensitive to changes in corporate organizational structure, which may require resources to be renamed as the company evolves. This in turn results in downtime while each resource is reconfigured to support the new name space.

In contrast, geographical naming is typically subject to fewer changes than the organizational naming strategy, as companies typically relocate less frequently than they reorganize. For example, a geographical structure may include domains for 'uk.company.com.' and 'fr.company.com.' corresponding to offices in the UK and France. However, this strategy typically requires users to understand the geographical distribution of company resources to specify resource URLs, and may not reflect the intended function of resources.

Functional naming utilizes the intended purpose of the resources, such as Intranet servers or e-business servers, to create the name space. For example, this structure may include domains for 'ebusiness.company.com.' and 'portal.company.com.' corresponding to e-business servers.

The functional naming strategy is suited for small to medium sized companies with few organizational or geographic structures and limited numbers of e-business resources. It provides simplicity for the addition of resources, and does not require alteration when the corporate organizational structure changes. However, with multiple similar resources, such as two portal servers, it may lead to the creation of a potentially confusing name space.

Finally, a hybrid naming strategy utilizes geographical or organizational categories, such as country code, and functional names for resources. For example, this structure could include two e-business servers named according to their function (e-business) and geographical location within UK and NZ offices, as depicted in Figure 14.3.

Figure 14.3 Hybrid name space strategy

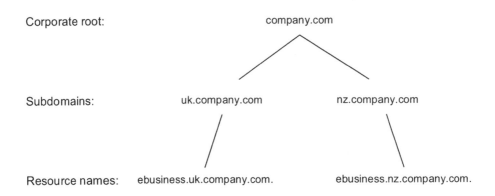

This strategy allows resources to be distributed and administered by regional or organizational local business units, and provides unique names for similar resources. If sufficiently broad naming categories are used, it can insulate the name space from broad changes in corporate organizational and geographical structures.

Once the naming strategy has been determined it should be formalized as a published corporate standard, and made available to users with administrative rights to the corporate DNS system. Procedures should also be enacted to enforce these naming conventions to prevent this standard from being modified.

Corporate zone files

Zone files are text files used to store DNS names and associated IP addresses. DNS servers then service DNS requests by reading the contents of zone files into memory, comparing these to the received requests, and responding with the appropriate IP address.

Zone files are created by assigning domain names to resources using the corporate DNS naming strategy, and then assigning them IP addresses in accordance with the corporate IP address allocation strategy.

For example, company.com utilizes a hybrid corporate naming strategy with geographical and functional naming. They create a domain corresponding to their branch offices, 'us.company.com.' and host an e-business Internet server, an Extranet proxy server, a transactional e-business server, and two ERP servers. A zone file is then created to contain entries for each resource and IP address, as depicted in Figure 14.4.

Figure 14.4 Forward mapping zone file – ebusiness.uk.company.com

```
company.com.        IN        SOA       ns.company.com    mail.company.com (
                              1         ; serial
                              86400     ; Refresh after 1 day
                              3600      ; Retry after 1 hour
                              604800    ; Expire after 1 week
                              86400     ); Minimum TTL of 1 day

; The following is the DNS Name Server for Company serving the company.com subdomain

company.com.                            IN      NS      ns.company.com.

; The following are addresses for Company server canonical names

localhost.uk.company.com.               IN      A       127.0.0.1
ns.uk.company.com.                      IN      A       172.34.2.2
www. company.com.                       IN      A       172.34.2.3
extranet.company.com.                   IN      A       172.34.2.4
shop.company.com.                       IN      A       172.34.2.5
erp1.company.com.                       IN      A       172.34.2.6
erp2.company.com.                       IN      A       172.34.2.7
```

This file is used by the company.com DNS server to provide IP addresses in response to DNS name queries, and is known as a forward mapping zone file.

Within the zone file, the header describes the start of authority (SOA), declaring this server as the authority permitted to serve this zone for the company.com subdomain. It also contains configuration parameters for the length of time the DNS information will remain valid. The body of the zone file contains the name and address of the DNS server for this domain (ns.uk.company.com), and a list of the names of each server (the canonical name) and their IP addresses.

Software occasionally queries DNS servers for the domain name of a resource based on a supplied IP address, in the reverse process to normal DNS queries. This requires the addition of an inverse (or reverse) mapping zone file, with a similar structure to the forward mapping zone file.

Inverse mapping zone files include similar structures to the forward mapping files, and name resources using reversed IP addresses for each resource, as depicted in Figure 14.5.

Figure 14.5 Inverse mapping zone file – db.172.34.2

```
2.34.172.in-addr.arpa.        IN      SOA    ns.company.com    mail.company.com (
                              1       ; serial
                              86400   ; Refresh after 1 day
                              3600    ; Retry after 1 hour
                              604800; Expire after 1 week
                              86400 ); Minimum TTL of 1 day

; The following is the DNS Name Server for Company

2.34.145.in-addr.arpa.        IN      NS     ns.company.com.

; The following are addresses for Company server canonical names

2.2.34.172.in-addr.arpa.      IN      PTR    nscompany.com.
3.2.34.172.in-addr.arpa.      IN      PTR    www.company.com.
4.2.34.172.in-addr.arpa.      IN      PTR    extranet.company.com.
5.2.34.172.in-addr.arpa.      IN      PTR    shop.company.com.
6.2.34.172.in-addr.arpa.      IN      PTR    erp1.company.com.
7.2.34.172.in-addr.arpa.      IN      PTR    erp2.company.com.
```

Distributing DNS within a company

Companies with many resources distributed across multiple locations frequently deploy additional DNS servers to those locations to provide local DNS facilities. This allows for high local performance and reduces dependency on centralized corporate DNS resources.

The DNS system provides a facility, known as delegation, to distribute the corporate name space throughout the company. Delegation is also used within DNS servers on the Internet to distribute the global name space throughout the world.

Delegation requires additional entries in zone files to point to the new DNS servers managing delegated domains. For example, company.com expands to include a UK division, who wish to manage their own DNS server. They intend to manage e-business systems providing email transport, a transactional e-business site, and an external integration server for supply chain management.

This requires the addition of the subdomain 'uk.company.com.' and the delegation of authority to manage all UK DNS resources within this domain to the new server, as depicted in Figure 14.6.

Figure 14.6 DNS name space delegation

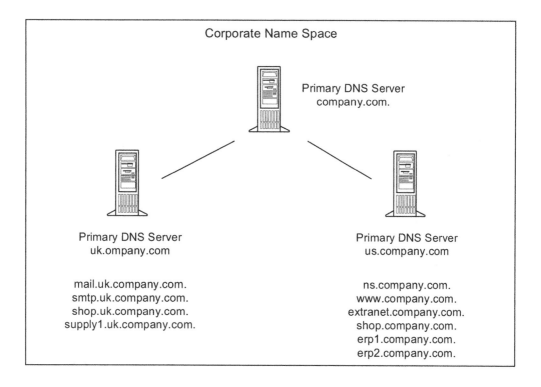

The delegated domain requires a new zone file stored in the UK DNS server, containing records for the e-business servers within the UK office, including the forward and reverse mappings for each resource. Zone files in the parent 'company.com' zone file are modified with the addition of 'Glue Records' to point to the new DNS servers for all requests to the new UK domain. These records provide the IP address for the London DNS server, and are depicted in Figure 14.7.

Figure 14.7 Delegating zones – forward mapping zone file

```
company.com.       IN       SOA    ns.company.com   mail.company.com (
                            1      ; serial
                            86400  ; Refresh after 1 day
                            3600   ; Retry after 1 hour
                            604800 ; Expire after 1 week
                            86400  ); Minimum TTL of 1 day

; The following is the DNS Name Server for Company serving the company.com sub-domain

company.com.                          IN     NS     ns.company.com.
uk.company.com                        IN     NS     dns.uk.company.com
                                      IN     NS     dns2.uk.company.com

; The following are addresses for Company server canonical names

localhost.uk.company.com.             IN     A      127.0.0.1
ns.uk.company.com.                    IN     A      172.34.2.2
www.uk.company.com.                   IN     A      172.34.2.3
extranet.uk.company.com.              IN     A      172.34.2.4
shop.uk.company.com.                  IN     A      172.34.2.5
erp1.uk.company.com.                  IN     A      172.34.2.6
erp2.uk.company.com.                  IN     A      172.34.2.7
dns.uk.company.com.                   IN     A      172.34.10.10
dns2.uk.company.com.                  IN     A      172.34.10.11
```

In Figure 14.7 the glue records are depicted in italic text, and point to the primary DNS server 'dns.london.uk.company.com' and the secondary server 'dns2.london.uk.company.com.' Similarly, changes are required in the inverse-mapping zone file of the company.com DNS server to direct requests for domain names to the UK DNS server.

The existing db.172.34.2 zone file is therefore modified with entries pointing to the DNS servers managing the new London network on the 172.34.10.0 subnet, as depicted in Figure 14.8.

Figure 14.8 Delegating zones – inverse mapping zone file

```
34.172.in-addr.arpa.        IN       SOA    ns.company.com   mail.company.com (
                            1        ; serial
                            86400    ; Refresh after 1 day
                            3600     ; Retry after 1 hour
                            604800; Expire after 1 week
                            86400 ); Minimum TTL of 1 day

; The following are the DNS Name Servers for company.com and london.company.com

2.34.172.in-addr.arpa.      IN     NS     ns.company.com.
10.34.172.in-addr.arpa.     IN     NS     dns.company.com.
10.34.172.in-addr.arpa.     IN     NS     dns2. company.com.
```

The inverse mapping zone file does not require glue records, as the new DNS servers are not part of this zone because they are located on different networks (i.e. the 'company.com' DNS server is in the db.172.34.10 zone and the new 'uk.company.com' DNS server is in the db.172.34.2 zone).

DNS server configuration

Once the corporate name space and zone files have been created, DNS servers must be configured to begin servicing DNS requests. DNS servers typically provide considerable configuration flexibility, supporting many options to control server behaviour. All solutions should support a minimum set of options, including control of the type of DNS server, creation of access control lists for regulation of zone updates, and support for split-level DNS.

DNS servers can be configured to service DNS requests in a number of roles. Servers can act as primary (master) authority for serving local zones, or provide redundancy through acting as a secondary (slave) authority for other zones. In addition, servers can act as a forwarder to channel DNS requests from local sites with minimal DNS requirements to central primary and secondary servers. For greatest flexibility, a DNS server should be able to act as all three types simultaneously.

Special configuration changes are also required to support split-level DNS systems for security and email transport, including modifications to the DMZ DNS server configurations. Typically, internal DNS servers are primary DNS servers and contain complete sets of records for all internal domains and their associated subdomains. To protect sensitive information, these internal servers are configured to disallow queries to these domains from external networks, including the DMZ.

In contrast, the DMZ DNS servers are configured to serve a public version of the company domain containing the externally accessible resources such as e-business sites. To preserve security these servers do not contain entries for the complete internal domain structure. This ensures DMZ DNS servers are able to serve name requests for the public DMZ resources, without exposing internal DNS information.

This configuration is also used to support email delivery into a company by removing internal email server DNS entries from public view. Configuration changes include the use of a single DNS MX (mail exchanger) record entry for the email relay server. The email relay server is configured to query the internal DNS servers for the IP address of internal email delivery servers. The internal DNS servers are in turn configured to accept these requests and respond with the correct internal addresses. This ensures internal addresses are not stored within the DMZ.

For example, if the relay server receives an email addressed to user1@uk.company.com it must locate the internal email server responsible for delivering this email to the user. However, the DMZ DNS servers contain entries only for public 'company.com' servers, and do not hold information on the 'uk.company.com' subdomain required for delivery to user1. The DMZ DNS servers include an entry in the 'company.com' zone file for a 'wildcard MX record' to direct all incoming email to the DMZ email relay server, as depicted in Figure 14.9.

Figure 14.9 Wildcard MX email DNS record

```
*              IN    MX    10      mail.company.com.
```

The internal DNS server configuration file requires modification to allow requests from this relay server for names of other email servers, as depicted in Figure 14.10.

Figure 14.10 Split-level DNS server configuration file, internal primary DNS server

```
acl internals { 172.34.0.0/24; };          // The internal 172.34.0.0 class C network
acl externals { DMZ-ips-go-here;};         // The DMZ network IP addresses
acl relay {email relay server DMZ IP;};    // IP of email relay server
options {
        forward only;
        forwarders { DMZ-ips-go-here; };   // forward to external servers for any other zones
        allow-transfer { none; };          // don't transfer zone allow-transfer (no one)
        allow-query { internals; externals; relay};  // restrict query access to internal and external ACLs
        allow-recursion { internals; };    // restrict recursion – no iterative queries
};
zone "company.com" {                       // primary (master) for the company.com zone
        type master;
        file "m/company.com";              // location of zone file
        forwarders { };                    // no forwarders, normal iterative name resolution
        allow-query { internals; externals; };  // allow queries from internal and external ACLs
        allow-transfer { internals; };     // only transfer zone information to internal DNS servers
};
zone "uk.compay.com" {                     // primary (master) for the uk.company.com zone
        type master;
        file "m/uk.company.com";           // location of zone file
        forwarders { };                    // no forwarders, normal iterative name resolution
        allow-query { internals; };        // allow queries only from internal ACLs
        allow-transfer { internals; };     // allow zone transfers to internal DNS servers
};
zone "mail.company.com" {                  // primary (master) for internal mail.company.com zone
        type master;
        file "m/mail.company.com";         // location of zone file
        forwarders {};                     // no forwarders used
        allow-query { internals; relay; }; // allow queries from internal and relay ACLs
        allow-transfer { internals; };     // allow zone transders to internal DNS servers
};
```

The configuration file from the primary internal server defines three access control lists for internal and DMZ networks, and the email relay server. It is configured to act as the primary (master) for the DMZ 'company.com', internal 'uk.company.com' zones, and internal email server zone, 'mail.company.com'. Queries to the sensitive internal 'uk.company.com' zone are restricted to internal networks only, while queries to 'mail.company.com' are restricted to the internal and relay access control lists. The company.com zone contains the DNS information from systems within the DMZ, and can be queried from the internal and DMZ networks.

The DMZ primary DNS server is also configured with access control lists specifying internal and DMZ networks, and is defined as primary for the company.com and ebusiness.company.com zones, as depicted in Figure 14.11.

Figure 14.11 Split-level DNS server configuration file, primary DMZ DNS server

```
acl internals { 172.16.0.0/24; };
acl externals { DMZ-ips-go-here; };
options {
        allow-transfer { none; };                    // sample allow-transfer (no one)
        allow-query { internals; externals; };       // restrict query access
        allow-recursion { internals; externals; };   // restrict recursion
};
zone "company.com" {                                 // Primary (master) for the company.com zone
        type master;
        file "m/company.com";                        // location of the zone file
        allow-query { any; };                        // queries can originate from anywhere
        allow-transfer { internals; externals; };    // zone transfer only to internal or external ACLs
};
zone "ebusiness.company.com" {                       // Primary (master) for the ebusiness.company.com
zone                                                 zone
        type master;
        file "m/ebusiness.company.com";              // location of the zone file
        allow-query { any; };                        // queries can originate from anywhere
        allow-transfer { internals; externals; }     // zone transfer only to internal or external ACLs
};
```

In contrast to the internal DNS server, this server has limited DNS entries in the company.com and ebusiness.company.com zone files, specifying systems within the DMZ network. In order to direct inbound email into the internal network for delivery, the DMZ DNS servers are also configured to use the internal primary DNS server for queries they cannot answer. This requires an entry in the resolv.conf files on the DMZ DNS servers to point to the IP address of the internal DNS servers when searching the company.com domains.

This configuration now allows internal users to access secure DNS information for internal resources, which are in turn hidden from external users. The DMZ DNS servers can now serve a limited set of information for the public resources on the DMZ, and also forward all inbound email into the internal network without themselves having to have the names and IP addresses of the internal email servers. In addition, internal users also gain access to the Internet, with all DNS requests for external resources forwarded to the DMZ DNS servers.

This configuration can also provide external name resolution for companies using the private addressing scheme on their internal networks. Use of the private IP address scheme restricts the ability of a company to resolve external DNS names, as private addresses are not routable across the Internet and therefore do not permit resolution of public Internet names and addresses. Internal DNS servers within a private address space network should therefore be configured to forward all DNS requests for external resources to the split-level DNS servers within the DMZ. These servers accept internal queries and attempt to resolve these using public DNS servers on the Internet.

For a detailed discussion of DNS server configuration options, consult the BIND Administrator Reference Manual.

14.2 High-level designs for corporate DNS systems

Organizations typically have highly variable requirements for DNS, including support for internal and external name resolution, queries to public e-business systems within DMZ networks, and protection of sensitive internal DNS information.

Corporate DNS systems must therefore provide DNS resolution for all users and systems within corporate Intranets and wide area networks, and be capable of resolving public DNS names through external connections such as Extranets or the Internet.

Designs must also accommodate the distribution of users and corporate e-business resources across multiple physical sites, including cities and countries, and provide secure name resolution for systems contained within secure DMZ networks.

In addition, DNS designs must provide high availability to ensure continued name resolution in case of network outages, and high scalability and availability to cope with demanding levels of queries. They must also allow for flexible deployment of DNS servers to support the different corporate naming space strategies.

Two designs are depicted in Figures 14.12 and 14.13, suitable for typical companies and companies with highly distributed networks of offices. Due to the considerable variability in corporate DNS requirements, these designs are intended as reference points for the creation of complete DNS systems. Detailed evaluation of corporate DNS requirements should be conducted to determine server placement and performance levels, zone structures, and numbers of primary and secondary servers required.

High-level design of a standard corporate DNS system

The standard corporate DNS design is intended for companies with several offices located within the same city. These companies typically have internal resources, such as enterprise applications and internal e-business systems, and externally accessible e-business systems, such as a public Internet portal presence or transactional e-business systems.

Such companies typically have private local area networks connecting offices in the same city. They also typically experience moderate levels of DNS traffic across these networks, and may have moderate to high levels of traffic to their external e-business sites.

These requirements dictate a DNS design for serving DNS to allow for location of these public e-business resources and for the provision of name resolution for internal resources across all internal networks.

This design features a simple topology with split-level DNS servers divided between DMZ and internal networks. Both networks include primary and secondary DNS servers for redundancy.

Additional availability and scalability features are provided using secondary DNS servers, ensuring continuous name resolution in case of failure of the primary servers or failure of network connectivity between offices. Secondary DNS may also be added within the main network to scale the performance of the DNS solution as request traffic grows.

This design is also extensible to the distributed corporate DNS design through the addition of primary and secondary DNS servers within remote branches. It also supports delegation of the corporate name space to local business units.

This design is depicted in Figure 14.12

Figure 14.12 Standard corporate DNS design

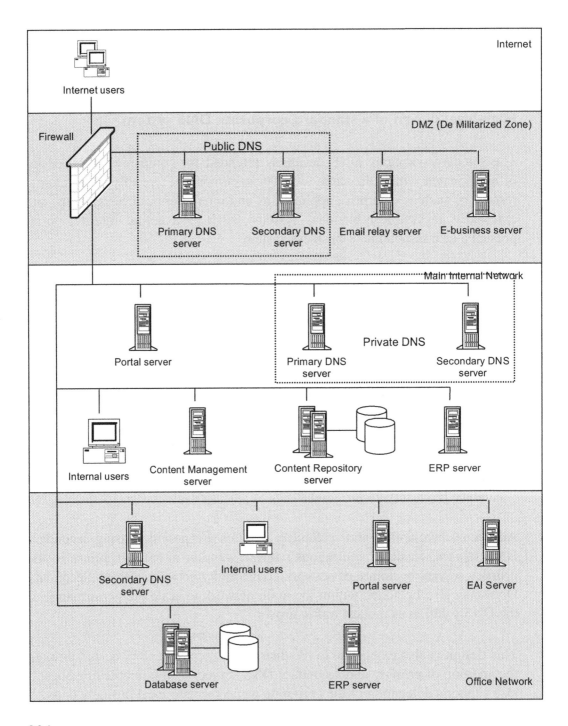

High-level design of a distributed corporate DNS system

The distributed corporate DNS design is intended for companies with multiple offices located across different geographical locations. These companies typically have large numbers of internal resources, such as enterprise applications and internal e-business systems, and multiple externally accessible e-business systems, such as transactional e-business systems and external integration systems.

Such companies typically have large numbers of internal local area networks connecting offices in the same city, and a wide variety of connections to multiple remote office networks, including virtual private networks and distributed wide area networks. Large groups of users are frequently spread across these different locations, and require access to local e-business resources and enterprise applications, in addition to company-wide common resources. This often generates high volumes of DNS traffic across these networks, in addition to high levels of DNS requests to external e-business sites from internal and external users.

These requirements dictate a highly distributed DNS design allow for provision of local DNS to large groups of local users, and to allow for local administration of DNS systems. It also requires provision of name resolution for internal resources across all company networks, and provision of external and internal location DNS names for public e-business resources distributed across multiple locations.

Due to the highly distributed nature of such companies, and the large numbers of systems and users, this design requires considerable extra redundancy to ensure continuous reliable operation. It therefore has a more complex topology with multiple primary DNS servers located at large concentrations of local systems and users, and multiple additional secondary DNS servers near large populations of users and remote networks to increase performance for local DNS queries.

Availability is assured using primary DNS servers configured as high availability systems, through server clustering or provision of hot-standby primary servers. Additional availability is provided through the deployment of the secondary DNS servers at remote network locations.

This design also supports a more complex corporate name space designed to accommodate the widely distributed e-business resources. This requires distribution of subdomains to local primary DNS servers.

This design is depicted in Figure 14.13.

Figure 14.13 Distributed corporate DNS design

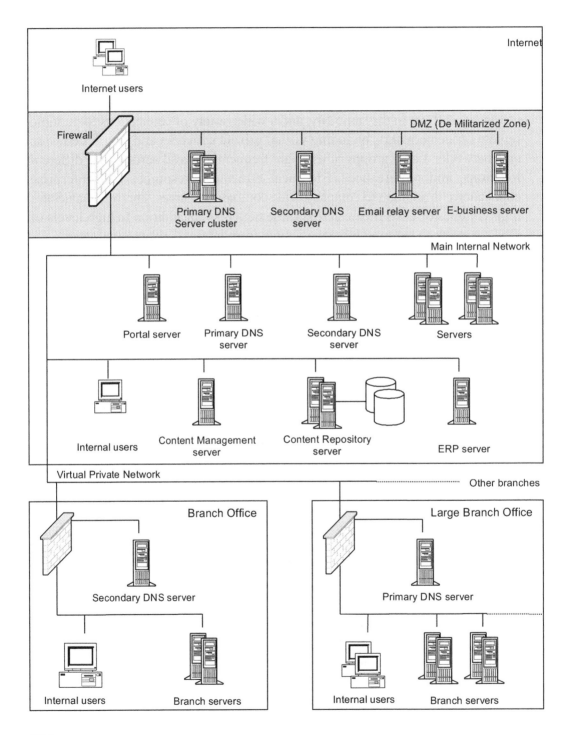

This design can be further extended to provide additional redundancy by deploying remote delegated primary DNS servers at the end of WAN links to also act as secondary servers for their parent domain. Thus, a remote DNS server configured as primary for 'uk.company.com' can also act as secondary for the US 'company.com' primary DNS server. Therefore, if the primary US DNS server fails, the remote users will still be able to access IP addresses for the remote US systems.

It should be noted that deployment into very large global networks requires additional design amendments, including multiple primary and secondary servers at each country. In addition, high levels of delegation of the company name space should be employed to partition the corporate name space according to the company organizational and geographical structures. Similarly, multiple secondary DNS servers should also be located across WAN links for smaller regional sites.

High-level design for Internet connectivity

Companies may have branches without connections to corporate networks, such as remote offices. Alternatively, a company may choose to deploy public e-business servers at a co-located site through an internet service provider (ISP), or instead deploy e-business systems internally for company staff.

The DNS system provides a configuration, known as the DNS forwarder design, to allow such companies access to the Internet for internal users. The forwarder design utilizes internal DNS servers configured to act as primary and secondary servers for internal domains, with the additional option to forward all requests for unknown resources to DNS servers on the public Internet.

This design requires the firewall to support stateful packet inspection to deny external DNS requests from entering the internal network, as this may allow for compromise of the internal DNS servers. In addition, internal DNS servers should be configured to disallow queries from, and zone transfers to, external sources.

This design is depicted in Figure 14.14.

Figure 14.14 DNS forwarder design amendment

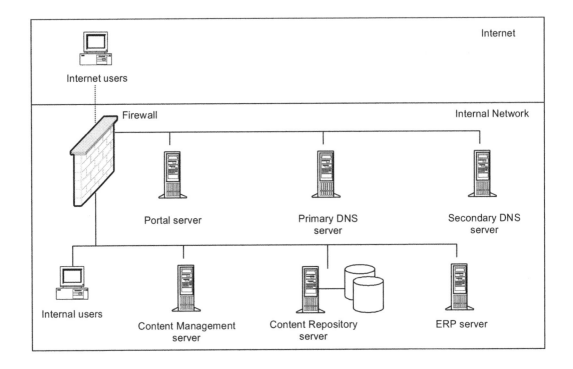

DNS systems migration

Many companies experience unplanned organic growth in their DNS infrastructure. This typically results in missconfigured DNS systems including the creation of complex and confusing name spaces, lack of consolidation of DNS resources such as widely spread servers and subdomains, incorrect zone file configuration and delegation of subdomains, and lack of redundancy in DNS systems.

It is therefore recommended that periodic audit of corporate DNS systems is conducted to determine the state of the DNS system. Such audits should also be conducted for companies planning to merge.

If an audit determines deficiencies within the DNS infrastructure, it is recommended that a migration plan be created to ensure compliance with the designs detailed above. A migration plan should incorporate the following stages:

1. Select an appropriate DNS design for the size and type of company, including a corporate name space and DNS architecture.

2. Select a DNS software provider from the list detailed in Table 14.10.

3. Determine the current DNS design and distribution of resources, including the location and configurations of all servers, the location and numbers of users within the company, and the network addressing scheme.

4. Determine the alterations required to these resources based on the expected final design.

5. Deploy new servers with appropriate domains, subdomains, zone files, and server configurations, populated with appropriate records for existing and new systems.

6. Pilot the new DNS design.

7. Switch to the new design by altering the DHCP configurations of client computers. These should include entries for the IP addresses of the new DNS servers in addition to old servers. This allows for parallel functioning of the two sets of DNS infrastructure.

8. Tune the new design to resolve any roll-out issues, and progressively remove legacy subdomains.

During the migration phase, disruption to resources can be minimized by using CNAME record types, to redirect requests for old resource names to new names.

14.3 Vendors of DNS systems

The industry-standard DNS software is known as BIND, the Berkeley Internet Name Daemon, with version 9.1.3 released in July 2001. BIND is available from http://www.isc.org/products/BIND.

Table 14.1 lists vendors of DNS software that utilize the BIND source code.

Note that this list is not exhaustive.

Table 14.1 Vendors of BIND compliant DNS systems

Vendor	BIND compliant DNS system
Bluecat Networks	The Adonis Server
Check Point Software Technologies	Meta IP
FBL Inc.	DNS Pro
Len Conrad	BIND 8 for NT 4 and Win 2000
Lucent Technologies	QIP Enterprise 5.0
Network TeleSystems	Shadow IP
Nortel Networks	NetID 4.2
Software.com	BindNT
Threshold Networks	EDGE IP

Open Source technology is a recent development in software development practices emphasizing the ongoing collaborative development of solutions, and the free availability of these solutions.

The traditional software development model focuses on the creation of software for profit. Development under this model creates periodic releases of new or improved products with enhanced features. Further development is financed from the sale or lease of the software to endusers, and support contracts, consulting and project implementation work.

In contrast to the for-profit model of software development, Open Source technology offers an alternative approach to software design, development and use that produces very low cost and/or free software. Utilizing standards-based Internet technology, Open Source products offer high levels of standards compliance, and strong support for e-business technologies. These attributes make Open Source technologies ideal elements in the implementation of e-business projects in companies of any size.

The degree of use of Open Source software within companies is difficult to assess, due to its free availability and lack of deployment restrictions. However, a number of indicators point to considerable uptake of Open Source software within the information technology industry. Research indicates that there may be up to 27 million users of Open Source software (Open Source Initiative, 2001). Statistics on server shipments reveal the open source operating system Linux held more than 27 per cent of the total market for server operating systems sold during 2000 (Connolly, 2001). The Netcraft survey of Internet sites reports that the Open Source Apache web server runs more than 50 per cent of all Internet web sites, and much of the primary infrastructure of the Internet utilizes Open Source software, such as email and ftp servers.

In addition, a number of reports have noted that the uptake of Open Source software has accelerated in recent years, due to increased charges from software vendors and a desire to have more control over technology solutions through access to source code. For example, InfoWorld reported a survey of chief technology officers, which revealed that around half of the survey participants used Open Source application development tools and application servers (Yager, 2001b). Nearly all participants reported savings in time and money from using Open Source tools.

15.1 Key technologies used

Open Source software is available across all software technology categories in use within the information technology industry. These include development languages and tools such as Java, C, C++ and Integrated Development Environments, productivity applications such as spreadsheets and databases, e-business applications such as content management systems and transactional applications, and enterprise-class software such as CRM systems.

15.2 History

Much of the early impetus and inspiration for Open Source software grew from the Free Software initiative, which originated in 1984 (Stallman, 2001). As a reaction to the restrictive licensing of early software, Richard Stallman sought to develop a compatible version of Unix known as GNU Unix (GNU denotes a recursive acronym, 'GNUs Not Unix'). GNU Unix included free software applications commonly distributed with operating systems of the time, including compilers, interpreters, text editors, and mail transport and reader programs.

The core tenets of this movement, encapsulated in the GNU Public Licence, focused on freedom for users. This included the freedom to run a program for any intended purpose, to have the right to modify a program to suit individual needs and hence to have the right to the source code of the program. It also including the freedom to redistribute copies of the software for free or for a fee, and to distribute a modified version of the software to allow the community of other users to benefit from improvements (Stallman, 2001).

As the GNU project progressed, it progressively replaced commercial Unix software components with Free Software versions, leaving only the operating system kernel. Although the Mach micro-kernel was initially selected as the kernel for GNU, work on adapting it to suit GNU was not completed when the Linux kernel was released in 1991. This kernel was adopted in 1992, resulting in the GNU/Linux combination, now frequently referred to simply as 'Linux'.

The subsequent success of the Linux kernel, and the widespread and well-reported collaboration to improve it, inspired the development of the Open Source initiative. This group focused on many of the same goals as the Free Software initiative, including providing freely available alternatives to commercial software but emphasized a more business-focused approach.

15.3 The Open Source development approach

The Open Source approach to software development emphasizes the free availability of software source code. As developers are permitted to modify this code, other developers are encouraged to participate in making improvements and customize the code for their own needs.

Development of Open Source projects proceeds in an iterative manner, with multiple contributors working on different sections of each project. Peer review of ongoing changes is actively encouraged among project participants during the evolution of the project.

As a project progresses, changes are incorporated into periodic releases or builds of the project. Builds are classified as either development builds, which are works in progress, or release builds, which are judged by project participants to be in a state ready for release.

The source code for each project is maintained on public Internet source code control servers. This permits open participation in the development effort by any interested party. Completed and development versions of code are then available for users to freely download from these sites.

As an alternative to the free download of Open Source software, companies may offer low cost packaged implementations of Open Source products, such as the Linux operating system. These packaged implementations typically include extra options such as free support or periodic updates.

In order to be classified as Open Source, a software product must conform to the Open Source licence terms. This requires a software product be offered free from licensing fees, even if it is included as part of a for-sale software distribution. All products must contain the source code in addition to the complete compiled software, and any software derived from this code must be distributed using the same terms as the licence of the original software product. It also permits the distribution of source code with subsequent update patches, and forbids the licence to discriminate against any individual, group, or field of endeavour. The licence must also not be made dependent on the product being part of a specific software distribution, and it must not place any restrictions on other software that may be distributed with the Open Source software.

15.4 Open Source software projects

There are currently a large number of Open Source software projects targeting most areas of software functionality. For example, the SourceForge Open Source development portal currently hosts 31, 690 separate software projects, with 326, 408 registered users either participating in project development or actively utilizsing their resources.

Typically, projects encompass broad areas of software functionality ideally suited to e-business initiatives. These include Internet site utilities such as the AFP NewsML news feed for websites, Internet infrastructure software such as Apache, and e-business development languages such as PERL and XML.

In addition, many Open Source projects are designed for deployment in a wide range of corporate settings. For example, Open Source projects provide software such as standard office productivity applications, including spreadsheets and databases, and enterprise-class applications such as financial, CRM and ERP systems.

Open Source operating systems

Open Source operating systems are ideally suited as core elements within an e-business initiative, due to their native inclusion of key Internet technologies and ability to host a wide range of e-business software.

Open Source operating systems are available in three major variations, including multiple versions of the GNU/Linux operating system, the FreeBSD operating system, and partial Open Source operating systems versions such as the Mac OS X/Darwin operating system. Each variation is characterized by a similar design approach first introduced in the Unix operating system, featuring a privileged kernel layer mediating controlling hardware resources and non-privileged operating system utilities and user applications, as depicted in Figure 15.1.

Figure 15.1 Open Source operating system design

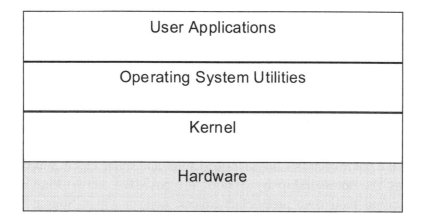

The Linux operating system kernel forms the core of most open source operating systems. Finnish student Linus Torvalds developed the Linux kernel in 1991 at the Helsinki University because of his dissatisfaction with the then current PC compatible operating systems. Torvalds therefore wrote his own kernel and associated components, but realized that he needed assistance to create a complete operating system.

Torvalds announced his project on USENET newsgroups, and received immediate feedback and suggestions for improvements. Following online placement of the source code for Linux, amendments began to arrive from contributors around the world in an early example of the Open Source development approach. Later releases of Linux source code under the GNU Public Licence (GPL) and the adoption of the Free Software Foundation GNU software library gave rise to a complete functional Unix clone adhering to the principles of the Free Software movement.

Multiple Linux variations, or distributions, are now available from vendors, providing support for different hardware architectures including Intel PC, IBM/Apple PowerPC, MIPS, SPARC, and Compaq/Digital Alpha. These vendors typically sell distributions for minimal cost typically in the region of $US 30 – 50, and permit free downloads of their software and installation of their distributions across an unlimited number of servers. These companies also gain revenue through the sale of consulting and support services.

Each Linux distribution is differentiated through offering combinations of GNU and other software. These typically include variations in applications such as fax software, Open Source productivity applications, additional bundled for-profit applications such as databases, and different management interfaces designed to make Linux more accessible to less technically minded individuals.

Linux has received considerable support from well-established for-profit companies such as IBM, Apple, and SGI. These organizations have embraced Linux as a means to sell more hardware, software and consulting services, and have begun porting much of their commercial software to Linux. In addition, they have sponsored development of Linux and other Open Source initiatives, such as the sponsorship by SGI of the SAMBA networking system, and contributed their own proprietary source code to Open Source development efforts, such as journaling file systems and cluster software.

Another common Open Source operating system is the FreeBSD project, the Open Source version of Berkeley Software Distribution Unix. FreeBSD arose from projects at the University of California in Berkeley in the 1970s to create a licence-free clone of Unix. Four variations of BSD have since been developed, including NetBSD supporting multiple platforms, OpenBSD offering very high security through a detailed operating system code audit, FreeBSD, an open community project with many contributors and the most popular variation of BSD, and BSD/OS, a commercial version of FreeBSD.

Due to their long development history, the BSD operating systems provide higher levels of proven reliability when compared to Linux systems. In addition, OpenBSD provides very high levels of security through an intensive security auditing process.

Finally, attempts in the past six years by Apple Computer to modernize the

Macintosh operating system resulted in the purchase of the NextStep operating system, another variation of BSD Unix. Subsequent development of NextStep by Apple led to the creation of the Mac OS X operating system. This system represents an amalgamation of technology from NextStep, GNU and BSD Unix, the Mach micro-kernel and a full copy of the legacy Macintosh OS 9 operating system for existing Macintosh software.

To gain the advantages of participation in the development efforts of the Open Source community, Apple has released many of the core components of OS X as the Open Source Darwin project. Formerly proprietary Apple technologies are also being released as Open Source projects, such as the QuickTime streaming server providing live streaming of multimedia content over the Internet.

The Darwin initiative offers developers and users major components of OS X as an Open Source project, including the Mach micro-kernel, device drivers and BSD layers. However, it omits some proprietary components such as the Aqua user interface. With the addition of an X Windows server to provide a user interface, Darwin users can utilize these components to create fully functional Unix compatible servers running on Macintosh hardware.

File and print sharing

Linux-based operating systems are suitable for direct integration and deployment within corporate desktop and server computing environments through their very high performance for file and print sharing functions. These functions are provided through the SAMBA and NetaTalk packages, which provide compatible implementations of proprietary Microsoft SMB and Apple AppleTalk networking systems. These packages transparently support all versions of Windows and Macintosh client systems.

SAMBA and NetaTalk typically provide comparable performance to the native file and print services available from Microsoft and Apple. They also offer advanced functionality such as Windows Primary and Secondary Domain Controller ability within Windows networks, allowing them to be utilized as Windows-based Domain Controller servers.

Deployment of SAMBA and NetaTalk allows companies to adopt high performance and reliable alternatives to existing vendor file and print services without requiring client and server software licensing. In addition, the modular nature of these solutions provides greater stability and reliability for file and print servers.

Deployment of these packages on very high performance hardware such as zSeries Linux mainframes or large-scale SMP Unix servers also allows for provision of file and print services to very large numbers of users.

Open Source office productivity software

A number of Open Source office productivity solutions have been created, offering features comparable to those found in the Microsoft Office product.

These products typically offer the most frequently used features of Microsoft Office, while maintaining file compatibility with the Office document formats. In addition, they can frequently be compiled to run on multiple platforms such as Intel, PowerPC and MIPS Linux, and often do not incur licensing costs.

Examples of these products include OpenOffice (the open Source version of StarOffice) from Sun Microsystems (www.sun.com), AnyWare Desktop from VitaSource (), and the AbiWord word processor (www.abiword.org). Open Source spreadsheets include the Gnumeric spreadsheet (www.gnome.org/gnumeric/), and the SIAG (Scheme in A Grid) project (http://siag.nu/).

Open Source databases

Databases are an important element of e-business systems. Several high performance Open Source database projects have created products suited to e-business systems, as well as typical corporate data-centric applications.

These products offer many of the features of enterprise-class commercial products including standard ANSI SQL command syntax, online backup, transaction management and clustering support.

The most advanced Open Source databases include Postgres SQL and MySQL. Postgres SQL is now available as a commercially supported product from a number of vendors, including Red Hat Incorporated.

Open Source e-business software

A considerable quantity of Open Source products suitable for deployment within e-business initiatives has been developed. In addition, a number of high profile commercial vendors have ported their e-business products to Open Source operating systems such as Linux.

These products include core Internet infrastructure functions, with many products currently utilized throughout the Internet. Other products provide enterprise-class e-business development systems such as application servers, Java solutions, development environments, and the emerging Microsoft .Net initiative.

Web servers

The Apache web server is a core element within the Internet infrastructure, and provides high levels of reliability and performance for serving static and dynamic web content. Apache is the most frequently used Internet web server product, currently responsible for running 56.5 per cent of all public Web servers as of December 2001 (source: www.netcraft.com).

Commercial web servers typically support a limited number of operating systems, and utilise proprietary programming models to provide advanced functionality such as dynamic web sites. In contrast, the Apache web server has been ported to all major and minor operating systems, and supports multiple e-business programming models including scripting languages such as Microsoft ASP, PERL and PHP, and Java Servlet support via the Tomcat project. This flexibility ensures e-business systems developed using Apache provide high levels of functionality and adaptability to changing e-business technology.

Apache has also been adopted as the preferred web server for the IBM WebSphere application server. This extends the reach of Apache into mission critical enterprise class e-business software offering high levels of reliability and performance. In addition, Apache offers very high performance comparable to commercial web servers for dynamic and static content serving.

Email servers

Open Source email software initiatives include projects for email transport, designed to transport and deliver email between source and destination email servers, and email client projects, designed for the storage and display of messages to users. Email transport products include the Sendmail email server, currently used to transport more than 60 per cent of all Internet email, and the secure Qmail alternative, designed in response to security weaknesses in the Sendmail product, providing a highly secure email server for DMZ environments.

Email client storage and display products include standard GNU products such as Pine and Elm, and the Evolution email management software from Ximian. This product provides an email client with similar levels of functionality to the Microsoft Outlook product, including calendar, scheduling and email management functions.

Typically, these products provide high performance and reliability, and are suited for deployments covering DMZ email relay to highly distributed, high performance mail routing and delivery across large distributed organizations.

DNS servers

The Berkeley Internet Naming Daemon (BIND) is the most commonly used software for providing DNS name resolution. BIND is currently maintained by the Internet Software Consortium, and is available for all computing platforms. BIND is regularly updated with new features and bug fixes, and is included in all Open Source operating systems.

BIND-based DNS servers are recommended for all e-business initiatives, including e-business systems within DMZ networks, internal networks, and within Internet service providers. BIND provides very high performance, proven reliability, and is available for all major platforms.

Linux and Unix-based BIND DNS servers are typically recommended for DNS systems, due to their highly reliable operation and support for highly secure deployment on hardened operating systems within Chroot environments.

Open Source application servers

Open Source application servers offer very low cost, scalable solutions for hosting e-business applications based on the Java J2EE platform technology.

Common application server projects include the Enhydra server from Lutris Technologies (www.enhydra.org), the JBoss project, and the Tomcat servlet engine. Enhydra provides support for the Java J2EE standard, XML services, and includes excellent support for wireless functionality and multiple country/language-based localization. However, Enhydra lacks some reliability features such as persistent session state management and transaction control.

Similarly, the JBoss project (www.jboss.org) provides a J2EE compliant Open Source application server with support for the J2EE standard, including Servlets, JSP pages, and Enterprise JavaBeans, and emerging Java specifications such as the Java Management Extensions.

The Tomcat servlet engine provides an open source Java servlet and JSP engine for the Apache web server. This addition to Apache provides for high performance Java-based extensions to the core Apache server for the creation of dynamic web and Intranet sites.

In addition to Open Source application servers, the commercial IBM WebSphere application server is now available for multiple Linux distributions, including RedHat Linux, Suse Linux, and TurboLinux.

CRM and ERP solutions

Open Source projects are increasingly targeting commercial grade systems such as ERP and CRM. These include the Linux Enterprise Accounting system (http://www.linux-kontor.de/), and the Kontor ERP system, focused on the creation of a Linux alternative to the SAP R/3 system. The QtTudo ERP project (http://www.bemme.de/index2.html) is designing an Open Source Enterprise Resource Planning product. The Relata project (http://www.relata.com/) is designing a web based customer relationship management system.

Finally, the Compiere project (http://www.compiere.org/) is creating an Open Source ERP and CRM system for small to medium sized enterprises using Java technologies. This solution is intended for small to medium sized businesses with revenue between $US 2 and 200 million, and covers customer management, supply chain and accounting functions.

Content management and portal systems

Open Source web content management and portal projects include the PostNuke and PHP-Nuke (http://www.postnuke.com; http://www.phpnuke.org) products, the Java-based Jahia Corporate Portal and Content Management System, and the Java-based Jetspeed portal system.

The PostNuke and PHP-Nuke projects provide a web-based portal system written in the PHP language, with the mySQL database back end. Features include threaded discussion groups, user polling, private messaging, downloads, and linking. They also provide add-on software components with additional features such as chat, event calendars, and bulletin board forums. See also http://www.nukeforums.com and http://www.nukesupport.com.

The Jahia project (http://www.jahia.org) provides a J2EE-based corporate portal system with integral content management and web-based publishing features. Additional features include security and profile management, template-driven content creation, and an aggregation engine to integrate legacy enterprise applications and data sources, cross-platform support through J2EE compliance, and integration with Macromedia Dreamweaver for template authoring.

The Jetspeed project has created a Java servlet-based portal environment. This includes support for template-driven portal creation, WAP support, syndication of portal content to other portals and websites, and integration with content publication systems such as Cocoon, WebMacro and Velocity. Jetspeed is available from http://www.jakarta.apache.org/jetspeed.

Development environments

A considerable number of e-business Open Source development tool projects have been created, offering a number of advantages including low cost access to a very broad community of developers, continual releases of new features and products, and rapid response to bugs.

Development projects include sophisticated Open Source integrated development environments (IDEs), such as the Kdevelop IDE and the new Eclipse project from IBM. Eclipse is designed to provide an Open Source tool framework supporting a wide range of development languages and target platforms. IBM intends to enhance Eclipse with leading edge e-business tools such as business process integration modelling components obtained through its acquisition of CrossWorlds in 2001.

Commercial Linux development is also catered for through the Borland Kylix Enterprise product. Kylix offers a similar development system to the Delphi environment for Windows, but targets software development on the Linux platform. It also includes the ability to generate software supporting the emerging web services standards for dynamic e-business.

Development using popular e-business scripting languages, such as the PHP, Perl, Python or TCL/Tk, is also greatly simplified using Open Source technologies. Such projects can utilize the vast numbers of existing modules created by other programmers to solve specific problems, or alternatively alter the language source code to produce the desired results. Open Source development also allows projects to be targeted to other platforms, such as Windows and Solaris, or embedded systems.

In addition, the Microsoft .Net runtime is being ported to the FreeBSD environment by Corel corporation, and another Open Source initiative (the Mono project available at http://www.mono.com) is creating a free version of the core .Net components to run under Linux systems.

Support and licensing for Open Source products

Support for Open Source software is available through online websites or news groups, which frequently offer comprehensive and in-depth levels of support. Open Source developers are frequently available to directly answer support queries regarding their products. In addition, in-house support within companies is also increasingly being addressed through the increasing availability of support staff who have gained exposure to Open Source technologies from university or commercial settings.

In addition, a number of commercial companies reselling Open Source solutions also provide consulting and support services for products such as the Enhydra application server, available from Lutris. This ensures companies are able to retain well-defined external accountability for support and product fixes for Open Source e-business solutions.

Finally, the retention of Open Source source code in-house allows companies to address licensing and accountability issues with Open Source products. This ensures companies can maintain ongoing control over the products they deploy, with the additional ability to hire contractors to modify the code in the event that in-house programmers leave.

15.5 Benefits and limitations of Open Source technologies

The Open Source software development approach typically offers a number of advantages when compared to for-profit development, including rapid development of product features, and frequent fixes for bugs and security flaws. It also typically produces stable products, which are available at low or free cost.

Open Source software is typically developed more rapidly than traditional software due to the ability of all participants to freely access and modify code without restrictions. This ensures that large numbers of developers can participate in each project. For example, when security issues are discovered with Open Source products, developers will often modify the product to fix the security hole within hours or days, in contrast to for-profit software vendors who may take months to amend security flaws in their products.

The large numbers of participants in Open Source projects also ensures Open Source software code is scrutinized by more developers, resulting in fewer security flaws. The peer review process used in Open Source development also encourages selection of the best code by project participants, producing more stable and bug-free products. Similarly, Open Source operating systems allow users access to frequent bug fixes and security patches, often only days after a threat has been identified.

Open Source operating systems also offer advantages such as very low costs for common distributions, the ability to purchase one copy of the operating system for deployment across multiple servers, and the wide availability of Open Source software. In addition, Open Source operating systems support an increasing range of commercial for-profit software products for Linux-based servers, including databases such as Oracle and Informix, ERP products such as SAP, and application servers such as IBM WebSphere. Therefore, deployment of Linux servers allows companies to capitalize on freely available Open Source software in addition to commercial products.

In addition, Open Source operating systems provide an affordable, reliable and scalable platform for the deployment of e-business functions such as database servers, e-commerce servers, and core Internet functions such as email, DNS and web-site serving.

However, deployment of Open Source products may be restricted due to a number of limitations. Open Source products may lack advanced enterprise-class features required for many e-business initiatives, such as specific business functions for particular industries, and may lack maturity in areas such as user interfaces, installation and configuration mechanisms, and product usability. They may also require considerable customization in-house to tune the solutions to corporate business requirements, and subsequent integration of other products to provide necessary features. Finally, the levels of support for many Open Source products may not be sufficient for enterprise e-business initiatives within companies.

Successful implementation of e-business solution architectures and supporting technologies gives rise to the creation of a company-wide corporate e-business solution.

This provides an affordable mechanism to reach businesses, consumers, and employees with products and services, improve customer service, decrease the time to market for products and services, and increase collaboration between employees and partners and suppliers. It also allows companies to automate and increase the efficiency and productivity of corporate business processes, to automate business processes shared with external partners and suppliers, and to outsource inefficient or non-core business processes to gain competitive advantage and dynamically respond to changing market conditions.

Figure 16.1 provides a summary that describes the e-business technologies that a company can adopt to support advanced e-business initiatives with customers, partners, suppliers, and internal enterprise systems.

Figure 16.1 Corporate e-business architecture

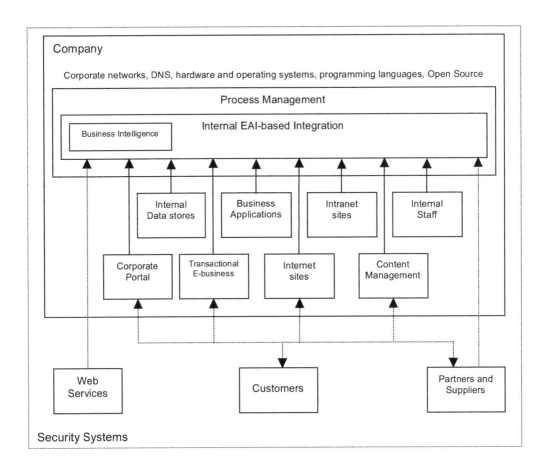

References

Chapter 1   Structuring an e-business project

Astels, D., Miller, G. and Novak, M. (2002). *A Practical Guide to eXtreme Programming*. Prentice-Hall.

Baird, S. (2002). *XP: A Project Manager's Primer*. InformitIt.com, March 22.

Bennekum, A. van (2002). A Human Being is not Equivalent to a Tool: Working with the Dynamic Systems Development Method. *Informit.com*, March 22.

Cockburn, A. (1997). *Surviving Object-Oriented Projects*. Addison-Wesley.

Johnston, M. (2001). A Methodology for E-business? *Informit.com*, February 9.

Palmer, S. R. and Felsing, J. M. (2002). *A Practical Guide to Feature-Driven Development*. Prentice-Hall.

Spitzer, T. (2001). Balancing Act. Reduce project development time by effectively capturing and managing requirements. *Intelligent Enterprise*, March 27.

The Standish Group (2001). *The CHAOS Report (1994)*.

Youngs, R., Redmond-Pyle, D., Spaas, P. and Kahan, E. (1999). A standard for architecture description. *IBM Systems Journal* 38 (1).

Chapter 2 Resourcing an e-business project

Spitzer, T. (2001). Balancing Act. Reduce project development time by effectively capturing and managing requirements. *Intelligent Enterprise*, March 27.

Chapter 3 The five phases of e-business adoption

Editorial (2001). BPM Deployments Still Immature. *EAI Journal*, December 11.

Gartner Group (2001). CIO Hotline: E-business is driving a new IT architecture. *Tech Republic*, June 8.

Seeley, R. (2001). IBM WebSphere Rises to Meet the Challenges of Dynamic E-business. *The Business Integrator Journal*, Winter.

Chapter 4 Phase 1: Internet-based e-business publishing

Custom Internet and Intranet publishing systems

Cox, K. (2001). A Web Development Studio in One Package. *WebTechniques.com*, May.

Editorial (2001). Top 100 Products of 2001: Software. *ZNNet.com*, October 5.

Jefferson, S. (2000). Automated Web site maintenance made easy. *InfoWorld*, November 17.

O'Reilly, D. (2001). FrontPage 2002 Gets Down to Business. *PCWorld.com*, July.

Segal, N. (2001). Macromedia Dreamweaver 4. WebDeveloper.com, April 3.

Reference sites:

http://www.webreview.com
http://www.webtechniques.com
http://builder.cnet.com

Portal systems

Bhatt, A. and Fenner, J. (2001). A Portal Odyssey. *Network Computing*, July 23.

Borck, J.. R. (2000). Beyond the hype, what will an EIP do for you?. *InfoWorld*, July 7.

Choksy, C., Sanchez, E. and Homan, D. (2001). Evaluating Portal Servers. *eDoc* (www.edocmagazine.com), September/October.

Fitzgerald, P. (2001). Tie it together and open it up with Enterprise Information Portals. *Intranet Design Magazine*.

Homan, D., Sanche, E. and Klima, C. (2001). Building a Portal? Vive La Difference. *Information Week*, November 5.

Mears, J. (2001a). Epicentric provides framework for multiple portals. *Network World*, October 16.

Mears, J. (2001b). IBM focuses portal effort. *Network World*, October 10.

Mears, J. (2001c). The New Enterprise Portal. *Network World*, September 24.

Mercy, J.-S. (2001). A Better Understanding of the EIP Market. *Owendo* (www.owendo.com), October 3.

Meta Group. (2001). Evaluation of Hummingbird Enterprise Information Portal.

Upton, M. (2001). Race for Portal Pre-eminence. *IDC*, June 28.

Content management systems

Aberdeen Group. (2001). Content Management: At the Center of e-Business: An Executive White Paper, July 2001.

Doculabs (2000). Enterprise Content Management: A Functional Assessment of 4i eBusiness Platform.

Gilbert, M., Drakos, N. and Latham, L. (2001). The Web Content Management

Magic Quadrant for 2001. Gartner Research Notes, August 28.

Heck, M. (2000a). Document Management fuels e-Business. *InfoWorld*, August 4.

Heck, M. (2000b). Eliminate Web Publishing Bottlenecks. *InfoWorld*, August 4.

Meta Group. (2001). Evaluation of: TeamSite. SPEX.

Moore, C. (2001a). Justifying IT Investments: Web Content Management. Giga Information Group, May 16.

Moore, C. (2001b). Vendor Viability is a Key Strength for Interwoven. Giga Information Group, June 11.

Pyles, M. (2001). The Three Steps to Content Management. *Transform Magazine*, January.

Sanborn, S. (2001). Content Management Moves Ahead. *InfoWorld*, February 16.

Shegda, K. and Weintraub, A. (2000). Documentum Inc Documentum 4i eBusiness Edition, Gartner DataPro, December.

Verma, G., Campbell, J., Turocy, P. and Andrews, L. (2001). Product Review: Content-Management Solutions. *VAR Business*, August 24.

West, K., Huff, R. and Turocy, P. (2000). Managing Content on the Web. *Network Computing*, October 30.

Chapter 5   Phase 2: Transacting with customers

Bettini, W. L. (2001). Microsoft Commerce Server 2000. *PC Magazine*, May 4.

Carr, D. (2001). Open Market Shifts Focus to Content Management. *Internet World*, March 12.

Connolly, P. J. (2001). BizTalk automates B-to-B. *InfoWorld*, June 15.

Cox, B. (2001). IBM Offers Digital Media Solution. *Internet News*, August 1.

Desai, G., Sanchez, E. and Fenner, J. (2001). Internet Infrastructure: App

Servers meet E-commerce. *Information Week*, February 26.

Fenner, J., Meister, F. and Patel, J. (2001). Evolution of E-commerce. *VAR Business*, June 11.

Fingar, P. (2001). Don't Just Transact – Collaborate. *CIO Magazine*, June 1.

Huff, R. and Fenner, J. (2001). E-commerce platforms take command of content. *Transform Magazine*, February.

IT Director. (2000). eBusiness for Traditional Companies – the Role of Enterprise Application Integration. March 5.

Kramer, M. I. (2001a). Blue Martini 4: How Blue Martini's Sell-Side E-Commerce Server Offering Stacks Up. Patricia Seybold Group, June.

Kramer, M. I. (2001b). Confident Commerce: IBM WebSphere Commerce Suite Version 5.1. Patricia Seybold Group, January.

Meister, F., Fenner, J. and Patel, J. (2000). E-commerce Platforms Mature. *VAR Business*, October 23.

Schultz, K. (2001). Click to WebSphere. *Internet Week*, April 16.

Stackpole, B. (2001). E-Commerce: E-commerce & Extranets Product of the Year 2000. Earthweb IT Management (INT Media Group), February 14..

Simmons, C. L. (2000). .InterWorld Commerce Exchange. Gartner DataPro Report (cited on ZDNet), August 24.

Tillett, L. S. (2001). Open Market, IBM Team For Content/E-commerce Offering. *Internet Week*, August 1.

Varon, E. (2001). The ABC's of B2B. *CIO Magazine*, August 20.

Chapter 6   Phase 3: Internal enterprise application integration

Barlas, D. (2001). EAI In The Spotlight. *Line 56*, November 5.

Britton, C. (2001). Classifying Middleware. *EAI Journal*, Winter.

Courtney, P. E. (1999a). Seamless, End-to-End Application Integration With BEA eLink. *EAI Journal*, July/August.

Courtney, P. E. (1999b). Business Process Integration from CrossWorlds Software. *EAI Journal*, May/June.

Courtney, P. E. (2000a). Control Brokers from Actional. *EAI Journal*, July/August.

Courtney, P. E. (2000b). Active Software's ActiveWorks Business Exchange Server. *EAI Journal*, June.

Courtney, Philip. E. (2000c). The iWave Solution – From NEON Systems. Delivering a Strategic Approach to e-Business Integration. *EAI Journal*, October.

Courtney, P. E. (2000d). NEON's e-Biz Integrator. Easing e-Business Pains Through Integration. *EAI Journal*, January.

Eck, J. R. (2000). Combining E-Commerce and EAI. *EAI Journal*, January 1.

Fenner, J. and Sanchez, E. (2001). EAI Users Go With The Flow. *Information Week*, March 26.

Gold-Bernstein, B. (1999). EAI Market Segmentation. *EAI Journal*.

Gonsalves, A. (2001). Value of EAI Grows As Integration Needs Expand. *Information Week*, May 28.

Hansen, M., and Mamorski, P. (2001). Java Connector Architecture: The Future of EAI? *EAI Journal*, May 15.

Hisham, A. (2001) Understanding Integration Strategies. *EAI Journal*, November 27.

Korzeniowski, P. (2000). EAI Tools Tie Business to Business. *EAI Journal*.

Linthicum, D. S. (2000). Application Servers and EAI. *EAI Journal*, July 1.

Linthicum, D. S. (2001). *B2B Application Integration. e-Business-Enable your Enterprise*. Addison-Wesley.

Longo, J. R. (2001). The ABC's of Enterprise Application Integration. *EAI Journal*, May 28.

Lublinsky, Boris. (2001). Achieving the Ultimate EAI Implementation. Part 2: Message-Level Integration. *EAI Journal*, February 1.

Lublinsky, B. and Farrell, M. Jr. (2001). .Enterprise Architecture and J2EE. *EAI Journal*, November.

Lutz, J. C. (2001). EAI Architecture Patterns. *EAI Journal*, March.

McGoveran, D. (1999). Architected Simplicity. *EAI Journal*.

Mann, J. E. (2001). Attunity. Transforming Legacy Applications to Support the Services Paradigm. Particia Seybold Group, June 7.

Moore, C. (2000). IBM's MQSeries Workflow Ecilipses FlowMark. Giga Information Group, February 29.

Open Systems Advisers Inc. (2001). CrossRoads A List Awards 2001: Peregrine Systems B2B (Extricity). January.

Sanchez, E., Beery, D. and Shehab, J. (2002). Review: EAI Systems Bring IT Together. *Network Computing*, January 21.

Sanchez, E, Patel, K. and Fenner, J. (2001a). Integration Powered. *Information Week*, May 28.

Sanchez, E., Patel, K. and Fenner, J. (2001b). Integration Platforms For E-Business. *Information Week*, June 4.

Sloser, S. E. (2001). Actional X - From Actional. Creating Direct Integration e-Commerce and Back-End ERP Applications. *EAI Journal*, February 20.

Stokes, N. (2001). EAI and Beyond: A Multi-Level Flow Model. *EAI Journal*, May 14.

Technology Trends (2001). iPlanet's New Web and Application Server Family Enables Web Services from Top to Bottom. D.H. Brown Associates Inc., March 5.

Chapter 7   Phase 4: External integration

Barrett, A. (2000). Making the B2B Connection: Why, and How, Companies are Linking to Their Customers and Suppliers. Editorial, *www.ebizq.net*, June 26.

Bolino, G. and Conti, E. (2001). B2B: Making Value Choices. *www.ebizq.net*,August 6.

Boughton, N. W. (2001). E-Business Messaging. *EAI Journal*, June.

Brox, N. (2001). The ROI of B2B Networks. Editorial, *www.ebizq.net*, 25 June.

Courtney, P. E. (2000). Sterling Commerce's e-Business Process Integration. *EAI Journal*, June.

Courtney, P. E. (2001a). First Impression: FuegoBPM 4.0 – From Fuegotech, Inc. EAI and B2Bi Without the Middleware Plumbing. *EAI Journal*, August.

Courtney, P. E. (2001b). First Impression: WorkPoint - from Insession Technologies. AppServer Independent BPM. *EAI Journal*, December.

Covill, R. (2001). The Future of e-Markets. Editorial, *www.ebizq.net*, September.

Cronin, C. (2001). Five Success Factors for Private Exchanges. *Business Advisor Magazine*, August 1.

Editorial (2000). e-Business Integration Drives EAI: An Interview with Aberdeen's Tom Dwyer. *EAI Journal*, July/August.

Frick, J. and Hyrne, C. (2001). Net Markets: Beyond The Basics. *www.ebizq.net*, March 5.

Gartner Group (2001). B2B Technologies and Initiatives Start Making Sense. *Tech Republic*, July 2.

Harrelson, W. B. (2001). B2B Trading Exchanges: Giving Suppliers and Buyers What They Really Want. Canopy International.

Helm, R. (1999). Extending EAI Beyond the Enterprise. *EAI Journal*.

Hildreth, S. (2000). The Marriage of EAI and BPM: A Conversation with Gartner's David McCoy. Editorial, *www.ebizq.net*, October.

Hildreth, S. (2001). BizTalk Talks Up Vertical Standards. Editorial, *www.ebizq.net*, June 11.

Jenkins, J. (2001). Customers Force Supply Chain Vendors to Change Gears. Analyst Corner, CXO Media, November 28.

Jennings, T. (2001). Application Deployment and Integration. Research Paper. Bowstreet Business Web Factory. Butler Group, August.

Jenz, D. E. (2001). Productivity Drives BPMS Acceptance. *www.ebizq.net*, July 23.

Korzeniowski, P. (2000). EAI Tools Tie Business to Business. *EAI Journal*, 2000.

Lawton, G. (2001). Achieving B2B Business Process Integration. *www.ebizq.net*, April 10.

Linthicum, D. S. (2000). Enterprise Evolution: Where EAI Meets B2B. An eBiz Q & A with SAGA software CTO David Linthicum. *www.ebizq.net*, May.

Linthicum, D. S. (2001). *B2B Application Integration. e-Business-Enable your Enterprise*. Addison-Wesley.

Linthicum, D. S. (2001). Solve the Integration Puzzle: Choose the Right Architecture. *e-Business Advisor*, October/November.

McDaniel, T. (2001). Ten Pillars of Business Process Management. *EAI Journal*, November.

McGoveran, D. (1999). Architected Simplicity. *EAI Journal*.

McGoveran, D. (2001). B2B Success Secrets, Part 1. *EAI Journal*, September.

Mann, J. E. (2001). Attunity: Transforming Legacy Applications to Support the Services Paradigm. Patricia Seybold Group Customer.com, June 7.

Mehra, P. (2001). Exchanges in the New Economy: Transforming The World Of Work. *www.ebizq.net*, July 23.

Morgenthal, J. P. (2000). B2B Integration: Marketplaces Vs. Point-to-Point. *EAI Journal*.

Nagaraj, N. S., Thonse, Srinivas., and Balasubramanian, S. (2001). Business Process Management: An Emerging Trend. SETLabs, Infosys Technologies Ltd.

Olsen, G.(2000). An Overview of B2B Integration. *EAI Journal*, May.

Sawhney, M. and Zabin, J. (2001). A Brave New B-Web World. The Bowstreet Business Web Factory. Delphi Group, August.

Scala, S. (2000). Don't Send an A2A Broker to Do a B2B Integrator's Job!. Editorial, *www.ebizq.net*, July 24.

Scala, S. (2001). Business-to-Business Integration: Participating in supply-chain initiatives and business exchanges. *www.ebizq.net*, March 26.

Schmidt, J. (2000). Enabling Next-Generation Enterprises. *EAI Journal*, July/August.

Schulte, R. (2001). Understanding the Convergence of B2B and Internal Application Integration: Questions and Answers. *Gartner Inc.*, April 12.

Smith, D. (2001). Gartner's Internet Strategies Research Note C-14-7199, 8 November.

Smith, M. (2000). The Visible Supply Chain. *IntelligentEnterprise.com*, October 20.

Smith, M. (2001). Business-Critical Prism. *IntelligentEnterprise.com*, October 4.

Tapellini, D. (2000). Negotiating B2B Exchanges: A Quick Tour Through Online Marketplaces. *www.ebizq.net*, September.

Ulrich, W. (2001). Critical Success Factors in a Business Process Initiative. *www.ebizq.net*, December 17.

Varon, E. (2001). The ABC's of B2B. *CIO Magazine*, August 20.

Verbeck, M. and Madda, T. Business to Business eCommerce Solutions. Epoch Partners, *www.ebizq.net*, July 2.

Yee, A. (2000a). Demystifying Business Process Integration. *www.ebizq.net*, July 24.

Yee, Andre. (2000b). Order Out of Chaos: Understanding B2B Integration Patterns. Editorial, *www.ebizq.net*, September.

Chapter 8   Phase 5: Dynamic e-business and web services

Borck, J. R. (2001a). Say goodbye to EDI. *InfoWorld*, October 19.

Borck, J. R. (2001b). Solving the Web services puzzle. *InfoWorld*, September 14.

Borck, J. R. (2001c). Supply-chain success. *InfoWorld*, April 20.

Bos, B. (2001). XML in 10 points. W3C Communications Team, November 13.

Colan, M. (2001). Dynamic e-business: Using Web services to transform business. IBM, IBM E-business, June.

Derome, J. (2001). Collaborative Commerce as the Ultimate Business Model. , *www.ebizq.net*, May 21.

Durchslad, S., Donato, C. and Hagel, J. III. (2001). Web Services: Enabling the Collaborative Enterprise. White Paper, Grand Central, July 1.

Ferguson, R. B. (2001). B2B Leaders Turn to Collaboration. *eWeek.com*, November 19.

Gilpin, M. (2000). XML: Standardising Data in Motion. Giga Information Group.

Gisolfi, D. (2001). Web services architect: Part 1. Introduction to dynamic e-business. *IBM developerworks.com*, April.

Harreld, H. (2001). Collaboration in supply chain management provides benefits. *InfoWorld*, April 20.

Jain, P. and Jain, A. (2001). The Competitive Advantage of Net Markets. *www.ebizq.net*, March 19.

Jennings, T. (2001). Application Deployment and Integration. Research Paper. Bowstreet Business Web Factory. Butler Group, August.

Karpinski, R. (2001). Inside UDDI. *Internet Week*, June 7.

Langabeer, J. (2001). Automating the Demand Chain. Editorial, *www.ebizq.net*, November 5.

Sanborn, S. and Moore, C. (2001). Collaboration comes together. *InfoWorld*, December 7.

Schwartz, E. (2002). Secure Web services a moving target. *InfoWorld*, January 17.

Schmidt, J. (2000). Enabling Next-Generation Enterprises. *EAI Journal*, July/August.

Seeley, R. (2001). IBM WebSphere Rises to Meet the Challenges of Dynamic E-business. *The Business Integrator Journal*, Winter.

Sullivan, T. and Scannell, E. (2002). Enterprises seek Web services platform unity. *InfoWorld*, January 11.

Sullivan, T., Scannell, E., and Schwartz, E. (2002). Second standards phase emerges. *InfoWorld*, January 10.

Uddi.org. (2001). UDDI Executive White Paper. November 14.

Udell, J. (2002). Web Services. *InfoWorld*, January 3.

Vaughn-Nichols, S. (2002). Fat protocols slow Web services. *eWeek.com*, January 7.

White, C. (2001). Analytics on Demand: The Zero Latency Enterprise. *Intelligent Enterprise.com*, October 4.

Woods, D. (2002). Web services: A skeptic's journey. *InfoWorld*, January 14.

Worthen, B. (2001). Collaborative Computing. *CIO Magazine*, October 15.

Chapter 10 E-business development technologies

Java

Berger, M. (2002). Survey: Java breezes by .Net for Web services. *Network World*, December 21.

Cutter Consortium. (2000). More Than Half Of Companies Using Java. *Cutter Consortium*, April 18.

Desai, G., Sanchez, E., and Fenner, J. (2001). Web Application Servers Come of Age. *Network Computing*, July 23..

Pawlan, M. (2001). Introduction to the J2EE Platform. *Java Developer Connection*, March 23..

Schaeck, T. and Hepper, S. (2002). Portal Standards. *TheServerSide.com*, February.

XML

Apicella, M. (2002). Side by side in perfect harmony? *InfoWorld*, February 22.

Borck, J. R. (2001). Building a better b-to-b marketplace. *InfoWorld*, September 14.

Boucher, R. (2002). XML needs more cohesion. *IT Week*, January 21.

Connolly, D. and Thompson, H. (2000). XML Schema. www.w3.org, April.

Editorial (2001). B2B and the standards issue. *IT-Director.com*, February 8.

Hildreth, S. (2001). BizTalk Talks Up Vertical Standards. Editorial, *ebizQ.net*, June 11.

Linthicum, D. S. (2001). *B2B Application Integration. e-Business-Enable your Enterprise*. Addison-Wesley.

Smith, D., Correia, J., Pring, B. and Plummer, D. (2001). Gartner's Internet Strategies Research Note M-13-3593, April 9.

Yager, T. (2002). The future of application integration. *InfoWorld*, February 22.

Reference sites

The XML & EDI Group - http://www.xmledi.com
XML.COM - http://www.xml.com
The World Wide Web Consortium - http://www.w3c.org
The RosettaNet consortium - http://www.rosettanet.org
The BizTalk homepage - http://www.biztalk.org
The OASIS group - http://www.oasis-open.org
OASIS &United Nations/CEFACT - http://www.ebxml.org
General XML reference - http://www.xml.org
Excellent comprehensive source of XML links - http://www.w3.org/XML/

Microsoft .Net

Ahmed, E. (2001). Introducing the .NET Framework and Jscript .NET. *EarthWeb Developer.com*, December 6.

Arnott, S. (2001). .Net battles against tough J2EE rival. *Network News*, vnu.net, September 26.

Berger, M. (2001). Survey: Java breezes by .Net for Web services. *IDG News Service*, December 21.

English, A. (2001). Microsoft .Net strategy pushes the Web application development envelope. *Network World*, November 5.

Yager, T. (2002). Microsoft .Net and C#. *InfoWorld*, January 3, 2002.

Chapter 11 Hardware platforms and operating systems

Anderson, R., Lee, M. and Chapin, S. J. (2000). Unraveling the Mysteries of Clustering. *Network Computing*, October 2.

Berger, M. (2002). Is Microsoft .Net coming to a platform near you? *Itworld.com*, January 10.

Connolly, P. J. (2001). The penguin swoops into the OS fray. *InfoWorld*, November 2.

Gray, D. F. (2001). Intel or Unix? Server Customers Face a Tough Choice. *ITworld.com*, December 11.

Lawson, S. (2001). IBM packages Linux clusters for e-commerce. *Itworld.com*, November 13.

Microsoft (2001). Introducing Windows Advanced Server, Limited Edition. http://www.microsoft.com/windows2000/64bit/, August 7.

Moore, F. (1999). Scalability and server selection. Horison Information Strategies.

Saltzer, J. and Schroeder, M. (1975). The Protection of Information in Computing Systems. *Proceedings of the IEEE*, 63(9), September.

Shipley, G. and Novak, K. (2000). The Linux Challenge. *Network Computing*, June 26.

Vance, A. (2002). Pall cast on HP Itanium leadership claims:, *InfoWorld*, January 4.

Yager, T. (2001). Inside Intel's Itanium. *InfoWorld*, June 22.

Chapter 12 Security

Article. (2001). The BS 7799 Security Standard: What is It?. C & A Security Systems Ltd.

Brooke, P. (2001a). DDOS: Internet Weapons of Mass Destruction. *Network Computing*, January 8.

Brooke, P. (2001b). Opening Your E-Business Perimeter. *Network Computing*, January 8.

Brown, K. (2000). *Programming Windows Security*. Addison Wesley, June 30.

Costello, S. (2001). Survey reveals one in nine IIS servers could be taken over by hackers. *InfoWorld*, November 2.

DeMaria, M. J. (2001). No Desktop is an island. *Network Computing*, November 12.

Eirich, B. and Shipley, G. (2001). Cisco Cures the Chicago Blues. *Network Computing*, November 12.

Forristal, J. (2001). Fireproofing Against DoS Attacks. December 10.

Fratto, M. (2001a). Defense Mechanisms. *Network Computing*, November 12.

Fratto, M. (2001b). The Survivors Guide to 2002. *Network Computing*, December 17.

Garfinkel, S. and Spafford, G. (1996). *Practical UNIX & Internet Security, 2nd Edition*. O'Reilly.

Messmer, E. (2001). Intrusion Alert. Gigabit-speed intrusion detection systems miss attacks on faster nets. *Network World*, December 3.

Mueller, P. and Shipley, G. (2001). To Catch a Thief. *Network Computing*, August 20.

Rapoza, J. (2002). Microsoft Still Suffers Insecurity Complex. *eWeek*, January 7.

Stacey, T. (2000). Toward Standardisation of Information Security: DS 7799. Sans Institute, September 22.

Shipley, G. (2000). Watching the Watcher: Intrusion Detection. Network Computing, November 12.

Viega, J. and McGraw, G. (2001). Building Secure Software: How to Avoid Security Problems the Right Way. Addison Wesley, September.

Wheeler, D. A. (2002). Secure Programming for Linux and Unix HOWTO. http://www.dwheeler.com/secure-programs/

Yocom, B., Brown, K. and DerVeer, D. (2001). Review: Intrusion-detection products grow up. *Network World*, October 8.

Reference sites

http://www.sans.org
http://www.securityfocus.com

Chapter 13 Networking systems

Andress, M. (2001). VPN's proving vital to corporate nets. *InfoWorld*, November 16.

Dunetz, B. (2001). Virtual Private Networks. *Network World*, September 3.

Galvin, P. B. (2000). Reliability without the cluster. *Sunworld.com*, March 24.

MacVittie, L. (2000). E-Commerce Security Gets a Boost. *Network Communications*, September 17.

MacVittie, L. (2001a). Content Switches. *Network Communications*, September 17.

MacVittie, L. (2001b). Scaling Your E-Business. *Network Communications*, February 5.

MacVittie, L. (2001c). Web Server Director Comes Out on Top of the Pile. *Network Communications*, February 5.

Chapter 14 DNS

BIND Administrator Reference Manual - brief treatment of some DNS design issues, good for BIND configuration file reference.

DNS and BIND: Help for System Administrators (O'Reilly).

Reference sites

http://www.dns.net/dnsrd/
http://www.isc.org/bind.html

Chapter 15 Open Source technologies

Baltazar, H. and Dyck, T. (2001). Tux: Built for speed. *eWeek*, June 18.

Borck, J. R. (2001). Taking the open road to Web Services. *InfoWorld*, November 29.

Connolly, P. J. (2001). The penguin swoops into the OS fray. *InfoWorld*, November 2.

Dyck, T. (2001). Apache 2.0 scales to Windows. *eWeek*, April 15

Hasan, R. (2000). History of Linux. http://ragib.hypermart.net/linux/, November 4.

Kegel, D. (2001). NT vs. Linux Server Benchmark Comparisons. http://www.kegel.com/nt-linux-benchmarks.html, July 31.

Open Source Initiative (2001). www.opensource.org, November 28.

Rapoza, J. (2001). Open-source portal radiates power. *eWeek*, September 13.

Scannell, E. and Sullivan, T. (2001). IBM connects its software layers. *InfoWorld*, December 14.

Schenk, (2001). Linux: Its history and current distributions. http://ww.developer.ibm.com/library/articles/schenk1.html, April 25.

Shipley, G. and Novak, K. (2000). The Linux Challenge. *Network Computing*, June 26.

Source Forge, www.sourceforge.net.

Stallman, R. (2001). The GNU Project. http://www.gnu.org/gnu/thegnuproject.html

Yager, T. (2001a). Developing in the open. *InfoWorld*, August 24.

Yager, T. (2001b). Open source takes hold. *InfoWorld*, August 24.

Yager, T. (2001c). BSD's strength lies in devilish details. *InfoWorld*, November 2

Index

Printed and bound by CPI Group (UK) Ltd, Croydon, CR0 4YY

17/10/2024

01775696-0003